CIRCULAR PASSAGE

A YOUNG MAN'S 480-DAY GLOBAL ODYSSEY

~A MEMOIR~

Robert V. Hardy

ISBN: 1-4392-1398-4
ISBN-13: 9781439213988
Library of Congress Control Number 2009905081

Visit www.booksurge.com to order additional copies.

In memory of Dad, a great competitor,
who by his example inspired me
to be the best I could be.

Table of Contents

Preface

For more than two years now, I have placed myself before the computer each morning in an effort to recapture the extraordinary events that unfolded during a sixteen-month adventure odyssey, one that encircled the world. I was encouraged to recall these experiences by family and close friends, who had heard my verbal accounts of these travel stories through the years and suggested I try to preserve them in writing. It is with a great deal of satisfaction that I see this long effort drawing to a close, and the chronicle at last complete. Aside from changing some of the names, as a matter of privacy, the episodes are set down exactly as I remember them.

An unexpected pleasure loomed up before me as I began the writing of this memoir. While sifting through the various maps, old letters to home, and reconstructed travel journals, I found myself reliving in memorable detail, the trials, the loves, and glorious occurrences that came together on this unusual quest. Suddenly these rich memories transported me back to the halcyon days of my youth, back to the years 1966–67, when I was only twenty-four, and the world was mine to discover.

You now hold in your hands a pocket global passage, one that encompasses much fascinating geography, the mysteries of different cultures, and the many personal reflections as I traveled through a host of foreign lands. The overall experience, that up until now was a tale much too long to tell any one individual, served to define my early years. It remains my wish that this story evokes in the reader the same level of wonder and excitement as it did for me at the time of the journey.

Let this be then, your armchair *Circular Passage*.

June 12, 2008   RVH

Acknowledgements

Gail Stovall and I met on a train in China, in the fall of 2005. Our small group of travelers had left Beijing for Xi'an, to see the Terra Cotta Army. She was a spark-plug of energy, and enjoyed hearing my travel stories from the old days. In the weeks and months that followed, she suggested I take the time to write some of them down. Soon I was struggling to connect ailing chapters into a book, answering Gail's persistent but gentle call to produce. She committed herself to the long haul, reading and rereading my work, pushing forward her points, logically, hopefully, always with precision. Gail has been a tireless and faithful reader, editor, and most of all, a remarkably good friend.

Linda Keller has been a fellow classmate in my Adult Education writing class for the last two years. She is one of twenty aspiring writers who gather around the tables in a bookstore once a week to work on their memoirs. Soon aware of her astute and discerning abilities, I asked Linda if she might lend another set of eyes to my budding creations. For the last year, she has generously applied her superior editing and computer skills, compiling and rendering sketches, formatting and expertly tending the manuscript as a master gardener. She has been a gem, donating her extra time with enthusiastic devotion that this project might live.

Marilyn Kregel is the great and humble leader of our writers' group, giving constantly of herself that the efforts of others around her might germinate, sprout, and bloom. I have been one of the many recipients of her extraordinary teaching talents, keen intellect, and tender educator's heart. She has thoughtfully passed on decades of experience while guiding with wisdom those of us who maintain desire but still struggle with proficiency. My classmates are the brothers and sisters who share in the joyful sessions of learning that she conducts each week.

Mary Cantrell taught me to climb mountains, when I wondered if I really could. She has smiled with me on the windy summits of Whitney and Shasta when it was frigid, miserable, and glorious. This dear friend, for years upon years, has read my scraps of prose, poetry, and letters, patiently waiting for my efforts to improve. She has professionally edited medical journals and grant proposals in her work, and then kindly exercised those same talents in nursing my writings along.

Then there is Barbara Durst, who delivered my mail for a number of years, before one day asking if she might read for me, engaging her adroit aptitudes for structuring, evaluating tone, and correcting timelines. These were the offerings acquired from her long experience with different writers' groups. Lucky for me, she came along at just the right time.

There are many more like Helen, Kirby, Pat, Niki, Kate, Laraine, Gordon, and Alaska Bill, who have sacrificed their time and energy, reflecting back to me what they saw in my writings, so that I might advance. All of their contributions, however large or small, have added to the whole, now greater than the sum of its parts.

To the dear friends, who have dedicated their long hours along the way with this undertaking, I express my heartfelt gratitude. Their work is an immense gift and I will treasure it forever. There is great doubt whether I ever could have completed such a daunting endeavor as this first book without their expert help and unending encouragement.

June 13, 2008   Robert V. Hardy

Global Route

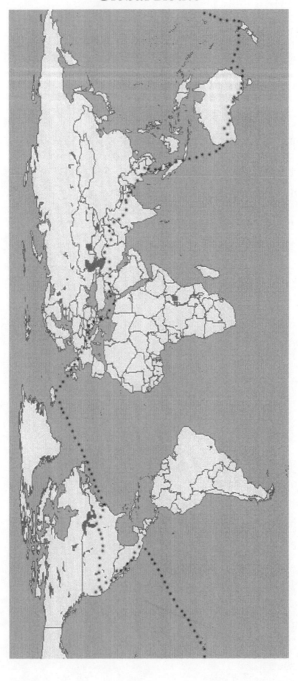

The World Is Round
Chapter One

Restless at home and ever prone to range. —Dryden

Forty years ago, I began a momentous journey that was to be a pivotal event in my young life, changing forever the way I viewed the world. Looking back, the crucial influences that persuaded me to purchase a backpack in the summer of 1966 and embark upon a sixteen-month trek around the globe seem apparent. However, at the time it simply appeared as the ideal antidote to the growing disenchantment of my humdrum life working as a mid-level loan officer in a finance company. Quite possibly, I was searching for a way to make a more compelling statement in what I saw as a banal existence. In the back of my mind, it had been my passion for as long as I could remember to see the world. I suspect it was a combination of forces, both environmental and perhaps those spawned from hereditary lines, which caused me to set off to explore foreign lands. In any event, it was something I had to do, something that I could no longer delay, and when the opportunity finally presented itself, I chose to loosen my grip on one existence and embrace another. For this, I have never been sorry.

My initial desires to see other countries grew from the vivid tales told to me by my maternal grandfather. The earliest recollections I have of him were those associated with the fragrant tendrils of smoke that rose from the bowl of his pipe. He smoked Prince Albert, and I was reminded when he had come to visit from his adopted Mexico by the pleasing odor that wafted through our house in Ashland, Oregon. Grandfather slept in the back bedroom, where he remained busy writing letters and shuffling through the papers he kept in an oak-ribbed trunk close to his bed. The whimsical grin he occasionally cast my way never ceased to warm my heart and left no doubt as to the pleasure he took in seeing me.

His name was Moray Applegate, a descendent of our family's pioneer ancestry who had come to Oregon by wagon train from Missouri in 1843. He was a tall man, with a gray mustache that matched his twinkling gray eyes. After college, Moray made his mark as an interpreter in the Spanish American War, a responsibility that took him deep into the interior of the Philippines. In this position, he became adept at negotiating with the fierce Moro tribesmen on behalf of our government. Later, in 1910, he once again seized adventure by the hand when he answered an ad in the *San Francisco Chronicle* for the manager's position of a large hacienda in the Mexican state of Nayarit. It was here, aside from his annual trips north to visit our family, that he spent the remainder of his life.

I can remember sitting on Grandfather's knee as a boy, wide-eyed and listening intently, as he narrated the colorful accounts of his exciting life. There were near-death experiences to digest and always the elements of intrigue that sprang from his involvement in foreign countries. He had a way of pausing to light his pipe precisely when the story had his listeners spellbound and hanging hopelessly on his next word. Among those who knew him, he had the enviable distinction and reputation of being a master storyteller.

The next major event that bolstered my dreams of experiencing faraway places came in the summer of 1962, when I had the good fortune to travel the European continent with Tom, a fellow classmate from the University of Oregon. I was nineteen, and it was the summer between my sophomore and junior years. For nearly three months, we followed the very complete itinerary laid out by his father. We visited the famous museums, ran with the bulls in Pamplona, Spain, slept in the haylofts of Swiss barns, and tirelessly roamed the romantic streets of the major capitals. There was some hitchhiking but for the most part, we toted our luggage to the various train stations, making efficient use of our Eurail Passes. These afforded us unlimited mileage on the European trains. It was an unforgettable summer, and it passed much too quickly.

Yet another inspiration took shape on a December night in 1964, with the chance meeting of a traveler in Omar's, a well-known roadhouse in my hometown of Ashland. While socializing one evening with friends, I saw the front door suddenly swing open bringing with it a strong gust of wet wind from the north. Stooping slightly, a tall lean stranger stepped over the threshold and out of the hard-driving rain. Just for an instant, flashes of lightning illuminated Grizzly Mountain in the distance. Then the portal slammed shut, and the man dropped his small backpack and bedroll to the floor. The rainwater streaked down his heavy canvas overcoat to puddle at his feet. He removed his jet-black beret, which was festooned with small amulets and medallions from different countries. Shaking it out, he placed it back on his head, cocking it expertly at just the right angle. He wore it proudly as a king would his crown.

The stranger revealed in conversation he was on the last leg of a solitary expedition around the world, which had taken him several years. His words ran like soft music to my ears as he told of periodically replenishing his grubstake by taking interesting jobs in the different countries along the way. As he spoke, I sensed this was a precursor of events to come. These stories fired my imagination, and I peppered this vagabond with questions until closing time when, like two ships passing in the dark, we parted. His tales continued to resonate within me, serving as a festering reminder that I had some unfinished business to address.

Another significant factor in stimulating this international quest was my introduction to a teacher in San Jose, California, my residence after the university years. I had taken a position with Pacific Finance Corporation and was renting a small apartment in an old converted two-story Victorian house. My landlady was a socially advanced, curvaceous blonde who lived in the fast lane. Upon learning of my interest in travel, she suggested I meet with Kirby, an interesting acquaintance of hers who had taught school abroad, a man in his late twenties who had proven himself a seasoned veteran of global exploits.

Our paths finally crossed on a fateful night at one of the frequent parties held by my landlady at her apartment. Kirby appeared somewhat younger than his years, calm in demeanor, and sporting a full head of sandy hair he wore in the style of James Dean. We soon settled in for a fascinating session of storytelling around the fireplace that lasted well into the night. Visions of foreign lands danced in my brain as this accomplished student of literature (who had taken his MA at San Francisco State) and budding young writer spun his humorous and romantic stories throughout the evening. He delighted me with his descriptions of life in countries like Pakistan, Japan, Switzerland, and New Zealand. Before parting, I mentioned to Kirby that should he ever break loose again and make for distant shores, I would be a willing travel companion who could share expenses. I went home that night, savoring the captivating images of foreign landscapes and singular adventures.

My grandfather's stories, the summer in Europe, the man in the beret, and the introduction to Kirby were the key motivating factors setting the stage for my future. Although my optimistic fantasies of going abroad once again lay dormant, they were poised for activation at the slightest nudge. I was determined to pursue this new course soon and continued to make regular contributions to my travel fund, preparing for the glorious day when I could depart. This fertile obsession led me to exist on grilled cheese and tuna sandwiches for extended periods in an effort to reduce my grocery bill and save money. Tomato soup was eight cans for a dollar, making me a great supporter of the Campbell's Soup Company! Then one day the call came—the call that would prompt me to take leave of the desk-bound discomfort zone that had gripped my life.

It was Kirby. He was leaving for Europe in August and asked if I were still interested in traveling. I answered in the affirmative and without hesitation. He mentioned that Franz, an old friend of his in Munich, would soon be traveling to the Middle East. He had offered his cold-water flat to Kirby during the upcoming months of September and October, for a nominal rent of five dollars a month. My new friend also told me he had been looking into the transatlantic flights of Icelandic Airlines to Luxembourg from JFK, finding a one-way fare to Europe for $162. Taking a deep breath, I instructed him to book an extra seat and I would send him a check. Having made this commitment in my mind long before that fateful call, I was relieved the wheels were at last in motion to travel again.

My heart pounded as I hung up the phone and then realized, from that brief exhilarating exchange, the course of my life would soon be drastically changing. Kirby and I had agreed to meet for further discussions regarding the staging of the trip once Icelandic Airlines confirmed. Our work would include reviewing checklists and discussing the different approaches to crossing the country to New York. I felt invigorated at having taken this first step, and now, in only six short weeks, we would be leaving the country.

New responsibilities gathered like storm clouds on my horizon, and all of them needed immediate attention. It was important to speak with my employer about my decision. Within days my branch manager and I were on the golf course as sometimes was the case on Wednesday afternoons. Playing through the links, I anxiously wrestled with the right words to inform him of what I was about to do. To my surprise, precisely at the moment I was ready to divulge my plans for resigning, the man began to praise me regarding my work at the office. In addition, he chose the occasion to offer a major promotion accompanied by a substantial raise in pay. This drove home the realization there would be a significant price to pay for my recent decision, one that would involve walking away from a rising and lucrative career.

I expressed my gratitude and carefully explained my confirmed plans to travel the world. Stunned at first, the older man soon regained his presence of mind. His eyes narrowed and a warm glow spread across his face as he grasped the full nature of what I was saying. Then he confided that he too had some of the very same desires in his youth. With his characteristic grin and a pat on my back, he then encouraged me to follow my dreams. We turned and walked towards the clubhouse together, both realizing change was in the air.

Soon after that, I engaged in another difficult conversation, one of informing my girlfriend of the plans to depart the country for an indefinite period of time. Though not without some heartache, the talk went better than expected as I had spoken to her previously of my wish to someday travel. This sweet girl was doing well at San Jose State and preparing for a career in teaching. Our physical relationship was over, but we would remain faithful pen pals for the next few months. Once again, I was aware of the emotional pain generated from dismantling yet another relationship.

There were other priorities to deal with, and these affairs took precedence over everything else. In the month that followed, I wound up my personal business in the Bay Area, closing bank accounts, selling furniture, and bidding farewell to old friends.

I visited a well-known outdoor store in Berkeley where I purchased a high-quality down sleeping bag. Who would have guessed then that within a year I would sell it to a Nepalese Sherpa, a seasoned veteran of Mount Everest expeditions? The bag would prove a wise investment. Later, I procured an inexpensive, lightweight, external frame backpack, in the sporting goods section of a department store. This pack would serve me well, in spite of enduring many repairs. Finally, it was time for one last visit with my parents in Oregon before my departure.

Kirby accompanied me north to Ashland where I had lined up a buyer for my car. It was here that I would do my final packing. The theme of simplicity remained at the forefront these last days, one of the many positive lessons gleaned from this stage of the preparation. I chose only to take with me those items that had multiple uses and ruthlessly eliminated those that did not. The list was concise: a change of clothes, a warm sweater, and of course a quality world map. Other items included a bag of toiletries, some vitamins, and a rain slicker with a hood. Efficiently loaded at last, I had gotten the backpack and bedroll down to thirty-three pounds, including a full water bottle, a few books, and some dried fruit and nuts.

What Mom and Dad ultimately thought about my venture remained somewhat of a mystery. From their occasional questions, I could see that making a sharp turn at this point in my life might not have been their first choice for me. My parents were from the WWII generation and had lived through The Great Depression. Steeped in the consciousness of utility and practicality, they held a high regard for financial security. There was some mention that my departure from a promising job for parts unknown was possibly an unnecessary jaunt away from the safety net of the established order. I acknowledged these concerns but immersed in the confidence of youth, I did not let such forebodings deter me.

Vietnam was in the headlines. I had a military deferment resulting from the serious knee injury incurred while playing basketball in Eugene. I was required to make contact with the draft board before leaving the country, and this I did. Back in my hometown, I visited one last time with old friends, noting that some had recently married and were beginning to build their lives together. Others were joining the military, soon to embark on journeys of their own.

The short visit to southern Oregon ended on August 21, 1966— the date that essentially marks the beginning of my global experience. My parents dropped Kirby and me off at the Highway 99 junction, just at the edge of town. The state was busy transforming the old highway into the new Interstate 5 freeway, an ambitious project that would be finished by the time I returned.

Mom stepped out of the car and, with a hug, told me to come back safe and sound. I consoled her somewhat nervously, saying, the world was round and as long as I remembered to continue moving east, I would eventually find my way back. The mask of doubt she wore betrayed her true feelings. I commented jokingly that the "safe and sound" part would largely be up to fate. She laughed, shaking her head, and with a parting smile, slipped back into the family sedan.

Dad and I shook hands warmly, and he wished me well. He was a serious and hardworking man, highly respected in the community. Dad had always taken a keen interest in my life, even showing great support for my summer in Europe, but I guessed he was somewhat perplexed over this latest venture. I watched as he and Mom drove away, the car fading into the distance, knowing it would be some time before I would see them again.

The thought that I was taking leave of family, friends, and all familiar lifelines stimulated a sudden flood of emotion inside of me. There were no real misgivings regarding my new direction. My initial concerns over the merits of this decision had long since dissipated and now the raw excitement of it all had me highly energized. Later, I would learn that freedom brings with it a certain amount of insecurity and, conversely, when totally immersed in the secure life, freedom diminishes. However, at the time of my departure these were lessons I had not yet come to fully comprehend.

For now, we were hitchhiking south, free and unencumbered. My pack was minimal and well-organized, leaving me with the comfortable awareness that I had whittled my material possessions down to the bare essentials. I basked in the pleasure of the moment, feeling liberated in the knowledge I was beginning a new and exciting chapter of my life.

Luxembourg Street

A Return to Europe
Chapter Two

I would rather be ashes than dust! I would rather that my spark should burn out in a brilliant blaze than it should be stifled by dry-rot. I would rather be a superb meteor, every atom of me in magnificent glow, than a sleepy and permanent planet. The proper function of man is to live, not to exist. I shall not waste my days in trying to prolong them. I shall use my time. —Jack London

We stood at the edge of the highway leading south with our thumbs extended. It seemed as though we were invisible to the passing motorists, as car after car streaked past us, failing to reduce their speed in the slightest. My hitchhiking experience was limited, having done a little in Switzerland and several other times in the States (after running out of gas). Now challenging the odds, we put an outwardly optimistic face on this noble experiment, while harboring a budding skepticism beneath. Would drivers really stop for two large fellows with backpacks? We continued walking along Highway 99 in the direction of the rugged Siskiyou Mountains. Pilot Rock, a southern Oregon landmark, sat on the ridge-line ahead as if placed there by a great hand. I remembered old-timers saying this was once the natural daytime beacon for every Oregonian leaving the Rogue River Valley by stagecoach or on horseback. It was thirty minutes later when our first ride rolled to a stop at the side of the road directly in front of us.

We quickly piled into the car without too much scrutiny of the driver. He careened back out onto the road before the doors were completely shut, which should have been our first red flag. We soon realized that we had been abducted by a wild-eyed lunatic, stressed out from having just left his wife up in Washington State. The poor fellow was beside himself, swilling his beer out of a quart bottle in a brown paper bag and appearing to be on a suicidal rampage. He muttered something about stopping for us in desperation just to have some company.

His erratic driving became worrisome, as both the speed at which we were traveling and the tenor of his lament continued to rise. The man was obviously on the edge, spewing venomous statements about the woman in Washington one moment and then becoming quite conciliatory with regard to her the next. It was not long before we convinced him to do his drinking in the back seat and leave the driving to us, something to which he reluctantly agreed. To our relief he drifted off into a deep slumber. This jaunt back into northern California took us the good part of the day, and we finally stopped at the fork in the road that was the old Winter's cut-off. There we separated from our new acquaintance, placing his life back in his own hands.

We continued into the Bay Area with the aid of two additional rides. One was in the bed of a dilapidated pickup truck leaving us exposed to the open air. Frigid winds swept off the San Francisco Bay, and with numb fingertips, I dug into my backpack extracting my trusted wool sweater. This ride would ferry Kirby and me as far as the Richmond turnoff. The next ride took us further south to Fremont and across the Dumbarton Bridge, to Menlo Park, and finally to Kirby's place. We had done it!

The following morning, Kirby's mom made us aware that the feelers she had put out on our behalf had reaped rewards. We now had a Volkswagen Beetle to deliver to her good friends, the Clarks, in Colorado Springs. This solved the immediate challenge of the next leg of the journey and provided the momentum we needed to start our eastern advance. After fueling up, we extended our parting respects to my friend's parents and then compressed our tall frames, loaded packs, and sack lunches into the small Bug.

We fled the congested traffic of the Bay Area eastward towards Stockton and Manteca, where we picked up Highway 120 towards Twain Harte, our first stop. Moving past Sonora, an area with which Kirby was quite familiar, we penetrated the western edge of the

Stanislaus National Forest. Finally we arrived in Twain Harte, a quaint little town nestled in the Sierras where Kirby's old friends from the community had offered to treat us to a *bon voyage* party.

This was a Gold Rush town, where tall silhouettes of conifers pushed their fingers high into the backdrop of blue sky. Historically, the lumbermen and ranchers had settled in this idyllic area, not far behind those with gold fever. Sequestered in the foothills, the location was favorable to the growing of apples and pears, with remnants of older orchards still in existence. The town was named after two well-known Mother Lode authors, Mark Twain and Bret Harte.

The going-away party progressed into the night, and fascinating people filled the rooms of the house that belonged to a local character by the name of Purdy. He was the perfect host. There were two other guests, Bill and Anne, who especially captured my attention. They had lived in Pakistan for two years where Bill had taught school. Anne had learned to play the *sitar* while there, later studying under the famous Ali Akbar Khan after their return to California. The sounds of this exotic Indian stringed instrument, and the *tabla drums*, played by Bill, held me transfixed that night, shattering all my previous conceptions of music. Extraordinary stories of world travel abounded, and there was a warm atmosphere of camaraderie throughout the evening with this special collection of Kirby's friends. It was the ultimate send off.

We departed later that night with the expressed intent of camping in the Sierras. Continuing in the direction of Sonora Pass, we drove through places with colorful names like Long Barn and Strawberry. After a short time, we pulled off the two-lane road into a grove of pines and made our camp near a small stream.

The moon, a shining white disk, rose slowly into a ceiling of stars sprinkled on a blue-black background. Like fireworks, celestial shooters sent streaks of light across the sky, a few transforming into red balls, before they melted into dispersing particles and dipped out of sight. It was our first real night on the road. I lay snug and warm in my new down bag, listening to the soothing sounds of falling water and taking in the fragrant smells offered by the Sierra Nevada, as I drifted off.

Dawn broke and the rays from the sun peeked through the timber, falling in patches of light on the kinnikinnik growing under foot. Like bonsai manzanita bushes, they provided an attractive carpet of ground cover. The vapors that hung just above the creek were beginning to rise into the arms of the surrounding trees.

The biting cold water of the clear mountain stream was refreshing, and I repeatedly doused my face from a small pool. Then, while I reclined on granite boulders in the sun, my thoughts drifted back to my days at the finance company. I mused on how liberating it was not to be at the office this morning, wearing a suit and perched behind a desk, anxiously answering the phones while talking to loan applicants. I would not miss thoughtlessly consuming those infernal jelly donuts and bear claws, temptations consistently bestowed upon our office each morning by our well-meaning secretary. Nor would I miss the repossessions and collection calls required of me on the way home from the office at night. This was now all part of another life that I was delighted to have left behind.

Recurring in the back of my mind was a sense of urgency regarding the plane we had to catch out of New York in only a few days. Constant movement was necessary if we were to see some of the country and still make our flight on time. After a breakfast of melon, dark rye bread, and honey we were back on the road. The plentiful farmers' markets along the way offered an array of healthy choices and we had stocked up. They provided pleasant roadside attractions, breaking up the long hours of driving.

As we pushed the Beetle ever higher, past Dardanelle and towards Sonora Pass, the blankets of forest that had once been evident began to fade. Tree lines became more apparent with the stunted pines now providing evidence of our gain in elevation. The topography, characterized primarily by an abundance of batholithic granite, exposed deep foundations of stone on all sides of us. Small alpine valleys supported flat basins of alluvium, appearing as dammed up lakes of gravel. Mammoth outcroppings bore enormous splits, a result of the seasonal campaigns of freezing and thawing that nature waged against them. Exfoliating granite skins pealed from the boulders like compressed layers of an onion. It was breathtaking country to absorb, and it served to validate my decision to travel again.

At an altitude of 9,624-feet, the Sonora Pass had been a historical route into California, allowing early settlers traveling west a passable track through the rugged Sierra Nevada range. Now we were migrating as those throngs of seekers before us, only in the opposite direction. After pushing over the summit, we started down the eastern slope, rolling through Leavitt Meadow and later coming to Highway 395. This main north-south thoroughfare skirted the eastern base of the Sierras, allowing us to turn north towards Carson City and Reno, where we picked up the main traffic artery to points east.

From Sparks, we traced the highway of many names in the direction of Utah. Early on, it had been a Pony Express route, and then it became the Lincoln Highway, later US 40, and most recently, Interstate 80. We moved on through Fernley and Battle Mountain, crossing high deserts and much dry terrain. Small mountain ranges like Stillwater, East, Tobin, and Shoshone pushed into view from the south. There were vast tracks of open land, and it gave me an exhilarating sense of the wide-open spaces. That night we camped in the desert outside of Elko, just west of the Ruby Mountains.

The nighttime aromas of sagebrush and tumbleweed were especially pungent and at 5,000 feet the high desert air was arid and sweet. The sky was again ablaze with heavenly bodies, casting down a phenomenal light show of brilliant stars. Critters scampered around the camp that night, letting us know we were not alone. I tracked a bright moon as it began the slow-motion arc across a dark sky, then I fell asleep.

Morning came, and we quickly gathered our bags and rolled up the ground cloths. We stuffed the puffy down sleeping bags into their small nylon sacks, compressing them for storage before loading up the Volkswagen. Kirby and I maintained our own gear and were becoming a bit more efficient each night with the tasks involved in setting up camp. I flashed back to the many times I had gone backpacking, first with the Boy Scouts and the YMCA, then later on my own, to explore the basins and mountain ranges of southern Oregon.

Reading from a brochure picked up at a filling station, I found that Charles Crocker of Central Pacific Railroad enjoyed tagging railhead towns with the names of animals. This was supposedly how Elko had gotten its handle. Crocker had added an "o" for ease of pronunciation. The town had originally evolved from a tent city, coming into its maturity as a stop on the Transcontinental Railroad line. The contingent of Basque people in the area had come from the Pyrenees Mountains of northern Spain to settle in the Elko region and raise sheep.

The truck stops along the way provided us with ample restroom conveniences, and some even had pay showers. Pushing our four-banger east, we found just such a facility in Wendover, the border town located on the Nevada-Utah state line. On my first trip to Europe, I had learned how to take a sponge bath, using water in the sink and then drying off with a small bandana. After that, I considered all showers on the road to be luxuries. We picked up some supplies before heading down the long straight line of highway that pointed to the Great Salt Lake basin.

With the Wendover range to our right, we glided over the ribbon of asphalt that parted the white sea of salt crystals that was the Great Salt Lake desert. This was a repeat, for I had seen this unique and dazzling wonder of nature before, but the vastness of the salty plain still remained a treat. The dry lakebed extended out to where it met the mountains. I could just make out the horizontal scars on their towering faces, denoting the engraved shorelines of the ancient Lake Bonneville. We passed by the turquoise saline waters of the lake, viewing the barren rocky outcroppings that made up Antelope Island. These rose from the gleaming surface of the water, appearing as a ghost ship fashioned from stone. From that point, we continued on to eventually find ourselves in the suburbs of Salt Lake City.

The beautiful country I had seen so far had left the big cities lacking, and I yearned to escape from the more populated areas quickly. That afternoon we motored diagonally southeast across the center of Utah on Highway 6 until it veered east at Green River, leading us to the western boundary of Colorado. Crossing over the border, this colorful state immediately yielded up vibrant contrasts with its red soil, green fields, and blue sky. We passed through Grand Junction and headed northeast in the direction of the White River National Forest just southeast of the Roan Plateau. There we spent the third night on the road, just outside of Rifle, Colorado.

The next morning we decided to take a detour and explore Aspen. The road climbed ever deeper into the national park, and soon the great peaks looked down over us from each side of the road. Sheered off tree snags and the wide swaths of forest cleared by avalanches indicated this was big snow country. Aspen, a winter ski resort, reminded me much of Zermatt, the alpine Swiss village I had visited near the Matterhorn where the same type of quaint little shops lined the main street. In the late summer of 1966, Aspen lay virtually undiscovered, and I marked it in my mind as a place to which I must return.

The winding road out of town led us through more of the imposing and picturesque mountains. The VW strained as we labored up and over the Continental Divide, that point where the inclination of a raindrop is fatefully determined, flowing either toward the Pacific Ocean or the Gulf of Mexico. At Independence Pass, under the shadow of Mt. Elbert, I got out and ran up a small hill, only to find myself seriously out of breath. We were now at 12,095 feet, and the air was amazingly thin.

Spectacular scenes and magnificent views flanked our descent down the eastern side of the divide. We passed by the South Platt River and near the well-known prominence of Pikes Peak. Then we dropped down into the city of our destination, Colorado Springs. We stopped to give the Clarks a call from a pay phone to let them know we had arrived safely with the car.

They invited us for dinner, and that night we told stories around the kitchen table, recounting our recent adventures of driving from California in the Volkswagen. Mr. Clark was thirty-two years old, a Major in the Army, and just back from a tour in Vietnam. He gave us firsthand reports of a conflict that was just then beginning to cause some protests at home. We were grateful for their hospitality and after dinner they offered us a guest room with twin beds—and real sheets!

The next morning we faced a new reality. Hitchhiking was illegal in Colorado and subject to heavy fines. Consequently, we voted to leave the urban corridor that lay nestled under the eastern crest of the Rocky Mountains and board a Greyhound bus bound for Kansas City.

In no time, we were rolling across the long, gradual, downward slope that led us to the Kansas state line. We blasted through the sparsely populated towns in our path, their water towers and grain elevators protruding from the dry landscape as their only defining monuments. These high plains gathered less than moderate rainfall, and it was an area given to the growing of winter wheat, dry-land farming and cattle ranching.

Being tall of stature, I took great pleasure in the additional leg room the bus offered over the Volkswagen. I was able to commandeer two seats for a good deal of the journey. I found the views through the large tinted windows of the bus to be hypnotically entertaining. The eastern parts of Colorado and the great plains of Kansas played out before me like an endless film. It was relaxing, and after nightfall, I draped myself as best I could across the seats and dozed off. Sleeping on a bus is anything but home, yet before this long world trip was over, I would sleep in places that would make the Greyhound seem like the Ritz Carlton.

The extended bus ride gave me the opportunity for a period of personal reflection. The emotional wave of deliverance that seized me upon departure was still very strong. I sensed that I was standing at the front end of an important quest that in some essential way tied into my destiny. Independence Pass was an appropriate metaphor denoting my passage from the old life into my new one. I felt myself becoming leaner, having greater vitality, and coming to life.

I thought about the words of my grandfather Applegate the last time I saw him, shortly before his death. He expressed to me his regret at not finding the time to step out of his daily routine long enough to write his memoirs. He explained that his active life had been so consumed with the chores of basic survival and fielding one big project after another that there had been no real opportunity. I thought of the old trunk he always had close by, which contained the papers and letters that documented his life. Different family members told me it still existed, down in Mexico. I pondered on what secrets it might hold and if my journey would lead me to the trunk, to discover the treasures inside.

For years, I had dreamed of a time I would not be compelled to conform to the constraints of my surroundings. First, there were the constant pressures and expectations involved with athletics, followed by the tedium of educational pursuits. Then there was the mad dash out of college to form the foundations from which to launch a career. It had all unfolded at much too quick a pace. I yearned for the opportunity to discover fundamental truths on my own rather than having them laid on me by parents, coaches, pedantic professors, and the managers of the workplace. I was left feeling rebellious, stifled, and unfulfilled. Now, I was looking forward to studying at my own pace and traveling with a relatively open itinerary. I relaxed in the back of the bus, composing my thoughts and feelings, while transcribing many of them into my travel journal.

The desire to break away from the metropolitan chaos and pandemonium of the Kansas City bus depot was overwhelming. With some difficulty, we made it to the edge of town where we could hitchhike. In a stroke of good fortune, the first ride came only twenty minutes later with an elderly couple who mistakenly assumed we were Boy Scouts, standing alongside the road with our packs. They were hauling their travel trailer across the state of Missouri and then up the Mississippi River on the scenic route towards Rock Island, Illinois. We could not believe our good luck in having caught such a long ride. Kirby and I deposited our backpacks in the trailer and then loaded ourselves into their backseat.

Our benefactors were decidedly sympathetic to our plan for staying in Munich and shared a story about their two sons who had once gone to Europe with backpacks. Their boys were now U.S. Marines, shipping out soon for Vietnam. We made good time that morning, making several stops at roadside campgrounds where our new friends served us soft drinks, lunchmeat sandwiches, and grapes. I remember catching some sleep in the back seat, stirring only once when a large bumblebee flew into the car, causing quite a commotion.

They let us out at Rock Island, a charming little Midwestern town with tailored neighborhoods, located on the Mississippi. We were now just 165 miles from Chicago.

Our next ride brought us to a suburb of the Windy City, where we called Doreen, an editor friend of Kirby's. She put us up for the next several days, preparing a number of delicious meals in the time we were there. I particularly recall a veal dish that was a sheer delight. She was another one of many great people we met along the way who contributed positively to our trip across the country. Her apartment became our base of operations for touring the city. We walked great distances and visited many sites that first day, including the central downtown area called "the Loop." Another day we rode the city buses, seeing Grant Park, the Field Museum, and the Art Institute of Chicago, where we viewed a showing of Pablo Picasso's works.

Our departure from JFK was approaching and the level of tension was rising, as we still had not found an economical means of reaching New York. I worked the phone trying to find an inexpensive mode of transportation. I nearly succeeded in arranging a hitched ride on a private plane with a pilot who wanted some company, but unfortunately he changed his plans at the last minute. Finally, one of my calls to a car dealership paid off and I secured a vehicle for us to deliver to Washington, D.C. This relieved some of the pressure that had been building and there was even a fair allotment for fuel with the delivery.

Back on the road, Kirby and I took turns driving as we progressed eastward through the night and for a significant part of the next day. Worn out, we at last pulled into the dealership and dropped off the car. The manager was congenial and offered to give us a lift to the Washington D.C. airport where we could catch the air shuttle to JFK. The airport had been renamed a month after the assassination of President Kennedy in 1963. We received a short tour of the city on our way, seeing the White House, the Washington Monument, Lincoln Memorial, Arlington cemetery and the Capitol building itself.

We boarded the shuttle flight first and then paid the $15 to fly to New York after we had seated ourselves. JFK was packed. The boarding gate for our flight to Luxembourg was a mess, over-crowded for the most part with traveling students and immigrants returning to Europe on holiday. Some people stretched themselves out on the floor to sleep, while others just sat on their gear in a daze. There were people nervously pacing the floor while looking at their watches in frustration. We were now experiencing the delays that we had heard about with the cheapest flight across the Atlantic. I noticed a crudely printed sign that read, "Flight delayed due to mechanical difficulties." If they wanted to shake my confidence in the flight, those were exactly the words to use. The agonizing delays went on for five hours—in one-hour increments!

At last, we were ready for takeoff. The Icelandic Airlines jet roared down the runway and thrust itself skyward as the G-forces set us back in our seats. We rose above the cloud cover to the clear, calm atmosphere that lay above. Later, freckle-faced sandy-haired flight attendants with large gray eyes served us reindeer-lunchmeat sandwiches, followed by lamb burgers at dinner, the appetizing choices of Iceland. All of these lovely young women were similar in appearance, betraying their common origin from the same narrow Icelandic gene pool.

We were in the air for seven hours before touching down at Reykjavik airport. There we disembarked to the passenger lounge just under the control tower while they refueled our Douglas DC-6B airliner. A short time later, the message we all were becoming quite familiar with came over the loudspeaker. There would be more delays due to "mechanical difficulties."

This time the airline offered the passengers free drinks in the passenger's lounge, and in the six long hours that followed, the nervous passengers consumed every drop of alcohol the bar had to offer, including the liqueurs. We sat staring out the lounge windows in horror as Lilliputian workmen struggled up and down ladders that led to the tail of the prostrate avian beast. Some were pounding on the ailerons with hammers while still others were pulling and adjusting the external guy-wires attached to the fuselage. It all seemed quite bizarre.

At last it was time to board. After all that free-flowing alcohol, none of us was much concerned with the flight safety factor, and passengers in various stages of inebriation staggered aboard the wounded bird. Once again, the noise of great engines filled my ears as the aircraft rose into the air, penetrating the forward edges of an oncoming storm.

I can remember how the turbulence tossed us around for the next five hours, and continued even as the plane entered the glide path that would take us down into the very heart of the European Continent. The violent buffeting increased as our pilots fully committed themselves in their attempt to push the craft through a thick cloud cover in zero degrees visibility. My grip on the armrest tightened, and I was certain this was how my life would end!

Then, miraculously, at the last instant, we broke through the stormy vapors to land safely in Luxembourg. Someone later said that the ceiling was only 300 feet. Everyone I talked to was quite relieved to be safely on the ground. However, the thrill for me was far greater, for I had at last fulfilled a promise made to myself years before—a return to Europe.

Rathaus Glockenspiel

Autumn in Munich
Chapter Three

To forget pain is to be painless; to forget care is to be rid of it; to go abroad is to accomplish both.—Mark Twain

The powerful lights reflected brightly off the wet pavement of the Luxembourg airport runway, burning painfully into my tired eyes. The boarding delays in New York and Iceland had led me to the periphery of exhaustion. Touchdown brought with it an immense feeling of relief, bolstering me with a burst of energy that would carry me through the ordeals of immigration and customs.

Progressing through the various lines, I was increasingly aware of how my backpack continued to prove a convenient and efficient luggage option. I flashed back to my initial trip to Europe four years earlier when I had lugged two Samsonite suitcases around for the summer. They were cumbersome and drained me as effectively as a ball and chain. In addition, the cases were identical in every way and I was never quite certain of just what was in each! The backpack was lighter and more expedient to carry, placing the weight on my back and hips, freeing up my hands.

After a visit to the airport currency exchange, we stepped aboard the shuttle bus that would take us into town. We were still in the predawn hours of the morning, and darkness shrouded the unlit neighborhoods along the way. Initially the view was colorless and austere but soon manmade structures began to emerge.

As we approached the city, I could feel a vibration in the bus from the uneven cobblestones beneath us. It reminded me of driving the rough corrugated country roads of Oregon as a teen. Multi-storied buildings grew out of the diminishing darkness, with fortress walls crowding the edges of the road. In the obscure light, I could make out chateau-like structures with mansard roofs that sloped steeply downward in four directions. Corner turrets, capped with pointed helmets of tarnished metal, towered above the edifices. On other buildings, dormer windows protruded from the roofs of attic garrets, like large eyes peering out from under heavy shingled brows. Everything seemed very quaint, and I expected to see a stork on one of the many chimneys. There was a storybook quality to the architecture and I recalled illustrations from books of nursery rhymes I had read as a child. The shuttle came to rest at the curb in front of the transit station, and we exited to explore our new surroundings on foot. My heart continued to pump new life into my veins, and suddenly I was not as tired and in need of rest. To the contrary, it seemed with each step I was more rejuvenated.

My guidebook informed me that Luxembourg was one of the smaller countries of Europe, less than the size of the state of Rhode Island and landlocked by its neighbors, Germany, France and Belgium. The rolling countryside with its broad open valleys and lush green landscapes supported a myriad of small family farms. These rural areas contained a vast network of waterways, rivers and small streams that connected the isolated hamlets. Many of these towns held festivals to celebrate their local harvests, and fortunate the visitor who happened upon them. Luxembourg had a high standard of living and a constitutional monarchy that provided a stable form of government for its well-satisfied citizens. From what I read, it seemed an ideal place to live.

Kirby and I strolled over rain-soaked cobblestone streets in the general direction of the train station, escorting two young women we had met on our flight. They were elementary school teachers on a travel break, preparing to tour Europe in the cool and less congested fall months. The aroma of fresh baked bread wafted through the streets, and we followed the scent like bloodhounds, soon coming up with some hot rolls dispensed at the backdoor of a bakery. Some of the more optimistic vendors, undeterred by the inclement weather, prepared to open up their sidewalk seating. Other proprietors simply swept off their wet walkways, and then scuttled back inside, forestalling the opening of their establishments.

Later that morning the precipitation increased, coming down in noisy sheets, with droplets bouncing off the sidewalks. We said goodbye to the girls and made a fast trek for the depot, agreeing without debate that the train was our best mode of transportation to Munich. I was starting to fade again, and I yearned for a dry warm place out of the rain where I could relax and catch up on my rest. We were in luck when we found a large vacant compartment in one of the passenger cars. We stowed our gear and stretched out. I was looking forward to viewing the pastoral scenes of the well-tailored European countryside from the window.

The slight swaying motion of the train blended with the rhythmic cadence of the wheels meeting the tracks, serenading me into a deep sleep. Sometime later, I awoke to see the extraordinary scenes of natural beauty that were streaking past me. As the train rounded a particularly sharp corner, I could see its long sweeping tail of carriage cars trailing behind us. Like a great silver serpent in search of prey, the train wound its way over arched bridges and paralleled the contours of the manicured valleys.

We traveled south from Luxembourg to Metz, then veered southeast in the direction of Strasbourg and the Rhine River, the leading waterway of Europe. To the northeast was Baden-Baden, location of those historically famous Roman baths with the legendary thermal waters reputed to have extraordinary healing qualities. We proceeded into the fabled Black Forest, a venue for enchanting nature walks. Here one could find numerous artisans, among them the creators of the world famous cuckoo clocks. The scenery was impressive, and I was completely charmed by the time we reached Stuttgart.

It was easy to communicate with the German students we met on the train, as most of them spoke some English. They proudly informed us Stuttgart was famous for two products, automobiles and beer. Carl Benz and Gottlieb Daimler had developed early versions of the four-wheel vehicle here that later became the Mercedes-Benz. In addition, Ferdinand Porsche had fabricated the first prototypes of the VW Beetle on this spot, calling it the "people's wagon." The Porsche name had been elevated to world-class status in the realms of the automotive world with the introduction of the prestigious 356 Speedster followed by its offspring the 912, which had just recently been introduced. The Stuttgart name was on the celebrated factory badges secured to the hoods of these responsive sports cars.

After Stuttgart, the train followed a route through a low range of mountains that delivered us across the Danube River. The water was not blue, as one might expect, but brown from the inordinate amount of silt it carried, the result of the autumn rains. Then we came to Augsburg, one of the oldest cities in Germany, founded by the Roman Empire in 15 BC. The most difficult concept for an American traveling in Europe to grasp is the incredible age of the structures as compared to ours back home. Coming from a relatively young country in terms of Western civilization, it strained my mind to conceive of the rich and lengthy histories of some of the cities we were encountering.

The train continued on, penetrating into the innermost hub of Europe, to Bavaria, the oldest state in Germany, with a history spanning 1,000 years. The many and varied landscapes included the majestic Alps to the south, where the Winter Olympics of 1936 took place. Munich, our destination, sat on the distant northern fringe of those rugged snow and ice-laden Bavarian peaks. I would soon come to understand that the geography of this area contributed to the independent and hard-working nature of the Bavarian people, who placed great value on their sovereignty.

I could feel our momentum slowing as the locomotive reduced speed, and prepared to enter the Munich train station. From Luxembourg, it had taken seven long hours, giving me a chance to nap and do some writing in my journal. I retrieved my pack from the overhead luggage rack and squeezed out into the crowded hallway. There was a full car of people disembarking, all of them moving in one continuous flow of human bodies to the platform outside. The large sign in front of me said *Munchen*, a name I would later learn had evolved from the establishment of local monasteries here in the eighth century. It meant "the home of the monks." This Bavarian capitol would become my home for the next two months, and there would be occasions during the rainy days to come when I would feel like one of those cloistered monks of olden days.

Kirby and I stepped out from the *Hauptbahnhof* (train station) onto the main street of *Schillerstrasse*, suddenly immersed in the presence of old-world architecture and Bavarian ambiance. Grand Gothic, Renaissance, Baroque and Neo-classical architecture all existed within a few city blocks of each other. Moving down the crowded sidewalks, I saw the stout and rosy-cheeked German people walking with authority among the local students and the few remnants of foreign tourists left over from the summer invasion. My initial impression was that Munich was a vibrant city, populated by a very determined people, following a definite plan, with somewhere important to go, and something significant to do.

We meandered through narrow alleys that eventually led to the broader avenues. I spied great church spires, protruding as silhouettes against the skyline ahead. A few blocks beyond, we stood mesmerized by the attractions of the Town Hall, where we observed the *Rathaus-Glockenspiel*. Here bells and life-sized figures built into the workings of a monumental clock interacted to create a historical depiction. These representations captivated all who viewed them from the plaza below. I had seen this before on my first visit to the city in 1962, and it was delightful to experience it again.

It felt invigorating to walk, and I could smell the fresh air that swept down into Munich from the snowy slopes of the Alps to the south. Stopping for wiener schnitzel and a beer at the *Hofbrau Haus*, I marveled at the strength of the husky serving maids as they carried armloads of beer steins to the long tables of anxious and thirsty patrons. The food was substantial here, with heavy potato salad and a variety of sausages the staples. I saw a heavyset man enjoying a large bowl of bouillon soup with raw egg yolks floating around in it. I learned this was *bouillon mit Ei*, and it soon became one of my favorites.

We purchased a city map and found the correct tram that would lead us out of the city to the flat, the ride taking slightly less than an hour. Soon Kirby and I climbed the narrow staircase to Franz's apartment in the suburbs, at *31 Leiberweg*. It was one of a multitude of minimal living sites embedded in a long, drab, two-story building, most common in design. I was somewhat shocked when I saw how small the two-room garret with the low gabled ceiling really was. One room served as a combination living room and bedroom, while the other held a small kitchen with sink and stove. A small closet off the living room contained only a washbasin, no tub or shower. Water for washing dishes and taking sponge baths would need to be heated on the stove, as there was no hot water from the tap. I smiled at the idea of this being my new home until our departure for Greece in early November.

After unpacking, we put water on for tea and had a meal of heavy dark bread with butter, liverwurst, and slices of a local cucumber called *gurke*, items we had picked up from the store on our way in. Later I climbed into my down bag to take refuge from the cold air that flooded the flat after sundown. I had not slept in a bed since Chicago, nearly five days prior. My bag was a cocoon of warmth, and I quickly slipped into dreams of the scenic wonders that had passed before me from the windows of the train.

Kirby was an aspiring writer, and I awoke in the morning to the sounds of the incessant pecking that emanated from his Baby Hermes portable typewriter. I admired his routine, one I would soon see him faithfully lock into at the beginning of each day. He sat in a straight chair at the kitchen table under the hanging light, leaning slightly forward with the body language of one aggressively reaching into his work. He paused at times to ponder a new idea or to mull over a phrase and then, after refocusing, produced a flurry of keystrokes. I learned much about the personal discipline that writing requires from my daily observations of him with his work.

A cold cloud of reality settled over me in the days that followed, and now I searched for a blueprint on how to use the next two months of free time productively. I reviewed the considerable number of books written in English that sat on the shelves of Franz's personal library and, in the ensuing weeks, I read them all. *Henderson the Rain King* and *Herzog* by Saul Bellow were among those I devoured. Still, I was aware of a growing personal restlessness, one that over time began to haunt me, causing some degree of distress. There was no job now to give me structure and no daily task to provide a base on which to build. I needed to form a plan. This uneasy feeling compelled me to stay busy any way I could. I had now come face to face with the liberated lifestyle for which I had yearned, and I was not completely sure of what to do with it. The rainy season had come to Munich as well, imposing certain limitations, but only if I chose to let it.

Many of my days commenced with the two hour walk into Munich, where I passed through the expansive green commons of *Englischer Gartens*, one of the largest urban parks in the world. Once reaching the old part of the city, I visited the *Volksbad*, or the "people's bath" where for one German mark, or about a quarter, I could take a shower and have a fresh towel. Although I had become proficient at boiling water and having a sponge bath at the flat, the facilities in Munich were much more desirable.

On these sojourns into the city, I would frequent my favorite establishments, finding a secluded corner in some ancient wood-walled *gasthaus*, isolating myself to feverishly write in my journal. This activity kept alive the dreams of writing while providing a daily measure of discipline on which to adhere. I did manage to compose several short stories from my early school days and other childhood camping adventures. I even made additions to the book of poetry started on my previous trip to Europe. Usually in late afternoon, I took the tram back to the flat, often joining Kirby for dinner at the small kitchen table. I continued to saturate the long evenings with a great deal of reading.

It took about three weeks for the patina of good feelings, which had been present since my exciting departure, to wear off. A strange melancholy overtook me, which was due in no small part to the deteriorating weather conditions. Occasionally, while taking the tram home at night, nostalgic tremors of homesickness would shake me. I quickly steeled myself to these attacks in an effort to be convinced such feelings were temporary and would quickly pass. At my stop, the tram jolted me back from these wistful and evocative dreams to the reality of the moment. Then I would step out into the cold and rainy night, and walk the remaining distance back to the flat.

The lack of a clear purpose turned my heart and head to thoughts of San Jose and the girl I had left behind. I found myself writing a barrage of letters to her, in a misplaced attempt to regain the past. It was not long before I learned that walking forward while looking back was very painful. I also missed my co-workers at the finance company and the fair-weather friends who frequented the dart pubs and gathered around the pool tables with me on weekends. Although I continued writing with determination, I one day fell to the sad conclusion that quite possibly I did not have anything noteworthy to say. Then I promptly discarded this discouraging thought.

The fall days of September soon gave way to the gloomy skies of October. The walls of the small apartment continued to be confining. Regardless of the weather outside, I did find some solace in going to town and made the journey nearly every day. It was pleasurable to take the crowded trams down the long wet streets that parted the repetitive rows of mass produced apartment houses.

There were some trips into Munich where I stayed late into the evening, favoring a walk down *Schillerstrasse* and losing myself in the various nightclubs that were abundant in this part of town. Sometimes I danced into the late hours with the local girls who shyly stood at the edge of the dance floor, neither of us able to speak the language of the other. More than once, I found myself catching the midnight tram back, sleeping well past my stop, only to feel the hand of the conductor shaking me at the end of the line.

On those rare days that were void of precipitation, I would seek out a secluded bench near the large lake in *Englischer Gartens* and watch the black swans motor serenely across the glassy waters like toy boats. It was tranquil here, and having decided early on not to bring a camera on my journey, I tried my hand at sketching. I enjoyed trying to capture these graceful birds with lead pencil in my tablet. Other times I labored at catching the lines of age on an elderly person's face, or duplicating the naked branches of an autumn tree gone dormant for the winter. Never having had the time to pursue such fancies, I began to welcome this period of experimentation. I carried journals and supplies with me in my small Icelandic Airlines travel bag. Writing down my observations and descriptions of Munich also gave me much pleasure, while reading more of the local history added meaning to all I was seeing.

I was coming to understand that most of the people of Europe had experienced living in close proximity with each other for centuries. This was a natural consequence of having less physical land within which to expand, giving way early on to a greater social consciousness. The evidence of socially minded efforts abounded, especially with their public transportation systems. There was an overall emphasis on the economy of space and an efficient use of natural resources. This would be a recurring theme as I continued to write down my observations of life on the Continent.

Books belonging to Franz, detailing Munich's history, revealed the city had always been a hotbed of political activity. In the 1890s, there was the *Wandervogel* movement, an idealistic group taken with the romantic notion of returning to nature and divorcing themselves from the materialism that had sprung to light with the industrial revolution. I marveled at how similar their sentiments were to those that had been brewing inside the subculture back home.

They longed to live off the land as their grandparents had, pursuing a healthier lifestyle and living closer to the earth. They shunned the short-term artificial gains and uncertainty offered by the cities. Moreover, they were extremely unhappy with what they called "the oppression of parental authority" and "the conformity fostered in the German schools." This was a male-only group that distinguished themselves by donning the robust attire of walking shorts and hiking boots. I mused to myself how, aside from the way they dressed, history certainly does repeat itself. My studies of German history continued.

In the beer hall back rooms of Munich, Adolph Hitler held the first meeting of the German Worker's Party on February 24, 1920. Here, from the most humble of political beginnings, he set a course that spawned cataclysmic events that would shake the existing world order. He used these nooks and crannies where the common people congregated, as a forum to clarify his ideology and political views. The consequences of the German defeat in World War I (1914–1918) and the terms of the Treaty of Versailles, among other things, had led

Germany into a period of severe inflation, giving rise to very high unemployment and an impoverished middle class.

After the worldwide economic crisis of 1929, conditions in Bavaria had become even worse. The political situation was confused; the people were desperate, and the mood was ripe for something new. A feeling of hopelessness existed among the populace as they experienced a complete and total economic depression. Simply put, the time was right for the coalescing of the many different political factions into two main parties. On one side was the Communist Party and on the other the National Socialists, later to become known as the Nazi Party.

Any mention of the Third Reich turned my thoughts to Dachau, a small medieval town about ten miles northwest of Munich. I had visited it in 1962 for a firsthand look at the infamous German concentration camp that had come to the world stage after the liberation of Europe. Opened in 1933 by the National Socialist government, it was the first camp exclusively built for political prisoners and became a prototype for the additional camps that followed. Tall and formidable electrified fences topped with barbed wire surrounded the camp, interrupted only by the guard towers with a clear view of the entire landscape. In addition, the walls and ditches placed around the perimeter of the camp further prevented a prisoner's escape. Here, I felt the distinct presence of the "heart of darkness" that once reigned, leaving lessons for all of humanity to take note of and never forget.

The same beer halls that once housed participants bent on transforming Germany and even the world were now the new tables of international goodwill. Here tourists from all over the world mixed with the local people in high celebration. Oktoberfest, the largest beer festival in existence, offered an exciting atmosphere that far exceeded any state fair or carnival that I had ever attended. The riotous laughter, gaiety, and even at times bacchanalian chicanery was intense and continued for sixteen long days and nights, ending the first Sunday of October.

I entered these great halls to see many local *Muncheners* wearing the traditional Bavarian apparel. Robust serving maids were everywhere, adorned in peasant blouses and tightly corseted vests that exposed remarkable cleavages while they served the beer in mammoth one-liter steins. Often they brought with them six to ten of these great vessels in their arms, slamming them down on the plank tables that were packed with anxious patrons.

The bands played on throughout the day and into the night from their elevated platforms. There were many large tents, some appearing to be permanent, with vast main floors, housing long parallel lines of tables. Outside there were sideshows, like a circus back home, with souvenir booths and food shops full of Bavarian specialties. Radishes, sausages, roasted chickens and large pretzels were available to all the celebrants.

Oktoberfest had been a welcome release for me, although there was still more bad weather to come in the remaining days of October. The advent of November brought with it the return of Franz and an end to our two-month stay in Germany. Franz was an excellent photographer and we enjoyed examining his incredible photos from his travels one evening before our departure.

Expressing our deepest gratitude to him for the use of the flat, we bid a farewell to Deutschland and boarded the train for Austria, to begin the next leg of the journey. I was happy to be traveling again and could feel my enthusiasm growing.

The Golden Roof

The Brenner Pass
Chapter Four

Afoot and light-hearted I take to the open road,
Healthy, free, the world before me
The long brown path before me leading wherever I choose.
—Walt Whitman, "Leaves of Grass"

Kirby and I journeyed south by train, away from Munich and into the Alps, piercing a geologic barrier of monumental proportions. Over time, layers of skewed and compressed stone had pushed heavenward, to display a vast horizon line of irregular forms. There were tall, pointed, saw-tooth profiles, cloaked in hoods of snow and ice, tilted up against the backdrop of gray skies. Glaciers ground their way down the steep ramparts, scouring, polishing and pressing their snouts forward, their solid forms eventually transforming into liquid. Frozen rivers then became streams and torrents, producing pure fountains of fresh water pulled ever lower by gravity to quench the thirsty valleys below.

The train was fast, smooth and efficient, moving with ease through routes that once created nearly insurmountable problems for Hannibal and his invading armies of men and elephants. We glided on lines of track laid over picturesque bridges that spanned gaps between rugged mountain towers, then disappeared into tunnels that burrowed through solid rock, blocking off the light of day.

Vistas of unspoiled natural beauty passed by as I peered out through the large windows of the car. The air was clear, and I could see for miles to the distant jagged edges of the Tyrollean Alps. For centuries, people had frequented the health farms and wellness sanitariums that thrived here, to avail themselves of nature's cleansing and healing influences. I could feel these effects even from where

I sat on the train, and the deeper we penetrated into the Austrian landscape the more vibrant I felt. I welcomed this revitalization after the two months in Munich.

The steady vibrations of the train left me tranquil, the desired state so many young people of my generation seemed to be seeking. I flashed back to a few years earlier, musing if only we all lived on trains, as a man I once met, who had his private railcar freighted all over the U.S. at his expressed whim. Willis was a fascinating individual who owned and maintained several small railroads. One of them was the Yreka Western in northern California. It serviced the railroad spur to Montague, where I had loaded boxcars with lumber by hand in the summer months, earning money to help cover the cost of college.

My mood remained elevated, and I yearned to be hiking on the network of pristine trails that occasionally came into view from the window of the passenger car. I wanted to hear the squeaks of the clevis pins in my backpack as they made their stressful calls in cadence with my boots. I felt it was time to push myself physically and again feel the blood rushing in my veins and hear my heartbeat strong in my ears. I was anxious to burn away the sediment formed from the rainy days in Munich. The loud whistle from the train announced our entry into the next major city.

The locomotive dramatically reduced speed, and then eased into the station at Innsbruck. I had discovered the name of the city meant literally, "Bridge over the Inn." This municipality, located in a broad valley between snow-capped mountains, enjoyed an international reputation as a wonderland for winter sports. It became a state capital in the early fourteen hundreds, solidifying back then its future stature in Austrian history.

Outside, I could see large groups of people, some in traditional dress, milling around the platform and the public squares beyond. The old-world shops and cafes beckoned me to come and explore. I yearned to disappear down the crowded walkways among kiosks stocked with a variety of treasures, and I quickly readied myself to disembark the train and investigate these new environments.

After a short stroll through the hub of Old Town we found a reasonably priced hotel, checked into our room and stowed the gear. Later we walked out into the streets to discover more about this landmark city. Amidst the excitement over being in a new location, I found myself eager to revisit the older sections of the city to view that classic mixture of Gothic and Baroque architecture, the Golden Roof or *Goldenes Dachl*. This well-known building has a long-standing reputation among ardent tourists and locals alike for displaying one of the more memorable and characteristic Tyrollean attractions in Innsbruck. The roof shed a reflection of golden light from the gilded copper shingles on the protruding addition affixed high on its two-story facade. I had come to view its unique and historical attributes in the summer of 1962, when traveling with Tom. The shadows cast on the town from the mountains around the rim of the valley were now enveloping us. I recalled one of these from my previous visit to Innsbruck.

The round-topped, 7,381-foot *Patscherkofel*, well-known for its exciting downhill runs, had played host to winter sport enthusiasts for decades. In early November, its exposed and scarred flanks offered an imposing presence to the south. Four years earlier, Tom and I had ridden the scenic gondola lift to the summit, and with a few apples, a loaf of hard bread, and some cheese, taken all afternoon to saunter back down the seemingly endless incline to the base of the prominence. The ground cover and sparse conifers at the higher elevations gave way to the thicker forests lower down. *Patscherkofel* was the mountain of the Olympic Winter Games where many champions had fine-tuned their skills on its steep slopes. Abundant opportunities existed here for all levels of proficiency, and this area remained a big draw for the European and international winter vacationers.

That night I located the same restaurant where I had first eaten "tarter steak" four years earlier. I again ordered this unusual dish composed for the most part of a half pound of uncooked ground sirloin with a raw egg sitting in a crater depressed in the middle. Encircling this were ringlets of raw onion, artistically arranged and spaced evenly apart, each enclosing a different spice, herb, or seasoning. There were even capers sprinkled about. I began to knead the malleable reddish ball with a fork and a spoon, mixing in the condiments as I went. I was slightly less apprehensive about consuming the raw meat this time.

Several relaxing days passed after which we were ready to continue our journey in the direction of Venice. This time we decided to employ the more romantic option of hitchhiking again. Forever optimistic, we walked out onto the road that led to the Brenner Pass Summit. The incongruities in size between the small European cars and us with our packs soon presented a problem. Unfortunately, the only car to stop in the first two hours kindly offered to take just one of us aboard, which was understandable due to the lack of interior space in the tiny vehicle. We discussed the notion of separating and then graciously declined the offer. Instead, we trudged uphill along the dusty apron of the road, inhaling an inordinate amount of exhaust fumes from the line of slow moving cars. This was very different from the visions of hiking in the Tyrol that I once held.

With diminished spirits and failing lungs, we took one of the inviting trails that led away from the emissions pollution of the road and disappeared into an evergreen tunnel of dense brush and trees. The path led ever deeper into the stands of dark green forest that wrapped around the lower ridges of the alpine slopes. Our relief from the switchbacks clogged with cars, freight trucks, and buses was instant.

Soon, we were trekking over a path that led across a narrow hand-hewn log bridge that spanned a small, clear stream. I removed my bandana from my back pocket and submerged it down into the cold glacial waters, which quickly caused my hand to ache. Then I wiped the wet cloth across my sweaty face and down my neck, suddenly feeling wonderfully refreshed. Later, we crossed other small streams on stepping stones edged with thick green moss, nourished by the same icy flow that trickled by. We came to places where the water fell steeply in a cascade, meandering around tree roots and through fertile troughs of mountain soil that led eventually to the valley floor below. The air was fresh with the scent of pine and fir.

Wildflowers were prevalent, spilling out in patches over the occasional fields and high prairies we encountered, adding colorful brocade to the landscapes we were discovering. Constantly changing, the narrow trail would wind through a dense growth of conifers and then open out onto yet another alpine pasture. Here I saw carpets of *Alpenrose* spreading out evenly around the bases of some of the derelict haystacks. My travel companion seemed as pleased with our new surroundings as was I.

Kirby had a quiet countenance about him, often maintaining a faint smile on his face when we were on the trail together. I supposed, but never was really sure, that his deep, active and well-educated mind traveled far, far away at times. He was a seasoned hiker and a veteran of many solo treks deep into the Sierra Nevada where he survived for weeks at a time while communing with nature. I had been impressed from the first time I heard him speak of these fascinating journeys. Later, he increased the intrigue by unveiling vivid stories of his solitary adventures in northern Pakistan where he traveled in search of the Wally of Swat, an obscure potentate who ruled a little known valley kingdom hidden away in the Hindu Kush.

These stories brought to mind images from the utopian fictional work, *Lost Horizon* by the English novelist James Hilton. The setting was Shangri-La, a city well-hidden in a secluded valley of Tibet and populated with spiritually advanced lamas, divorced from the troubles of the world.

There were other stories Kirby told, of teaching in Japan, writing for a newspaper in New Zealand and the exploits associated with living and teaching in Switzerland for a year. I was learning more from Kirby, seeing where he often understated himself and his accomplishments. He seemed very content with his lifestyle.

Hiking farther up the mountain, I redirected my reflections to the current surroundings and how they related to my own path. I speculated on the astounding contrast between the more desirable track through the woods we were now on and the one along the congested mountain road from which we had just escaped. I could not help but ponder the fascinating parallels to life in general with regard to the many choices we sift through in seeking a direction. At times in my life, I had expended great amounts of energy towards making the wrong path appear to be the right one, apprehensive of making a change. After sufficient pain, it was obvious I needed something different, possibly even something involving more risk. Stepping into a new venue and situation, I soon found it was exactly what I needed all along. Increasingly, I was coming to believe in the adage that, "as one door closes so does another one open." Circumstances I once viewed as insurmountable almost always looked better after I took that first small step in making a change. So it had been with this trip.

There was a vague degree of familiarity in these landscapes. Where had I seen this remarkable country before? This sensation nagged at me while my mind reviewed early memories of movies like *Heidi* and *The Sound of Music*. The cool mountain air sanitized my lungs. Occasionally we came upon an unlocked hut stocked with provisions for the lost or injured trekker. Larger rustic lodges came into view, inhabited by local families that lived on the premises. Constructed of stone and timber, we usually found them nestled at the edge of small clearings with the dark forest providing a pleasing background. These structures supported slate roofs and displayed large log porches full of evenly stacked firewood. There were ornately carved flower boxes projecting out from under windows like oversized drawers. Some of these were artfully tole painted. There were Tyrollean designs scrolled into the window shutters and on the fascia boards that sloped up to the roof peaks.

We soon realized these were commercial hostels, made available for overland hikers like ourselves. Exhausted from an uphill climb lasting most of the day, we decided to stop and take a room for the night at one of these lovely country mountain inns. We were eagerly welcomed by the proprietor and his family.

That evening it became very cold outside after sundown, and we were wise to stop when we did. I soaked up the heat from the fireplace after a heavy dinner of sausages and potatoes. It was good to have the time to bring my travel journal up to date, and I wrote by the light of candles and the flickering light that glanced around the room from the fireplace. There were a great number of framed black and white photographs on the walls of the lodge, depicting the bygone days when wooden skis and hemp ropes had been used by the skiers and climbers. Some of the old sports equipment hung from the log rafters, making interesting curios and lending a special atmosphere to the old lodge.

I walked down the dimly lit hallway and found the common restroom where I washed up before turning in. My bed-frame was composed of heavy wooden planks mortised into a thick headboard with a mountain scene carved across its face. A heavy down comforter, wrapped in a white duvet, covered the bed. I cracked the wood sash window open and settled in for one of the best night's sleep I had ever known. I vaguely remember the sound of cowbells in the night. I did not wake up until the morning light poured through the windows and the pleasing aromas of breakfast drifted in from the kitchen. We ate heartily and then, after paying our pleasant hosts, resumed the long trudge up the mountain.

The high altitude pastures and meadows were breathtaking and I recalled the innkeeper talking about this general area at dinner, the night before. He revealed to us that the dairy cattle grazed at the higher elevations while crop cultivation and harvesting took place lower down in the valley. This explained the presence of cows we had begun to see. In the distance, the craggy peaks of the Alps lanced the sky with their sharp pointed hats of stone and ice. In our second day of trekking, we followed our innkeeper's instructions and climbed steadily in the direction of the pass. Finally, after many hours hiking, tired and soaked with sweat, we found ourselves approaching the Brenner Pass border station, the point where we would be crossing into Italy.

The pass, named after the border village of Brennero on the Italian side, had been a strategic location throughout history. This route had been a coveted possession since Roman times, later becoming a key invasion route used by the Germanic tribes as they moved into northern Italy. Once a pathway for mule trains and crude carts, it was opened up for carriages in the late seventeen hundreds. They completed the transalpine railroad in 1867, allowing it to become a vital link between points north and south. The international borders had relocated some throughout history, but after World War I, the control of the pass came to be shared by Italy and Austria, connecting Innsbruck, Austria, with Bolzano, Italy.

The Brenner Pass, at an elevation of 4,495 feet, is one of the easier of the Alpine passes to negotiate by car, but on foot, we could now testify to having a slightly different experience. I calculated we had made an invigorating trek with full packs of some eighteen miles uphill in the two days before reaching the border.

We picked up our pace as we approached the border station and prepared to hand over our passports to the official at the sentry shack. Apparently he had seen us walking toward him for some time. He asked if we were Germans, erroneously supposing only they would attempt hiking the Brenner Pass all the way from Innsbruck! With a measured sense of pride from our accomplishment we answered, "No, we're Americans!"

I had gotten the energetic stimulus from the physical activity that I had needed. I felt renewed, and ready for the next stage of the trip that would take us into Italy. A hard rain had begun to pelt us, and it seemed from our previous trials that hitchhiking here had proved an unsatisfactory option. We decided to board the train at the Brenner Pass Station. It was rewarding to find ourselves settled down once again in comfortable seats and anticipating another scenic ride that would deliver us to our next stop, Venice, that celebrated city of canals.

The Rialto Bridge

Canals of Venice
Chapter Five

*There is something so different in Venice from any other place
in the world, that you leave at once all accustomed habits and
everyday sights to enter an enchanted garden.* —Mary Shelley

The Italian train rolled steadily along, transporting us deeper
into yet another country. I reclined on the comfortable cushioned
seats, savoring the tide of pleasurable sensations produced from the
long climb up the Brenner. The laborious trek over the shoulders
of the Austrian foothills had made one thing obvious; it was time
to eliminate any surplus weight I was carrying. This was the ideal
occasion to take a discerning physical inventory, a judicious review
of everything that I had accumulated in the dark crannies of my
backpack since Munich. Extracting my limited belongings, I placed
the individual items onto the seat next to me and then, with intense
scrutiny, I analyzed the necessity of each. We were passing into the
winter months, so I chose to keep my excess clothing. Nevertheless,
there was nearly always an extra book or a sacrificial hat that I
could pass on. I seemed to attract books and hats for some reason. I
weighed the pain of loss against the pleasure gained from the purging
process, then made the difficult decisions needed.

The feeling associated with traveling freely through Europe
toting most of my worldly possessions on my back was exhilarating.
"Know what you have," a wise friend had once told me. However, in
all honesty, there was a bit more. There remained back home a trunk
full of books, some fishing gear, a couple boxes of extra clothes, and
$500 on deposit with the Bank of America to give me a start when
I got home. Already on the trip, I had parted with certain favorite
items not long after acquiring them, the result of constantly reducing

the burden of weight and the stress of attachment. My discarded baggage often made suitable parting gifts for those I had met along the way. "Less is more," was becoming my traveler's credo, my new philosophy of life.

I admired the words, thoughts, and disciplines of Henry David Thoreau. His writings, which passionately addressed topics such as economy and simplicity, were now influencing me as a traveling man. Personally, I had always been interested in improving methods and streamlining living techniques towards a desired goal of minimalism. Now, with my new vocation, it had taken on an even more significant meaning.

I continued to reflect as the train streaked on, eating up the many miles that lay before us en route to Venice. I had grown up immersed in the great outdoors and working in close proximity to natural settings. These were some of the benefits that small town living provided, coming of age in the sleepy hollows of rural Oregon. My post-university initiation to the fast pace of suburban life in San Jose had now led me to reach for new alternatives. The high rents, crowded environments, and the hectic freeway commute each morning were all tie-downs to a lifestyle that I had increasingly found questionable. It seemed that city-life brought with it a host of complications and it was good to be free of it.

I gazed out the window, admiring the pale and chalky protrusions, reaching high into the sky like the decaying spires of stone cathedrals. These were the Dolomites, glorious and breathtaking creations fashioned by the slow and steady hand of the elements through the ages. Towers of compressed stone had grown out of the ancient seabeds, now resembling the contorted shapes of castle walls and flying buttresses. Colors faded and brightened from moment to moment as the sun appeared and then hid itself behind the sweeping ranges of clouds. Here and there, I could see a turquoise lake or a patch of snow among the alpine meadows that lay beneath the pinnacles. The valley of treasures soon passed and these few fleeting glimpses were all I would see.

The train snaked away from the city of Bolzano towards Verona, the ancient provincial capital of northern Italy and a favorite transportation crossroads since Roman times. Early writings have indicated that Julius Caesar chose this city for his extended vacations. William Shakespeare had used Verona as the setting for his timeless tale of lovers, *Romeo and Juliet*.

I recalled enrolling in Shakespeare classes one summer in Ashland, location of the famous Oregon Shakespearean Festival. The respected Angus Bomer had first initiated the idea of the festival in the 1930s, completing the construction of a theater resembling London's Globe, in lovely Lithia Park shortly after that. I was fortunate to have Angus as my professor, and he actually conducted some of our classes on the stage of the theater itself. Angus had committed to memory a great number of the parts in his long productive life. My thoughts moved away from Shakespeare and back to the gentle motion of the passenger car.

We had turned eastward, later stopping for a short time in Padova where more passengers boarded. Soon we resumed full speed for the final segment of the trip to Venice. I was anxiously awaiting my entry into this historical wonder that had been the cultural magnet to artists and travelers for centuries. There was barely time to gather my backpack and use the restroom before I heard a proud little man in a black coat and conductor's hat calling out a familiar name, "*Venezia!*"

Leaving the train, Kirby and I proceeded into the mazes and labyrinths that led away from Santa Lucia Station. After crossing the Ponte dei Scalzi, one of the many bridges in the city, we followed walkways along the large inverted S-curve that was the Grand Canal. Our route then veered off onto side streets where we lost ourselves deep in the commercial tangles of small shops in the central district. The footbridges were works of art, ornately decorated in stone relief and gracefully arched to accommodate the gondolas that silently glided under them. I reflected on what I had recently read on the train about the city of canals.

Venice is one of the most unusual cities on earth, as it has canals in place of streets and boats in place of cars. The impressive palazzos, or palaces, faced the canals, reflecting the once grand residences and headquarters of renowned Venetian families.

Long ago men of vision raised this city out of a marsh, building it over a foundation of pinewood pilings driven deep into the earth. These were hardened with layers of impermeable stone supported on an archipelago of low-lying mud-bank islands. From these humble beginnings, approximately 1,200 years ago, the city gradually rose to prominence as an important trading center. This sizable colonial empire evolved as Venice, the "Queen of the Adriatic," and soon cast a wide net of commercial and political influence over the entire eastern Mediterranean. The full force of the city's glory manifested itself during the fifteenth and sixteenth centuries when a multitude of fateful influences melded together to produce an age of opulence. The original interlocking network of canals eventually became the most defining feature of the city.

My history courses had imparted the theory that all great powers reach an apex, after which their essence begins to wane and modify. Venice was no exception. The city slowly began to change its role from the purveyor of economic and political authority to something much different. Over time, the slow evolutionary search for identity yielded something new for the city. Venice's incredible art treasures and its important cultural heritage began to dictate an ideal future direction. The Venetians became the restorers of objects of art and with this, the rightful custodians of their own rich heritage. As a result, great schools of restoration came into existence and flourished in the city.

It was now dusk, and we walked footpaths in a subdued light, created by the long shadows that stretched between the multi-storied facades. This was a search for anything that might resemble a hotel or inn. We came upon a suitable place adjacent to a small plaza, where a quaint outdoor cafe adjoined the front office. I quickly negotiated our lodging, and they led us to our hotel room. It was a relief to find a place, and I leaned my pack against the wall. I opened the weathered green shutters to provide a view of the narrow canal below. Ignoring the temptation to collapse on the spot, I made the extra effort to go back out to do some exploring. To my delight, the evening held more discoveries, as I found Venice to take on new life bathed in the light that reflected off the canal waters.

The stair steps leading to the marble footbridges elevated me up and over the manmade channels of water as I followed the soft sounds of bells from Saint Mark's Campanile. This was a bell tower, a simple brick shaft adorned at its crest, pressing up into the air some 300 feet. As I strolled casually along, I looked up to see great oversized windows, framed by the elegant stone facades of the ancient palazzos. Through them, I could see enormous chandeliers hanging from the frescoed ceilings of grand ballrooms. These displays reflected the warm light of earth tones from the faceted glittering crystals. I envisioned the spectacular social events that must have taken place within those selective walls. My senses overrun by the countless evening charms of Venice, I decided to return to the hotel. With some luck, I found my way back through the narrow alleyways, guided by the light of a luminescent moon.

The preserved Venetian architectural wonders were a testament to the traditions of a city that graciously hosted its perennial visitors. There were Gothic, Renaissance, and Byzantine legacies, all within close proximity of each other. The city itself was a living and working art museum that constantly attracted a new and never-ending stream of devotees. Antiquated convents had become important locations for art restoration, housing the various institutes involved with this important work. Some of the larger commercial warehouses of the past were now prestigious museums displaying the countless treasures of a city that hovered just above the sea. Many Venetians partitioned their once grand style palazzos to produce additional sought-after apartments. Shops and hotels had grown up inside the walls of ancient structures, replacing, restoring, and combining the new and the old in the same original facility.

The city, while resilient, was still fragile and continued to find itself threatened by the seasonal peril of flooding as rivers filled and overflowed the lagoon. Nevertheless, many of the Venetian buildings were surprisingly healthy, continuing to withstand the punishing effects of the elements for many hundreds of years due to age-old efforts towards preservation. The primary layout of the city itself had not altered much in the last two centuries, with change taking place slowly and gradually from within the original walled perimeters, undetectable from outside viewing.

The next morning we enjoyed a motor launch ride down the Grand Canal in a *vaporetto*, or water-bus, viewing more of the magnificent facades. This was a major corridor of marine traffic. The *traghetti*, or small foot passenger ferries, crisscrossed the canal both in front and behind us. The light in the daytime was spectacular, rendering resplendent colors off the buildings and proving yet another visual treat. The boat passed under the Ponte di Rialto (the Rialto Bridge), completed in 1592. It was the renowned architectural marvel of Antonio da Ponte, engineered and constructed during the Renaissance. This archway has maintained its span across the Grand Canal for more than 400 years. Its footings sit on thousands of subterranean wooden pilings and accommodate the numerous adjoining shops on the main body of the bridge. This remarkable achievement projected a striking image, an archetype of pure form, forever memorable as a Venetian landmark.

Our well-designed *vaporetto* cut smoothly through the water, taking the right of way over the smaller craft to each side of us. This was the ideal method to tour the major attractions. We stopped at the Basilica di Santa Marco and got off the craft. This famous structure was undergoing major repairs from damage from the disastrous floods that had struck Italy just that spring. We walked around the Piazza San Marco as best we could amongst the hordes of tourists, photographers, and pigeons. We had to negotiate through some standing pools of water that sometimes inundated the plaza certain times of the year. This trapezoidal-shaped *piazza*, properly described as one of the great drawing rooms of Europe, was one of those special places on earth where travelers love to congregate.

We motored out to Lido Beach, stopping for a long walk, and then again boarded the water-bus for the return to the Grand Canal. The skyline of the old city before us, I marveled at how fortunate I was to be living through these memorable experiences. Each new day brought with it novel and stimulating sights. It was good to be on the move again.

Some mornings Kirby stayed behind at the hotel writing, while I investigated the city's seemingly endless web of walkways, making fascinating discoveries along the way. Small and active business enterprises and cottage industries flourished behind the thick walls and plank doors. Each housed a treasure trove of different manufacturing skills and products. One such specialty that particularly raised my curiosity was the blowing of glass. I devoted an entire day to learning more about this traditional Venetian profession.

The Venetian glass shops have maintained this practice dating back some 700 years. Their artistic creations kept me fixated for hours. Most of these artisan skills were gifts from father to son, master to apprentice. I watched as they pulled globs of hot molten-glass from the furnace and fashioned them into finely detailed artifacts, vases, and tableware. I was most intrigued with "end of day," a product made from the colorful bits and pieces of leftover glass that had accumulated on the floor and workbenches at the end of the shift. This random collage of spun colors in the finished pieces was always original and stunning. The work looked difficult. The grimy faces of the heat-scorched artisan workers showed lines of age, their hands scarred and their leather aprons baked into hard shields from the constant heat of the raging furnaces.

Venice cast a wonderful spell over me, filling my soul with wonder and delight. After a few days, I could feel the rhythm of the canals as they perpetually cleansed the city, providing a matchless existence of renewal for the populace here. The ocean's relentless heartbeat pumped in new waves of vitality, nourishing this historical jewel. But now, it was time to leave.

On my last morning, I stepped outside to greet the cool sea breezes and invisible currents that swirled between the old stone buildings bordering the constricted streets. Street signs had been of little use to me in my early wanderings, challenging me to memorize my route based on landmarks. Later, I had succumbed to the pleasure of just being lost in this paradise. Now I was more familiar with the city, and I walked briskly along, confident I could find my way back to the hotel. I would miss the sounds of water lapping at the edges of canals. It would be hard to forget the splendid sights and smiling people that filled the narrow streets.

The travel itch had struck again and suddenly the memorable visit to Venice was at a close. Far too often, the experienced joys of one location conflicted with the need to continue on to the next. On numerous occasions, I had to leave a place just as I began to feel at home. A slice of Venetian life would have to do for now, as it was time to look ahead, to a new country—to Yugoslavia.

Dubrovnik

The Yugoslav Route
Chapter Six

We travel, some of us forever, to seek other states,
other lives, other souls. —Anais Nin

Our decision to travel the length of the Yugoslav coastline on our way to Greece weighed heavily on my mind as the train left Venice for Trieste, Italy. One of the primary reasons for choosing Yugoslavia as our next country, was the intriguing prospect of it being a Communist country. Although it was legal for Americans to pass through this principality, it still remained taboo. However, the opportunity to see this forbidden territory was hard to pass up, and I thought it just might offer a chance to satisfy my nagging curiosity regarding the lives of people living under a different political system. How would it compare to ours? Was it better? Was it worse and if so, why? Yugoslavia presented a perfect occasion to expand the boundaries and to learn more.

We had been under the mistaken notion that it was possible to travel overland to the Peloponnesus of Greece through Albania, that unfriendly satellite country that butted up to the southern end of Yugoslavia, where the two nations met the Adriatic. We soon learned there was another option, that of taking a small passenger steamer from the Yugoslav port of Dubrovnik on to Greece by sea.

The train delivered us across the northern shoreline of the Gulf of Venice and finally to the Italian port town of Trieste, located on the northern Adriatic coast, just southwest of Ljubljana. It was here we prepared for the trip down the western edge of the Balkan Peninsula. Hitchhiking was illegal, so we cut short the mental gymnastics associated with deliberating on what punitive measures Marshall Tito might exact on us and decided to take the bus. It was a pleasant surprise to find there were regular lines from Trieste to Rijeka and points south. This route followed the irregular rocky coastline that began at the top of Kverner Bay and extended on down the coast.

Soon we were passengers on an overloaded bus, listening to the enchanting harmonics of Serbian folk music emanating from the speakers attached to the four interior corners of the vehicle. Though Serbia was located in the southern interior, one of six republics that made up the country, the music was quite familiar to the locals aboard. The captivating high-pitched female voices profoundly and emotionally touched the hearts of the people, who swayed in their seats to the music as we rode along. These melancholy rhapsodies mesmerized the riders, at times causing a calm and quiet mood to descend over them. Other songs were more energizing with themes of patriotism and ethnic pride warming the blood.

Folk songs had played a significant and unifying role in this country's long history, with these clarion serenades especially stirring the common people. The melodious chanting of the vocalists followed the synchronistic resonances of the *gusle*, a well-known one-stringed musical instrument that resembled a fiddle. These sweet calls appealed to a vision of national glory and respect, effectively connecting the past to the present. Many on the bus sang along with the music.

There was a warm tingle in my belly left from the bottle of clear plum brandy passed to me by one of the commuting workers. I sat immersed in the influences of this new culture, one completely apart from what I had experienced in Italy only a few hours before. The constant catapulting into new cultures was one of the many things I loved about traveling.

The world traveler, bombarded with new information and impressions, is continually processing. These perpetual encounters with changing scenes, different customs, and new languages, present a constant revolving door of things to absorb. Even the money can be challenging. As a cultural stew pot that is always percolating, the travel experience is ongoing. I was approaching the trials of each new country, as I would the first day of a new job or playing a card game for the first time. I set aside my musings as we pulled into our first Yugoslav city, Rijeka.

My extensive walks through the city that afternoon revealed a bleak and urban landscape most devoid of color. Some of this may have been due to the apparent diminished role of capitalism. There was little or no advertising in the streets. The bland nature of the surroundings, accentuated by the lack of detailed signage, was a stark contrast to what I had grown accustomed to in my world. The streets were stone, the buildings were stone, all the walls were stone, and as far as I could see, it looked like a master painter had completely brushed the place in different hues of gray. My first impressions of this drab community reminded me of leafing through the pages of a black and white photo album. However, these feelings would soon change as I moved farther south.

Boarding another bus in the morning, we continued down the shoreline, following the Dalmatian Coast on a winding and picturesque road, isolated and blockaded from the interior by the high walls of the Dinaric Alps. We passed by towering sheer cliffs of limestone *karst* that overlooked the many Adriatic islands, themselves the tips of submarine mountains. These plentiful offshore outcroppings were interruptions in a calm sea of blue and green clarity. The Dinaric range made up the entire spine of the country, curving south to Greece, over into Bulgaria, and eventually reaching Rumania. The mountains ran parallel to the Adriatic Sea and limited the coastal access from the interior. They were a natural barrier creating geopolitical divisions of the towns that had spouted up along the coast.

Small stone houses sprinkled on each side of the road blended perfectly with the natural surroundings, causing me to look closely to distinguish the manmade structures from those created by nature. Even the fence lines for the goat pens were composed of the same native gray stone.

This was in direct contrast to Rijeka, where the boarded up churches, restless workers in the streets and cloudy weather reflected the bleakness in tone and opportunity. The existence mirrored by the northern city was much different from the way of life we were now seeing in these agrarian coastal communities. This was a rugged and lonely land. Here shepherds and goat men watched their flocks and sensed the changes in the weather while patiently leaning on their sticks or squatting under a rock overhang. Families eked out livings on small farms, goat stations, and from fishing the sea. Now we were coming upon villages more frequently, and soon the bus pulled into Zadar, our next major city.

Here again, men in dark overcoats huddled in the streets, clustering in small groups to share their newspapers and cigarettes, talking among themselves in low voices. I sensed a certain air of hopelessness in the mood of the populace, as if the people just existed rather than lived to get ahead and change their station in life. The young boys were dressed in overcoats and proletariat garb cut from the same cloth as their fathers, looking much like smaller versions of the older men who stood next to them.

I wanted so much to speak their language and ask questions about their lives. Looking around, nothing prominent stuck out, only mediocrity and stifled opportunity. I could see fear and suspicion in the eyes of the people around me, as if they were curious but apprehensive about speaking with us. As a foreigner, I could not help feeling shunned yet somehow I felt this was an inaccurate assessment.

Hotels in Zadar seemed non-existent. Kirby and I walked the monotonous streets the first hour in search of food, maintaining equal portions of optimism, curiosity, and desperation. The spell was broken that evening when an old woman wearing a black shawl that covered the top of her head scurried out from the shadows and pulled us quickly back into the darkness. Whispering fearfully in broken English, she asked if we needed a room. We were delighted at such an opportunity and followed her along cobblestone streets and through dark alleys to her small house. She led us to a room with two beds, a table and chair, a water pitcher, and a photo of Marshal Tito on the wall.

In fact, a picture of this sponsor of the post-war Yugoslav independence was hanging in every room of her home. I could never quite determine if this came from a sincere heartfelt gratitude for their leader or merely the result of compliance with a proclamation of state. I suspected the latter. Before she left the room, she made us aware that it was illegal for the locals to solicit foreigners to rent rooms. She obviously felt it was necessary to engage in this risky business in order to survive.

It was raining hard, and we turned in early that night. The beds sagged in the middle like a hammock and sleep did not come easily. In the morning, I found I had come down with my first case of bed bugs! In the days that followed, the bites from these vicious and annoying little creatures kept me in a constant state of discomfort. The only choice was to ignore the incessant itching they caused, something that took a great deal of concentration.

We enthusiastically explored the impressive archaeological treasures of Zadar. I was surprised to see prominent and extensive Roman ruins here. The Church of St. Donat, the Roman forum and the Church of Anastasia were all remarkable examples of Romanesque architecture and the gleaming visions of a glorious past. The spread of the Roman Empire was extraordinary, and I was impressed to see the evidence of this nearly everywhere I had been on the trip so far. After walking the city for a couple of days to view the sights, we bid goodbye to the old woman and boarded a bus south in the direction of Split, a new and different kind of Yugoslavian city.

As we traveled along the coastline, the small bays and inlets lent a pleasingly irregular appearance to the waterline. I would occasionally get a glimpse of a pristine beach, secluded and tucked away, stretching around large boulders. Native roses decorated the rocky outcroppings and wildflowers flourished in the fields along the road. Aged olive trees with thick gnarled trunks, twisted by the weather stood as timeless sentinels over the stony landscape. I could not remember ever seeing any place quite so beautiful.

I sat next to a professor who was on vacation from the University of Ljubljana and traveling to visit his relatives in Split. It was an excellent opportunity to question him about the long history of struggle and hardship surrounding Yugoslavia. I mentioned it may have been a socialist utopia for some but my initial impression was that the north was a profoundly cold, repressed, and impersonal place. He seemed eager to enlighten me and spoke enthusiastically of a country still looking for workable answers. He began with some history on the leader of the country.

Marshall Josip Broz Tito was one of the original partisan commanders who had successfully expelled the Germans from the country during World War II. He was now the absolute ruler of this diverse and complex mixture of ethnicities. Under Tito's rule, only the Communist Party existed. He had nationalized farms, factories, and businesses in a plan to move Yugoslavia from an agricultural existence to that of a modern industrial nation. To the dismay of the Soviet Union, Tito had refused to take sides in the Cold War, playing off the adversaries to his country's advantage. His efforts had unified factions of Serbs, Croats, and ethnic Albanians into what was now an uneasy truce. Yugoslavia had found some solutions to the severe problems that had beset them during the war, but progress was slow. The conversation then turned to Split.

Continuing south, we began to see thriving communities, with definite signs of greater human endeavor. The weather was better and the landscapes became even more appealing than what we had seen in previous days. The professor told me the Romans must have liked the area too, as their interests and influences in Split surpassed even those of Zadar. The Emperor Diocletian had settled this ancient walled city in 300–304 AD, leaving some of the best-preserved Roman ruins of Europe in the Cathedral of St. Dominus and the spectacular remains of his main palace. Split is the largest of the Adriatic cities and acts as the appointed curator of these imposing ruins. Legend has it that Split's pure water, beautiful women, and absence of earthquakes played a large part in Emperor Diocletian's decision to make it his retirement home.

Soon it was time to leave the bus and the professor. I said goodbye to the educator from Ljubljana and stepped out into the streets. We spent the next several days walking the city and viewing the Roman ruins. It was a marvelous place, much different from the northern coastal cities. Here there was some evidence of European tourism, interest in antiquities, and a populace with greater means. There was less indication of state suppression and the atmosphere was more cosmopolitan. The people seemed friendlier and less suspicious. I heard English as well as French spoken in the streets, and I guessed vacationers would be eager to seek out Split even more as time went by.

Several days passed before we were once again back on the road, this time to Dubrovnik, and the "Pearl of the Adriatic." Rolling down the coastline, I pondered on the information the professor had shared with me. He had dissected the mythical and ethnical underpinnings of this region and of Yugoslavia as a whole.

For a host of complex reasons, strife had existed since man first set foot on the bedrock of Yugoslavia. Mountainous physical barriers had isolated communities and given birth to a diversity of languages and cultures, leading to ancient and unresolved conflicts. These had left their scars on the people. As a politically naïve American youth just passing through the country, I found the historical dynamics of these ethnic diversities incredibly fascinating.

Our bus entered the walled fortress city of Dubrovnik. It struck me as both timeless and awesome, like peering back at history through a spyglass. There were monumental stone structures everywhere, utilitarian but graceful. The city was a citadel by the sea, proudly displaying its ramparts, bastions, and strongholds to thwart any would-be invader. It sat on the southern edges of the Croatian coast where it had been ruled and administrated by various regimes throughout history. Among these were the Byzantines, the city-state of Venice, and even Hungary. The city had survived by the wits of shrewd merchants, the skills of master shipbuilders, and politically astute city leaders who negotiated and paid exacting tributes to their overlords. This effectively bought their independence and retained their relative sovereignty. I was anxious to probe further.

Evening strolls through this stone municipality revealed an entity enclosed by mammoth walls, designed to protect its medieval churches, palaces, and monasteries through the centuries from outside forces. I walked the *stradun*, a promenade that began at the city gate and led through the uneven cobblestone streets to the clock tower. Dubrovnik seemed to speak to me in gentle sea breezes that carried voices reaching out from its vibrant past. The city pulled me ever deeper into its soul.

Old stone buildings supported aging red tile roofs and flanked the mazes of narrow passageways. These led to enticing squares featuring artistically sculptured fountains. I surveyed the alleyways and streets absent of automobiles, compelled to walk on and to explore even further. On one occasion, I heard the soft serenade of a gypsy's violin reverberating from wall to wall down through the constricted stone corridors. Later, the sounds of folk music and laughter enticed me to descend steps of rock, seeking their source in the cellar café below. At the foot of the stairs, I entered through the wide plank door into another world, one of live music, folk dancing, and people eating and drinking, using old wine barrels for tables. Charmed, I joined them, allowing the experience to transport me into the very heart of Dubrovnik and her people.

Late in the evening, I departed the joyous cellar, in an attempt to clear my head with a walk to the harbor before returning to the hotel room. I strolled towards the stone breakwater that pointed out to sea, this time pursuing a different kind of music. In the moonlight, I spied the dark profile of a great four-masted ship moored at the pier, her sails trimmed smartly for the night. It was from here the new music came. In the lantern light, I saw sailors dancing on the main deck to the accordion-like sounds of a squeezebox.

These were Russians sailors on their training vessel. They did not hesitate to invite me aboard, and soon, in a spontaneous mood of fraternity, the vodka bottle came around and we were all dancing. Young men with names like Dimitri, Leonid, and Shirov introduced themselves to me. It made no difference to them I was an American. Some of the sailors were wearing their long black boots and doing the "Cossack Kick." Squatting very low to the ground they would kick their legs straight out in difficult maneuvers that made the cartilages in my knees ache. For this night, the Cold War was over, and there was only dancing, music, vodka, and camaraderie. It was just that simple.

I had a frightful headache the next morning. The vague memories of the night before began to recycle through my foggy mind, and then a smile broke out on my face. I wondered how I found my way back to the hotel. I felt compelled to return to the ship, to see my new Russian friends one last time. I walked to the port. Upon arrival, I was disappointed to find their ship had sailed, "vanishing into the dawn" as one man at the dock put it. However, in close proximity to where the Russian ship had been, there was another vessel, one of even greater interest to me.

This was a forty-foot sloop, her lines frayed, her sails torn, and, much to my amazement, displaying a number of large caliber bullet holes down the side of her hull. Two very thin and badly sunburned fellows were lying about on the deck. They looked completely done in, and the flag they were flying told me they were my compatriots.

Unshaven and sallow of cheek the younger of the two men asked me if I had any food with me. I told him I was going back to town and could show them where the market was. They revealed their weakened condition and begged I bring them something to eat as they were not comfortable leaving their boat. I quickly walked to town and picked up a loaf of hard bread, a block of cheese, and some fruit to keep them going. After returning, I spent an hour listening to their incredible story.

They had engine trouble off the Strait of Otranto and decided to shut everything down in an effort to make repairs. The strong currents caused their craft to drift into Albanian waters. Heavy gunfire from shore had ripped holes in the hull, causing them to start taking on water. They had barely gotten away with their sloop and with their lives. After this, they had lost engine power again and sailed for days before coming into the Dubrovnik port under wind-power alone.

Their story was a powerful testament to the dangers of world travel. I wanted to stay and talk but since we were leaving soon I could not spend any more time with them. I wished my compatriots well and took my leave. The story of their encounter assured us we had made the correct decision, taking a small passenger vessel to Greece.

The next day we paid our respects to Yugoslavia and sailed out of the small Dubrovnik harbor. Our route was around Albania, to Corfu, through the Gulf of Corinth, with our final destination the Greek port of Piraeus. In leaving Yugoslavia, I could not help but feel I had uncovered another rare and exquisite jewel that yielded memorable stories I would treasure throughout my life.

The Acropolis

My Greek Island
Chapter Seven

The world is a great book, of which they that never stir from home read only a page. —St. Augustine

The crew cast off all lines and our small passenger vessel sailed due south, away from the high walls that were so characteristic of the port of Dubrovnik. Italy and Yugoslavia had been countries of transit, and I looked forward to Greece where I could settle down for a few months. Our vessel was now steaming towards the Strait of Otronto, that body of water that lies between the heel of Italy and the forbidden shores of Albania. Corfu, a coastal city located on the landward side of Kerkyra Island, would be our first stop. It was one of a series of rugged islands protruding out from the northeastern edge of the Ionian Sea.

Keeping me company were a score or more of young Yugoslav middle school students who occupied the main deck of the ship. They were taking an educational holiday, making the three-day voyage to Greece, where they later would meet their assigned docents for different tours of Athens. They were fresh and active, smartly dressed in their crisp school uniforms. I enjoyed the sound of their pleasant melodic voices. Their wholesome energy was contagious, and they encircled me like curious puppies, asking questions in French and English, their second and third languages respectively. I entertained them as best I could, with my world map and stories of America. I even sang for them the few popular songs that I could remember.

I enjoyed sitting up in the prow of the ship and feeling the air currents generated by our forward momentum blowing in my face. Liberating emotions ran strong in my veins at times like these, and I delighted in the knowledge I was on the move again. I reflected on how comfortable traveling had become for me as I moved into my third month abroad. All vestiges of homesickness had vanished for now, and I realized it was much healthier to look forward than to look back. Reaching out to meet life left me feeling alive, while spending too much time in the past grew painfully tiresome. I rolled out my sleeping bag in the sun on some canvas rigging, where I relaxed and took pleasure in the gentle undulating motion of the small ship moving across the water.

A day at sea brought us to the narrows at Steno Kerkiras, near the southern tip of the Albanian coastline. Here the islands broke out of the waters like the serrated tail of some deep-sea monster. The captain maneuvered the ship into the great inside channel that led to Ormos Potamos, the old town and the port of Corfu, where we would dock for the night. As we entered the port, I could make out the old citadels perched on the high ground, fortifications built up by the Venetians in the fifteen hundreds. Under these, I could see the lighted produce markets and tailored garden pathways that led through to the inviting beaches at the edge of the water below. I happily disembarked to explore.

This region had been a whirlpool of turbulence throughout history, leaving a legacy of strongholds tactically positioned all over the island. The intricate networks of narrow streets in old Corfu were remarkably well-preserved. Though too restrictive for vehicles, these passageways allowed for pleasant sauntering between the various shops and outdoor bistros.

Following an attractive esplanade along the water, I was pleasantly surprised to discover even more promenades by the seashore. I went for a late evening swim, allowing the salt water to work its healing magic on my bedbug bites. Later I stopped for a seafood dinner in an outside patio before returning to the ship.

Dawn found us sailing southeasterly through the chain of Ionian Islands that would eventually lead to the entrance of the Gulf of Corinth, an inlet of the Ionian Sea. Beyond that, we would come to the Corinth Canal where, from 1881 to 1893, men cut a vertical slice through limestone nearly 70 feet wide and four miles long, severing the Isthmus of Corinth. This once solid isthmus divided the Saronic

Gulf, an inlet of the Aegean Sea, from the Gulf of Corinth. The narrow width of the canal precluded the passage of modern ships of wider girths. In ancient times, men dragged the ships in transit overland, across the full width of the isthmus.

Another day of sailing brought us to the canal itself, a monumental work that raised equally monumental questions. I was captivated, wondering how men could accomplish such an incredible feat. Precisely carved, the near vertical sides of the canal looked as if a colossus had slashed his sword down in two mighty blows, cutting through the compacted desert sandstone to separate the Peloponnesian peninsula from the Greek mainland. The canal was the greatest technical achievement of its time. Looking skyward, as our ship passed slowly through the narrow passageway, some 300 feet high in spots, I spied a railroad trestle stretching from rim to rim far above. A ribbon of blue sky presented an attractive backdrop to the Rion-Antirio Bridge. Then, as if on cue, a locomotive blasted across the chasm with its many cars in tow. This was one of those occasions when I yearned for a camera.

Having passed through this manmade cut in the earth, our vessel maneuvered out into the Saronic Gulf, home of the Saronic Islands. Familiar island names, like Hydra and Poros, came to mind. Our vessel passed close enough to the island of Salamis to have a clear view of the whitewashed habitats that blanketed the hills. They were randomly stacked and fastened to each other, with one person's patio acting as another person's roof. Many of them had blue trim and shutters, pleasantly accenting the preponderance of white. I would later learn blue and white were the two national colors of Greece, proudly displayed on their flag. Our voyage terminated in the Bay of Phaleron, where we docked at the ancient port of Piraeus, the third largest city in Greece, about five miles southwest of Athens.

It was enthralling to be close to Athens, the epicenter of Greek culture and the birthplace of Western civilization. My heart raced in anticipation of seeing those marvelous points of interest that up to now I had only studied in history classes. After leaving the ship, Kirby and I stepped onto the subway that whisked riders on a half-hour sojourn from the port of Piraeus into the heart of Athens. We soon found ourselves seated in a quaint outdoor café, reading the *New York Times* and drinking Nescafe in the colorful *Plaka* area. Here I learned more about the country that was to be my home for the next three months.

Athens lies at the southern end of a long plain stretching over the irregular peninsula of Attica. Historically, the city was a nucleus for such mercantile interests as shipping, tourism, textiles, and the mining of marble. The Acropolis, that enduring testament to classical Greece and Athenian democracy, sat on the venerable high ground looking down over the capital. At its center sat the Parthenon, the most prominent building of antiquity in the world, constructed on this site in the fifth century BC. This monumental temple, built in the name of Athena, the patron goddess of Athens, characterized the zenith of the architectural period and order known as the Doric. The great fluted vertical columns exhibited unique qualities, sculpted to bulge slightly in the middle, as a cigar. These optical refinements, referred to as *entasis*, served to "enliven" the appearance of the building to the viewer. Built true to the ancient builder's calculations and golden ratios of aesthetics, the structure reflected the maximum harmony of its parts to the whole.

My travel companion and I agreed that Greece was an ideal venue for spending the winter, as it presented a temperate climate while still manifesting some seasonal changes. We scouted out the new territory while assessing the resources of this exciting metropolis. The physical surroundings were inspiring for the history alone. Availability of such delights as libraries, museums, and parks was important to us. I became intrigued with the prospect of living in Greece and was sure that this location would be much more satisfying than the confining autumn just spent in Germany.

We stayed the first night in a small inexpensive hotel located on a side street in the *Plaka*, the oldest section of Athens. It was like a village within a city. Under the Acropolis, the narrow streets directed us into a neighborhood featuring a variety of antique shops, jewelry stores, and *tavernas*. A kaleidoscope of color encircled me from all corners: Byzantine jewelry hanging from racks; hand-painted curios spread out on tapestries; brightly lettered signs; and the ubiquitous postcard shops. There were coffee houses with their chairs spilling out into the street, packed with writers, artists, and expatriates from many different countries. Fashionable kiosks occupied by merchants selling handmade copies of ancient and famous museum pieces were present throughout.

Eclectic shops teased and tantalized tourists, all to the mesmerizing sounds of the Greek music. *Tavernas* and cafes displayed menus in the front windows, alongside the revolving vertical rotisseries, with slowly roasting cylinders of ground lamb. This was for the *souvlaki*, or pita gyros, those conically wrapped sandwiches that included *tzatziki* sauce, tomato, onion, and meat. They were delectable and melted in my mouth. Other aromas came from the heavily seasoned lamb, pork, or goat meat stacked in slices and revolving slowly on spits. These smells saturated the air and beckoned all who caught the scents to draw closer. Occasionally a shop owner would reach out, take my arm, and usher me into his restaurant where the *bazookia* music played loudly and men danced like Zorba, breaking plates on the floor and waving their arms wildly in the air.

That night the Greek wine, *retzina*, ran freely. It was aged in barrels sealed with pine-pitch and tasted much like turpentine. I would come to know its foul taste well in the months ahead, as it was very cheap, mere pennies for a half-liter. Near the stunning displays of the Acropolis, illuminated by powerful spotlights, we absorbed the vigorous nightlife. Later, dodging street musicians, flower sellers, and photographers, we made it back to the hotel near Kidathineon Street.

The following morning Kirby and I walked to Amonia Square for very strong coffee in very small cups at one of the many outdoor cafes. This was another Greek pleasure I would cultivate. Here, close to the subway terminal to Piraeus, we sat outside in the sun and pondered our next move. In the hour that followed, we tossed about the notion of investigating life on an offshore island. Kirby had considered sending for Doreen to join him once we found a place. Soon we were on the subway train to Piraeus, dreaming of life on one of the Greek isles.

The short one-hour voyage to Aegina by ferry was an adventure in itself. This was the first island out from the mainland. The ship was filled with traveling families carrying their sack lunches and blankets, fishermen returning home from the port, and island folks loaded down with supplies from shopping in Athens. There were also small businessmen with bags of wares to sell on the island. Old men sat calmly fondling their *komboloi*, or worry beads, while looking out over the white caps that pelted the hull.

The sea remained rough the entire trip, with great swells holding the craft poised between the crests of waves, rendering it immobile at times. I sat quietly, resisting the sensation of seasickness that was passing over me. I observed the passengers around me not so fortunate. I focused on formulating a plan of action upon arrival with regard to our lodging. Finally, the northern edge of the island appeared off our port side.

There came into view great rectangular two-storied mansions with long balconies and tall, shuttered windows. They looked old and weathered, but not quite abandoned. I imagined these structures had stood tall against ferocious storms from the sea, battered hard since first built up from the rocky flats that supported them. I speculated about the interesting history that each house held within its walls. What were the great stories hidden here, those exuding romance and intrigue, of fortunes made and lost, of life's age-old struggles? Already I was developing an affinity for the island. Rounding the Hill of Kolona, Aegina's small picturesque harbor came into view. It was stunning.

As we docked, I scanned the open-air restaurants that lined the street facing our incoming ferry. My eye came to rest on a small well-dressed man standing in the doorway of one of the larger restaurants with outdoor tables and chairs. He looked a likely prospect for inquiry.

His name was Elias Karagandis. After properly introducing myself, I explained our desire to secure several months lodging at a reduced rent. Obviously, Elias was a consummate businessman. He smiled broadly and then rubbing his hands together, replied in heavily accented English, "Yes, I know just the place for you!" At his request, we followed him into the dark recesses of the stairwell of an old three-storied structure close by, something he called, "a condemned hotel." We climbed the squeaky staircase to the top floor, while speculating on just how bad it would be.

Although absent adequate plumbing or electricity, the space was massive, with the main room of the top-floor having huge windows that faced the sea. These glass expanses flooded the room with natural light. They extended all the way across the front wall, framing a panoramic view of the small harbor, the incoming boats, and a horizon line profiled by the offshore islands. A glass-paneled door led to the balcony that hung out over the main street below. It had a rusty but well-placed wrought iron railing and was just wide enough for several chairs and a small table.

Elias explained that Aegina's water came from the mainland and was available for only one half-hour, every other day. At those specific times, we could fill the large earthen jugs and pour from them as needed. The toilets would flush if we used buckets to fill the bowls with water. This cold water was available for sponge baths but there were no working showers in the building.

The time to conduct business was at hand and, much to my surprise, everything fell into place quickly. We established the rent at $15 a month! Kirby gave his approval, and I searched no further for lodging. The entire matter, including paying our first months rent, took less than an hour. After this initial business transaction, I spoke at length with Elias.

He had started waiting tables for the hotel-restaurant on Dimokratias, the crescent shaped street bordering the harbor, when he was a small boy. He did well and moved up through the years. Elias was now in his forties, and the proud owner-manager of the very same business. In the months that followed, he would become our patron saint, solving any small problem that would arise. I later came to realize that vacant places on the island were quite rare, and we were extremely lucky to have approached him and to have found even these minimal facilities.

Life on the island took on a momentum of its own in the weeks that followed. Doreen, Kirby's editor and girlfriend from Chicago, came to the island, and together they rented a charming little whitewashed cottage with a pomegranate tree in the front yard. She was the lovely woman we had stayed with during our trip across the country. I now had my own space, retaining the top floor of the old hotel through the winter.

Soon after settling in on the island, I began making weekly trips into Athens, stopping at the American Library to check out books on the reading lists Kirby had helped me to prepare. I loved to read, and with his background in literature, he was able to aid me in filling in the gaps. I read voraciously, devouring several books a week. Herman Melville, Joseph Conrad, Theodore Dreiser, Sinclair Lewis, Charles Dickens, James Joyce, Thomas Mann, Henry James, and Nikos Katzanzakis were just some of the authors I pursued in my time on the island.

On one visit to the city, I found a leather shop where I commissioned a cobbler to fashion a sturdy pair of sandals for me on his aging metal last. These were destined to become my only footwear for the next year, even when walking on the high snowy plains of Afghanistan. He ingeniously used the tread of discarded tires for the soles and even carefully fitted me for an arch. The longer I wore the sandals the greater of a treasure they became, molding perfectly to my feet over time.

I enjoyed the bohemian aspects of the *Plaka*, and would hang out for half a day at a time in the coffee shops, those smoke-filled dens that attracted vagabond intellects from all over the world. Poetry readings, art shows and the discussion of politics abounded among this random cast of characters. This was the longest I had stayed in one place, and I soon had a sense of a home away from home. Living in Greece was much more than a hotel room for me. As I made new friends, island life brought to me a sense of belonging. I wrote home how pleased I was to be there.

Aegina, Greece   *November 20, 1966*

The people are very friendly and I have made a number of friends. They are anxious to speak English. Many of them have relatives in the States and are very proud of this. I met a fellow last night who jumped ship in Los Angeles and spent an interesting year in California, working under the name of a friend and using his Social Security card. He was doing well until the immigration authorities caught up with him, and after a few weeks in jail, exiled him from the country forever. Even so, he made enough money to start a small furniture business on the island. He invited me to the soccer match between Aegina and Athens this afternoon and to his house for dinner next week.

Meandering through the Acropolis, I listened in on the English-speaking guided tours, learning what I could of such interesting topics as the Golden Age of Pericles, Greek architecture, and philosophy. I spent long days in the city and nearly always found myself on the late subway train from Athens to Piraeus and invariably returned by ferry in the dark hours of the evening. On clear nights, I walked the length of the Aegina seawall and entered the tiny whitewashed chapel near the end of the jetty. There I would light a thin beeswax candle as I had seen so many of the Greek people do. It gave me a sense of peace. This was one of the hundreds of small chapels on the island. The sounds and vibrations of the pounding surf on the breakwater always left me inspired.

While on Aegina, I found work with the village boat-maker. One of my tasks was to carry lumber down to the sea and then submerge it under the weight of large stones. After allowing the lumber to age a week or more underwater, I then brought it back to the shop, where I would help the master craftsman fashion it into the shape of a hull. The boards were much easier to bend around the unfinished vessel's timbered ribs after they had soaked in the briny waters for a few days. He used a fascinating array of blocks and tackles with which to coax the slats into position before he clamped them. Another aspect of my work was to help him repair his damaged fishnets and floats. This was merely a part-time job and I took it more for pleasure than for the meager pay.

Aegina had several island mascots. One of these was a dog by the name of Rusty. Not long after my arrival, the dog and I became friends at the small price of an occasional crust of bread passed under the table at an outdoor cafe. These tidbits were leftovers from my near daily trip to the island baker for a fresh loaf of bread at a cost of five cents or one Greek *drachma*. Rusty was a mongrel island dog, a survivor of the general animosity displayed towards animals by the population. He was exceedingly effective in sidestepping the predictable "swift kick" invariably offered by community members passing him on the street. I had come to presume this gesture was a sign of misplaced affection for the dog, as some islanders stopped to feed him after missing with their kick. Whatever the case, Rusty had found a home here, although his origin was an island mystery.

The island was also the sanctuary of a one-legged stork-like creature. Island legend had it the bird flew into town one stormy night, landing on a power line, damaging a wing and frying one of its spindly legs. The result being, the large bird was now earth-bound, hopping around town and competing with the stray dogs for handouts. He was a favorite with the tourists coming off the ferries, as well as the constant object of harassment by Aegina's children. The stork was not completely without recourse, however. Its very long sharp beak was a formidable weapon when it came to matters of self-defense. Over the weeks of observing the bird from my lofty perch on the balcony, I saw swift justice meted out more than once to the dismay of many a mischievous young Greek lad.

Then there was that person affectionately known by the islanders as "the village pest." He was a simple man in his twenties. Unpredictably, this pathetic fellow stood out in the cold near the incoming ferry in a long overcoat, posing himself in a position of maximum exposure. At just the right moment, he unveiled the private parts of his anatomy to the unsuspecting tourist arrivals. The island authorities had taken action numerous times to quell his obsession. They found it impossible to compel the man to alter his behavior, and not wanting to keep him in jail all the time, where they had to feed him, as well as endure his exposures, they decided to incarcerate the fellow on a case-by-case basis only. But, it was not long after each release that he was at it again.

I took pleasure in viewing the incoming island visitors deposited daily on our shores who came to experience the many charms of the island. I often made my way down the hotel staircase to meet the influx when the ferry arrived. They fanned out into the various seaside cafes at the water's edge. Some rented bicycles, while others just walked the shoreline. On one particular day, a middle-aged and mild-mannered Englishman by the name of Bill came to the island. I accepted his invitation to sit down at the small round table in front of Elias's hotel.

Bill revealed he was on holiday from his job with the railroad in Britain, having come to Aegina at the direction of his physician. His purpose was to ease the pain caused by a distressed bowel that had devastated him after a painful divorce. The man was planning to take a few relaxing days at the far side of the island, to view the Temple of Aphaea, and spend a full week at the quiet and secluded resort of Aghia Marina.

I offered to buy my new friend a glass of *ouzo*, the Greek national drink made from anisette and served with a small assortment of snacks called *mezedes*. These usually included an olive, a piece of feta (goat cheese) and a cracker. All this was a mere ten cents, including the *ouzo*. Bill made it clear he preferred not to drink, fearing once he started, he just might not stop. So, I was surprised when later during his second night on the island, the pledge of sobriety vanished into a bacchanalian whirlwind of descent at the Blue Barrel and other island haunts. This riotous evening finally concluded in the early morning hours.

Nursing a *retzina* hangover, Bill boarded the small bus the next day for the resort, disappearing up the dusty road that wound over the backbone of the island. Life went on as usual and I nearly forgot about him entirely. After a week's time, he suddenly emerged, a new man, bubbling with stories of a lovely German woman whom he had met at the secluded seaside facility, falling in love at first sight. As I walked him to his ferry that would take him to the mainland, he told me that they had already made plans for a future rendezvous in Europe.

One month later, I received a letter from him stating he had safely arrived back in England, with his stomach problems and depression now miraculously cured. Furthermore, he had already gone to see

"Ursula" in Germany and was currently planning to go see her again. Romantic inclinations abounded around the Greek island, touching in some small way all that walked its shores. The warm memories of Bill faded in time and sadly, I never heard from him again.

One day I encountered an attractive, well-dressed and sophisticated woman seated at one of the outdoor cafes. Eager to speak with someone I assumed to be an American, I introduced myself, mentioning I had seen her around the hotel in previous days. Her name was Darlene and she had come from New York. She was quick to direct the conversation towards me, revealing very little information about herself.

I could not help but notice her sensitive mouth and the dark eyes that matched her long chestnut hair. I assumed she was slightly older, but from our initial glances, there was little doubt a certain chemistry was beginning to build between us. In the days that followed, we became friends, taking several extended island walks along the shoreline to view the jellyfish hanging suspended in the remarkably clear waters.

One afternoon, foul weather drove us inside the hotel, whereupon she invited me to her room for a drink. Upon entering I could see the ceilings were tall as were the elongated windows looking out to the harbor. There were several pieces of furniture comfortably placed about the room and a balcony protruding out over the street, much like mine. After a casual inspection, I turned from the balcony door to comment, only to see this shapely American woman standing close behind me.

Instinctively, I put my arms around her in a gentle embrace. Many tender kisses followed and I felt catapulted into a new dimension. Moments later she responded further by slowly unbuttoning her silk blouse, revealing her lovely cleavage that fell open before me. Her fleshy twin globes were perfectly formed in every way. Resistance was not an option at this point, and we came together on the large feather bed, enclasped in passion. A great sense of peace flowed over me as my long unintended period of abstinence came to a delightful end. We spent the rest of that rainy-day-afternoon secluded from the world in her cozy room. That night over dinner, she told me of her intended departure the following day. I could not say it was a big surprise.

In the morning, during our farewells, Darlene confessed she was forty-two years old, eighteen years my senior, and had voted for Dwight D. Eisenhower! We each laughed warmly. Later I walked her to the boat where she quickly boarded. Looking back over her shoulder, she gave me a sexy wink. As the ferry pulled away, I noticed two menacing looking characters standing at the handrail close to her. They had long black beards and wore lengthy dark overcoats. I had seen them around the hotel, nicknaming them the "Smith Brothers" from the images on the cough drop box. I would cross paths with these mysterious men again, months later in Herat, Afghanistan.

I took great pleasure in exploring what had now become "my island." On one such extended walk, I followed a narrow winding dirt track over dry and rocky terrain to the crest of the island in the direction of Aphia Marina. The road followed stone fencerows that effectively funneled me through picturesque olive and pistachio orchards. There were some gates through these fences near the roadsides, covered by lattice atriums and the leafless grapevines of winter. As I passed one such entrance, I heard the faint and familiar sound of piano music floating through the stands of gnarled olive trees.

I opened the gate and followed the hypnotic harmonies up a stone path leading to a small stone cottage. After my knock, the door opened. I immediately recognized the man as a patron of the same bakery I frequented in Aegina. I told him I was just following the music. He invited me in, and we walked into the piano room, where his wife sat demurely playing. She smiled while continuing to perform flawlessly, her nimble fingers dancing skillfully over the keyboard of the baby grand.

After an exchange of pleasantries, she asked me if I played. I was happy to rehearse the few respectable pieces I had memorized from the lessons taken as a boy. They were Americans, from the East Coast, and had lived on the island for several years. Students of music, they had purchased the piano in Athens one day after discovering it hidden under a dusty tarp in the back of a furniture warehouse. They had it delivered to their house at no small cost and with considerable difficulty. First, it had come to Aegina by ferry, and then the townspeople had loaded it onto a donkey cart and hauled it to their country home. At their insistence, I came to visit them several more times to play my few selections, tell stories, and take tea with them.

Christmas was approaching, and Kirby, Doreen and I hatched a plan to treat ourselves to hamburgers for the main course on that special day. We had often fantasized about this good old Yankee mainstay, and now the time had come to see if they could be prepared away from home. Almost simultaneously, we conceived of a great scavenger hunt, with each of us assigned to procuring one or two of the different hard-to-find ingredients.

Having once taken mechanical drawing, I dropped off my specifications and sketches of the buns to the local baker. This fascinated the man to no end and he took a personal interest in our project. On my next trip to the Athens, I found a food specialty shop in the *Plaka*, where I purchased a tube of mayonnaise that had come from France.

The other participants in this master plan had not been idle. Doreen negotiated with the butcher for some ground lamb patties, as beef was not available. Kirby rounded up the *morulli*, a leafy green vegetable that the locals used for salad lettuce, and some brine-soaked carrots for pickles.

The big day finally came. I always enjoyed visiting their cottage, as my old hotel was without heat and frightfully cold at nights. Our Christmas dinner came together perfectly and the flavors of the Greek burgers were unsurpassed. We had a holiday reading of the Dylan Thomas poem, *A Child's Christmas in Wales*. Kirby had studied Dylan Thomas in his Masters program. Later in the evening, while walking home between the narrow stone buildings, I came upon some religious processions.

People were carrying candles, chanting, and making their way to one of the many orthodox churches on the island. I was shocked to see some of the older women following an island tradition of crawling on all fours over the cobblestones to their destinations. They were wailing and some were even leaving trails of blood from the abrasions on their knees. I pondered the degree of devotion these impressive acts of faith reflected.

The weeks of January passed quickly, and I continued with my literature studies. I did make one side trip to the island of Poros and, upon returning, spoke with ticket agents on the waterfront in Piraeus regarding the continuation of my world trip. Egypt seemed the best next move for several reasons, the first being there were small passenger vessels to Alexandria weekly. From there, I could catch an inexpensive freighter from Port Said or Suez, through the Red Sea, and on to Bombay (as Mumbai was then called). Others mentioned crossing the Mediterranean again to Beirut and traveling overland to India from there. I checked my world map and naively calculated a possible crossing of the Sinai Peninsula, as there definitely appeared to be a railroad track across this historical stretch of land.

On January 27, 1967, I was walking the waterfront of Piraeus after securing arrangements for my upcoming voyage to Egypt. After talking with one of the travel vendors, I stopped in one of the seaman cafes for a Turkish coffee and some *baklava*. This was a delicious Greek pastry made with *phyllo* dough, honey, walnuts, and the spices of cinnamon, nutmeg, and cloves. I gravitated to these sweet delectable treats when I came to town.

Suddenly, I became aware of Greeks approaching me to ask my nationality. When I answered, they promptly expressed their sympathy for the loss of our three astronauts that day in the tragic Apollo fire on the launch pad at Cape Kennedy. A spark had ignited an oxygen-filled capsule, killing Gus Grissom, Ed White, and Roger Chaffee within seconds. I hurried down the street to pick up a *New York Times*. I was so impressed with the outpouring of emotion by the people on the streets who showed respect and sympathy for our lost astronauts. The people of Piraeus have stood tall in my eyes since that mournful day.

Just as there was a time to arrive in Greece, so too was there a time to depart. It was now February, and my funds were diminishing. If I were to make my way around the globe, I needed to get started.

Kirby had made it clear that Greece was as far as he was going this trip and that he and Doreen were comfortable on the island. There was much celebration on the day of my leaving, with Kirby, Doreen, and my landlord Elias seeing me off at the ferry as I departed for Piraeus.

I remember well my emotions as the vessel pulled away from the tiny island port. My friends continued waving until we could no longer see each other, and the backdrop of the town became gradually smaller as the stretch of water between us widened.

I would soon experience a new brand of freedom, one that I was eager to explore. A sharp wave of emotion hit me as I realized I was now completely alone. I paused in my solitude to ponder the exhilarating fact that the next day I would be boarding a small passenger vessel for the voyage to Egypt.

Pyramids & The Sphinx

Voyage to Egypt
Chapter Eight

Security is mostly a superstition. It does not exist in Nature, nor do the children of men as a whole experience it. Avoiding danger is no safer in the long run than out right exposure. Life is either a daring adventure, or nothing. —Helen Keller

Still a little unsteady from the rough sailing into Piraeus after leaving Aegina, I ducked into the small ticket office to take shelter from the rain that was drenching the port. I swung my backpack down to the floor, threw back the hood of my rain slicker, and rang the bell that sat on the counter. The agent appeared from the recesses of the back-room, adjusted his spectacles, and, recognizing me, extended his warm greeting. We had spoken the week before about my taking "deck passage" on the three-day voyage across the Mediterranean to Alexandria, Egypt. I handed him the twenty dollars in Greek *drachmas*, along with my passport displaying the visa I had obtained from the Egyptian Consulate in Athens. After close inspection, he gave me a hand-stamped, official-looking ticket. I was to board a small ship the next morning. The vessel was equipped to accommodate passengers in one of two ways, first class, of which there were several cabins available, with the second choice being deck passage. I chose the latter, which offered some hammocks below and a variety of random locations topside on the main deck.

The waterfront of Piraeus was a wild place at night. Tough men drank hard, danced, fought, and then staggered away, cursing the sea wind that blew out of the night. After securing a room in an inexpensive hotel, I entered several of the bars to mingle with the sailors and fishermen. My six-foot five-inch frame invariably attracted attention and occasionally drew challenges. Spreading my map of the globe over a table usually defused the most ardent inquisitors, with their eyes following my progressive circuitous route across the flat world before them. For this night, there was nothing more exciting than some arm-wrestling and storytelling. I turned in before midnight, aware the next day would be a demanding one.

I stepped aboard the vessel in the early hours of the morning, with plenty of time to explore the layout before we cast off. She was trim, with plain wooden decks, a massive bow that curved up high above the deck, and a raised helm from which the captain and first mate could navigate. There was a fair sized galley below, with some tables and chairs, then a large open room lower down in the hull referred to as the bilge. It sported a number of hammocks attached to the great ribs that supported the bulkheads. The captain and crew quarters were located in the small bunk-appointed compartments off the main deck.

I moved below deck to test the hammocks for comfort. Finding them somewhat lacking, I proceeded topside to scout locations for my sleeping bag on the main deck. Soon more passengers came aboard. I met two German fellows, an Englishmen, several French students, and two more travelers from Denmark. There was also a young student from Khartoum, in the Sudan, who had been away studying in East Germany. I would come to know all of my new shipmates much better in the days to come. It was not long before they all disappeared below to claim their respective bedding areas.

Whistles blew, and the responsive crew busied themselves making ready to leave the Greek port, stowing the stores of new supplies. One weathered-faced seaman cranked up the gangplank while still others disengaged the tethers from the dock piers, fore and aft, securing them in great neat coils. We slowly maneuvered away from the Piraeus dock to begin the first leg of the Mediterranean crossing, south into the Sea of Crete.

I could not help thinking back on one of the authors I had been reading during my time on the Greek island, Nikos Kazantzakis, the man from Crete. I still carried his fascinating novel, *Zorba the Greek*, in my pack. I had done extensive research on his life while in Greece. It added greatly to my interest when I found that Elias, my landlord, had waited tables for this famous writer, scholar, and ascetic in the same cafes of Aegina in which I sat. Elias was but a young boy then, and remembered Nikos as a quiet, thoughtful man who always wore sandals, even in the wintertime.

As a philosopher, Kazantzakis explored the highest circles of an intellectual and spiritual experience that was his life. His profound works chronicled the continuous odyssey of a man in search of the divine. These writings take the reader on a long journey through the wondrous mysteries of life. The Nobel Prize for Literature escaped him by the narrowest of margins in 1949, when they gave it to William Faulkner instead. They denied him once again in 1957, when Albert Camus received the honor. The epitaph on the tomb of Nikos in Crete reads, "I hope for nothing. I fear nothing. I am free." It seems he had finally shed himself of the earthly bondage that so restricted him.

Heavy rains were upon us by mid-day, interrupting my pleasant reflections. I took my backpack below, planning to post new descriptions and musings into my journal in the small room that was the deck class lounge. Here I met with the other contingent of voyagers. They were sitting at the tables sharing their lunches of hard bread, cheese, fruit, and canned meat.

Soon, I was actively engaged in conversation of a most stimulating nature. Four or five languages flew around the room with translations offered where needed. In this well-educated group of individuals, diversity of opinion seemed to be the rule rather than the exception. There was a wholesome, if not misguided, search for the truth. Several had embraced Communism as a viable political philosophy, apparently a natural backlash to the extreme nationalistic ambitions of Germany's Third Reich. In the days to follow, we broached topics such as Vietnam, Israeli-Arab relations, the student traveler, philosophy, and music. As the lone American in this assemblage, they eagerly asked for my opinions.

In the evening, I returned topside to stake out my territory on deck, a great coil of rope that I had earlier fashioned somewhat into a lounge chair. The seas were rough that first night as we plied through what seemed like a typhoon. I made one trip below to the head where the foul sour smell of vomit was strong and evidence of rampant seasickness was quite visible. Back on deck and getting soaked from the pelting rain, I pulled a deck tarp over myself and receded deeper into my down sleeping bag. Great waves slapped the hull hard all night, sending water high into the air and filling the gunnels. Several times, I felt myself dislodged from my nest in the ropes and became concerned that I might roll away into the tempestuous seas that held us hostage. I remembered Kirby's story of losing a good friend who rolled overboard in a Mediterranean storm, sleeping bag and all. The violent and explosive wave action abated about daybreak, and there was a change for the better in the weather.

The second day at sea I propped myself up on my backpack in the sun, allowing the warm penetrating rays to vaporize the moisture that had gathered from the previous night. The clouds continued to dissipate, and I relaxed topside as we steamed further south. I pulled out my world map to plot the new segments of my journey. It remained my trusty companion, my identity, as I moved from country to country. I was becoming thin and efficient, having lost some thirty pounds since leaving home, and my heart continued to soar in the knowledge I was finally realizing a major lifetime dream. Kirby had expressed reasonable doubts regarding just how far the $450 I had remaining would take me after I left Greece. He was skeptical of me reaching one of my desired goals, Kathmandu, Nepal, on such meager funds. His reservations served to remind me to be frugal with my remaining resources. I decided to talk to the young man from Khartoum about what things might cost in Egypt.

Mustafa Kamal was a twenty-two-year-old engineering student returning from West Germany to his hometown of Khartoum, on the upper Nile, in the Sudan. From the moment we met until our parting in the streets of Alexandria, we communicated almost non-stop on a multitude of subjects. For the next two days, it was like two thirsty minds intensely drinking up information from each other. He graciously gave me lessons in basic Arabic, which I used after we arrived. We seemed destined to become memorable friends, at least for the duration of our short voyage, and I have never forgotten his name in all the years since meeting him.

Mustafa's education funds had run out, and he was traveling home from Europe to prepare an application to one of the East German Universities that offered scholarships. Though not partial to living in a Communist country, he was pursuing this avenue as a last resort. The Sudan had no institutions of higher learning at this time, and Sudanese students had to seek their college education in what other countries would have them. He sensed mistreatment in Germany due to his skin color, and he felt Switzerland had denied him entry also for racial reasons. I do not remember the specific details of his concerns but he did seem to be sincere in his claim of injustice. I found each traveler had his or her own story, about which I could not help pondering the validity in passing. The perceived intentions of others are not always what they appear to be, and many times, we only see what we are looking for. At least I had found this to be true for myself.

As we steamed closer to Alexandria, my thoughts turned to its complex history, a subject I had researched on my weekly trips into Athens. Founded on orders from Alexander the Great, 300 years before Christ, Alexandria became a city that would contend with Athens and Rome for greatness. Alexander commanded Ptolemy, a trusted general, to develop the city to the highest degree of architectural splendor, while Alexander himself pursued his campaign into India. The general's efforts in Alexandria continued even after Alexander's death, and the city flourished culturally and economically, becoming a prominent center of learning.

History gives us accounts of Alexandria's great library, one charged with acquiring all the knowledge of the known world. It had accumulated more than 700,000 volumes towards this purpose before being destroyed by fire. History is vague on the cause, but there are several candidates in line for blame regarding this great tragedy, among them Julius Caesar.

The great minds of the day came to Alexandria to live, to work, and to create. Others came to translate the massive quantities of information that came in from foreign lands. The discoveries of Euclidian geometry, the knowledge that the earth revolves around the sun, and the calculation of the earth's circumference all came from Alexandria. This great city was also the home of the legendary *Pharos*, the lighthouse referred to as the Seventh Ancient Wonder of the world.

Alexandria fell into decline in the time of Cleopatra and degenerated even further when the conquering Muslim armies swept into Egypt in the seventh century. Although impressed with the city, the residing Arab general passed it over for renewal, and instead concentrated on settling a new capital to the southeast, on the banks of the Nile. There were further major setbacks for Alexandria from the outbreak of the plague in the sixteen hundreds. When European forces led by Napoleon arrived in the year eighteen hundred, this once glorious city had mysteriously regressed to the status of a humble fishing village. Napoleon's men did find something there of great value, to later share with the world.

Hieroglyphics, civilization's oldest known writing system, were inscriptions that had mystified language specialists for centuries, if not millennia. Egyptians engraved into their monuments a flowing pictorial script, conveying complex religious beliefs. A black granite stone discovered outside the village of Rosetta by Napoleon's army in 1799 was to unlock these mysteries some twenty-three years later. It held the text of a single passage written in the three scripts of hieroglyphics, Egyptian Demotic, and classical Greek. The Rosetta Stone laid the foundation for future translations of a system that had evolved into a compilation of more than 6,000 characters.

Our three-day voyage to Egypt would soon be at an end, and now it would be my turn to enter Alexandria and taste the results of her long convoluted chain of historical events. As we approached the busy seaport, I could see it shrouded in a haze of black smoke. I wondered if the great city was once again on fire. Soon I found the answer.

The large gray battleships of Gamal Abdel Nasser's Egyptian Navy sat in rows at the Port of Alexandria. Their mammoth grey stacks were pumping great clouds of dark smoke into the air, in preparation for departure. Mustafa made me aware that President Nasser was a major leader of important standing in the Arab world, espousing a pan-Arab ideology. This nationalist movement, with an anti-colonial foreign policy, had won him a great following since his takeover of Egypt in 1956.

I thought it odd that the first scenes I viewed in this historical and second largest city in Egypt were gray battleships. This was very different from the lighthouse or library that the inbound traveler might have beheld in a bygone era. From the seaport, Mustafa accompanied me in a horse-drawn cart into the Old Quarter of the city. There he insisted on seeing that I had a decent room before he departed for Cairo where he would board a river taxi that would take him up the current of the Nile to Khartoum. We stopped in a small street-side café for a lunch of turnips, pickled carrots, and alfalfa-like greens stuffed in pocket bread, costing only a few pennies. The price of my hotel room was one U.S. dollar a day, and it included a veranda with a view of the beach, framed by arched palm trees. I would only reside there for one night, feeling it far too expensive. Mustafa and I bid a sad farewell in the knowledge we most likely would never see each other again.

I was coming to realize that with traveling, one is rarely completely alone, as there are always people to communicate with around you. Yet with these developing friendships on the road, though intense, comes the knowledge they are likely to conclude shortly after they begin. This required some emotional preparation and contributed to more of a "live in the moment" philosophy.

That night I ventured deep into the street bazaars, becoming lost in my first true exploration of the Third World. All manner of goods were on display, from jewelry to medicinal plants, to Bedouin garments. My innocent Western eyes suffered non-stop assaults from swirling visions of poverty, chaos, and human suffering. Everywhere I looked there were small cafes filled with raggedly dressed men who all looked alike and sat on Persian carpets smoking their "hubbly-bubbly" pipes. The more formal name was *hookah*, a solitary or multi-stemmed water pipe, with a base of ceramic, glass, or brass. I went into one of these cafes without a second thought and sat down. One man came up to me and said in broken English that the café was not safe for foreigners. Mustafa had told me the same thing when he had helped me to find a room. Nevertheless, I stayed at the café for several hours, trying unsuccessfully to become invisible in the crowd of coiled turbans and tasseled *fez* hats. I squatted down and smoked with all the others, blending in as best as any Anglo could. Of course, a whole host of curious onlookers continued to survey me.

Later that night, dizzy from the strong tobacco, I slipped back out into the noisy streets of the bazaar. It was not long before I felt myself pulled into a dark alley by a man with bad teeth, selling sugar cane juice. He gestured that I sit on a small stool in his stall. He had a crude machine resembling an old wringer washer, which squeezed juice from the short cuttings of cane stocks he fed into it. I drank down the brown juice from the fly covered glass he presented, not realizing that I would pay for this indiscretion with severe dysentery a short time later. The man told me many stories of how good things were under British rule, that he could buy a pound of beef for his family at a reasonable price then, that he had a good job as a bureaucrat in a government house. He lamented his life was now reduced to selling juice in the streets. There was much more.

His eleven-year-old daughter had been making tea near by, smiling at me occasionally with big brown oval eyes by the light of the kerosene lantern that hung from the roof of his *souk*. I was unprepared for what happened next. The man came closer, appealing to me in subdued tones. At first, I thought he was merely begging. Then I realized he was endeavoring to negotiate with me for the favors of his young daughter. Revolted, I rose to my feet and left his shanty immediately, anxious to get back to my hotel. I had been overwhelmed with all I had experienced my first night in the streets of Alexandria. I felt the telltale cramps in my stomach beginning a familiar and painful cycle. It was more than enough for one day, yet somehow I knew there would be additional trials to come.

I checked out of the hotel and boarded the train for Cairo the next morning. From the start, the railroad car was overcrowded, certainly far too overburdened to find a seat. It only got worse with each stop. Eventually, I was standing in an aisle with only room for one of my feet! My fellow passengers stared at me with those deep brown eyes for the next several hours as I stood up straight, holding my backpack over my head as the blood ran out of my tired arms. I was hungry, and there was absolutely nothing to eat. The warm bodies all around immobilized me, pushing, shoving, and conversing in a language that I could not understand. Making my way to the restroom was out of the question. My intestines were in a knot from the sugar cane juice that continued to eat its way through my system like acid. A sense of helplessness broke over me as I fully realized how restricted I was, caught in a miserable trap. Cairo could not come soon enough.

Cairo lies at the end of the great Nile River delta, a fan of fertile alluvium that spreads outward ninety-three miles in width. It is the African continent's largest city, hosting millions of commuters who invade each day, some to work, and others to bring their goods to market. There are foreigners as well, who have come to view the numerous historical treasures and roam the colorful if not hectic streets. I tried to make sense of it all as we pulled into the Cairo station.

Upon exiting the train, I stepped out into a menagerie of desperate looking souls making their way through the streets. Buses passed by clogged with passengers, much as the train had been. I aimlessly followed the crowds while my mind struggled to accept this new environment. I was soon to discover the overcrowded conditions in Cairo had placed enormous strain on the transportation and housing services, causing me great difficulty in getting around and even finding lodging. At last, my trek through the hot and dusty streets brought me to the American Consulate.

Here they made me aware of a youth hostel, located on a boat moored on the eastern bank of the Nile. I used this opportunity to discuss my options for making the journey to India. They shared some crucial pieces of information with me. First, for political reasons, land passage to Israel or Jordan was not possible across the Sinai Peninsula. Second, they informed me there were no freighters leaving in the near future for India, from either Port Said or Port Suez. I walked back outside into the hot sun, still hungry and feeling somewhat depressed.

Exhausted from the stress, I continued walking towards the El-Gamaa Bridge, and then crossed over the Nile in search of the youth hostel they had mentioned at the consulate. I looked out over the water to see the many *feluccas* sprinkled out across the great river. These lateen or triangular rigged sailboats were of a traditional design that had remained unchanged for over 3,000 years. The youth hostel was no more than a small barge, with different sleeping areas below deck, partitioned off by dirty sheets of cloth. I stowed my gear and collapsed on the wooden floor that was to be my bed for the next week. I drifted into a light sleep, lulled ever deeper by the sounds of prayers called from the towers of the ancient mosque near by. I remembered Mustafa's words about the Nile being a site of continuous human habitation since the Paleolithic era, and now, I was one of those inhabitants.

Every day I arose and made a gallant effort to make the trip to the pyramids, only to find the buses packed with riders and no seats available. There were men standing on the bumpers, sitting on the roof of the bus, and on its fenders. They were even hanging out the open and missing windows. On some days, the buses just sat at the bus stops in a non-operational status, no reason given. The pollution on the streets from the older vehicles made it difficult to breathe. On the fifth day, I was successful in squeezing aboard one of the crowded carriers. My heart raced when we approached the Sphinx and the Great Pyramids of Giza, wonders I had studied and yearned all my life to see. In the parking lot, there were several vendors offering to photograph me on a camel. I refused, first because of the unnecessary expense and secondly for fear of being perceived a common tourist.

The distance to the Pyramids had been deceiving, the result of their great size. I could see they were composed of large cubes of stone, stacked in tiers, and forming an over-sized receding staircase to the pinnacle, some 400 feet above. Energized, I strode across the sand to the base of the larger antiquity and initiated the difficult ascent up its sides, desperately clutching the stone blocks, as I moved ever higher to a comfortable viewing point about a quarter of the way up. I took mental snapshots during this most pleasurable moment. I marveled at sitting on the sole survivor of the Seven Wonders of the Ancient World. From this point, I looked out upon the great Sphinx, half human and half lion, a sagely poised protectorate on the scorching sands. Just who carved the world's largest statue, and when, remained an unanswered riddle.

Ensuing days found me wandering the halls of the many great museums of Cairo. Most notable of these was the Egyptian Museum, established in 1835, and possessing more than 120,000 objects dating from prehistoric times to the Greco-Roman period. I tracked small groups of *Egyptologists* through the tall corridors, listening intently to the guides as they imparted the history of Egypt with great expertise and clarity. The museum displays were fascinating, especially the mummies.

As far back as 10,000 BC, cultures were present that worked the pastoral lands of the area known today as Egypt. Migrations to the Nile River, probably facilitated by climate changes, gave way to the more centralized and agriculturally based societies. Following this period, several pre-dynastic cultures flourished, maintaining contact with each other through trade. The earliest hieroglyphic writings appear during this period, dating back to about 3250 BC. The Kingdom of King Menes, circa 3150, grew from these historical seeds, spawning cultural influences uniquely Egyptian in language and custom. From there a succession of dynasties followed, extending into the Old Kingdom (2700–2200 BC) and finally to the Fourth Dynasty of Pharaoh Khufu, also known as Cheops, from which came the Pyramids of Giza. This reign extended from 2589 BC to 2566 BC.

Throughout my stay in Cairo, the constant gnawing pain of hunger was with me. Try as I might, cauliflower and pickled vegetables in flat bread did not satisfy it. Once, by mistake, I tried fried goat brains. I should have known as much when the vendor pointed to his head while serving me the odd tasting, heavily spiced dish. Taking up notches in my belt, I knew I was losing body weight fast and the water continued to make me sick. My body was telling me, it was time to leave Egypt.

I did not relish the trip back to Alexandria on the train, but from there I could secure sea passage to Beirut, Lebanon, where I could make my way south to Jerusalem and from there across to India. After some thought, I decided to take the bus back to the Mediterranean port. This avenue of transportation was also overflowing with wall-to-wall people. It was very hot, dusty, and nearly as traumatic as the train trip, but I survived, checking into the Alexandria youth hostel shortly after I arrived.

The hostel had a thriving population of remarkable world travelers, as well as those dreaded little creatures from hell that I had previously encountered in Yugoslavia—the bedbugs!

Jerusalem

Beirut to Jerusalem

Chapter Nine

A traveler to distant places should make no enemies.
—Nigerian Proverb

The Alexandria Youth Hostel played host to some fascinating occupants, most of them falling into one of several categories that had been taking shape in my mind. First, there were the scholars, usually students from Europe, who had come to study the cultural history or archeology of the region or to examine its antiquities. They were often following an educational agenda in pursuit of an advanced degree. Some of these were associated with a university and had stipends or grants to assist them.

Then there were the adventure tourists, usually clad in shorts and wearing hiking boots, who for one reason or another had fashioned a particular goal to achieve or challenge to surmount. For the most part, this group was committed to completing their itinerary before flying safely home. They were frequently exuberant in speech and action, drug-free, and the first ones up in the morning.

Finally, there were those whom I would identify as the seekers, more spiritual in nature, usually evolving from one of the previous categories after too much time on the road. These souls were in various stages of insolvency, increasingly divorced from the material world and, in many cases, losing their health. For them, the travel experience had become not just a personal quest, but an ongoing lifestyle. These individuals had no definite plan for returning to their native homeland, preferring to wander from country to country, immersed in the game of survival. Many sold their blood or their passports, two items always in demand, for subsistence money. The farther east I traveled the more I would encounter travelers of this particular type.

The mix at the hostel was constantly changing, and new stories were quick to replace the older ones. The free exchange of information usually proved useful, as some had already been where others were going. The cast of characters staying here produced a host of unusual stories, some of them quite bizarre.

It was around these tables on one particular day that I first met Morgan. He was British and traveling to Ceylon where his brother was involved in some way with a large tea plantation. He was of medium height, thin with dark hair and intense eyes. He was annoyingly too well-educated, precise, determined, and unwavering in all his dealings with those of us around him. In time, I shared some of my experiences with him regarding Alexandria and Cairo. Oddly enough, we would meet up again in Jerusalem, eventually traveling east together.

One of the more interesting temporary residents at the hostel was an American in his late forties, who had just completed riding his motorcycle to Alexandria from Cape Town, the southern most tip of the African continent. This ordeal had taken him a full two years and his face reflected the toll of the journey. The man had been incarcerated numerous times while crossing different borders, where he was suspected of being a spy. Once he had even enlisted as a mercenary soldier, for a short interval, to make ends meet. His motorcycle had given up twice on the journey, making it necessary for him to stop and forge new parts for his machine over village fire pits. His lengthy white beard and complementary long hair only enhanced his persona, and he exuded a powerful presence. A veteran of many confrontations, it was evident he was a one-of-a-kind, self-contained individual. We broke bread together at the lunch table, and I suspected his gnarled and scarred hands provided flesh and blood testimony to the validity of his remarkable stories.

There was also a Dutch fellow, in his early twenties, with long silky blonde hair and a slight build. He was rather withdrawn and, after hearing his story, it was easy to understand why. In halting speech, fraught with emotion, he chronicled an account that astounded us all. Hitchhiking across the hot and dry deserts of North Africa, from Marrakech, Morocco, he had been accosted by a small band of nomads and gang-raped. Observing him from their hiding places behind sandy outcroppings, they had caught up with him, bent him over a large rock and had their way with the young man. Humiliated, he pulled himself together and continued onto Alexandria, where he now unveiled his horrid tale. The element of danger was never far away when traveling in foreign lands.

On a lesser note, but worthy of mention, were the annoying bedbugs that populated this part of the world. These small wingless insects voraciously fed in the early morning hours on the ill-fated lodgers tucked away on their infested sleeping pads at the hostel. The bugs usually left a track of three or more bites either close together or in a line. Primarily, they flourished in the primitive bunks at the hostels, frequented over time by multitudes of international travelers. Though bedbugs rarely transport themselves with the host, they can easily travel in the dark recesses of a sleeping bag or clothing. I came to understand that DDT powder or seawater provided the only relief from these miserable pests.

The small passenger ship across the Mediterranean to Beirut was again a mere $20 for deck passage, but this time the vessel was overflowing with passengers. I boarded and quickly searched the main deck for a spot to claim as my own. After securing my place topside, I explored the levels of the ship below. A hush fell over a room when I peeked in on a group of female Muslim pilgrims shrouded in black headscarves who were returning to the Middle East. Our three days at sea would bring with it wails and chanting from these women, cloistered below, as seasickness spread its misery among them.

I was impressed by how strikingly similar the procedures for getting underway were between the three different vessels I had now been on. The ship's crew reacted smartly to the loud chimes of the large brass bell affixed on the main deck at the bow. Hearty men cast lines, rolled barrels, and coiled up oversized ropes, all choreographed to the clarion sounds of the bell.

I had gradually lost my appetite in Egypt. However, hunger now invaded my entire being. I was living on a stack of dry pita bread disks and a bag of pickled vegetables, which I had purchased in the open street market shortly before boarding the ship. The daily ritual of journaling kept my mind off the hunger pangs, but lack of food caused the next three days to pass slowly. I rested up for the new country I would be entering in the days that followed.

Upon arrival in Lebanon, I passed through a lengthy customs process. Those of native origin passed through the gates quickly, but I, obviously a foreigner, found myself escorted into a small room and thoroughly questioned by two military men. Once again, my world map was crucial in answering questions and providing me with a legitimate reason for being in the country. It supported my account of traveling around the world on a shoestring and even sparked occasional interest from my persistent interrogators. In this part of the world, they were always stout men with thick mustaches.

The beautiful city of Beirut unfolded before me, offering ever-widening vistas of appeal. The sun was warm and people were smiling as they scurried down the narrow stone walkways, toting bundles of flowers, fruits and vegetables from the various farmers' markets. There were impressive sights everywhere I turned. Attractive squares, ornate gates, and intriguing shops filled the margins of the wider avenues. The momentum of the crowds pushed me through the streets and out into the quadrangle of the city center. I smelled something delicious cooking, and focused intently on the several street vendors roasting dozens of whole chickens on spits. Others were squeezing out extra large glasses of orange juice from crude hand presses. I dropped my backpack at a park bench and immediately purchased a chicken for about a dollar. I completely devoured the delectable fowl at one sitting, while at the same time downing several glasses of juice. I could feel the nutrients running through my veins, replenishing my depleted body. Nothing had ever tasted so good. My hunger satisfied, my thoughts turned to another matter, a special friend I had met back home who came from Beirut.

Nafisa was a foreign exchange student who had lived for a year with family friends in Ashland, Oregon. She often wore her alluring veils and lovely embroidered gowns of silk that were a tradition in her cherished home. I had met Nafisa several times before leaving on my world trip. She had given me the telephone number of her parents, insisting that I contact her family when, and if, I ever came to Beirut. I hesitated to make contact with her family due to my somewhat tattered condition, so I reserved that decision for another day. Instead, I chose the long hike to a youth hostel outside the main city, in the village suburbs.

The following morning an event transpired that could have put a quick end to my young life, but instead provided me with one of those valuable life-lessons in awareness. With visions of more roasted chicken and orange juice on my mind, I naively strolled through some of the most dangerous neighborhoods in Beirut, en route to the city square. At this point in the journey, I had acquired a certain air of invincibility, mistakenly assuming no harm could come to me. After all, was I not merely a humble and compassionate citizen of the world minding my own business?

Walking down a dusty side street, I encountered a shopkeeper, who seemed relentless in his desire to chat. He addressed me in heavily Middle Eastern accented broken English, questioning if I were "Joe." Not sure of what he was getting at I nodded greetings to him, announcing my name was Robert. The man quickly called to his friends who materialized out of nowhere, making a small closed circle around me. Soon more men filed out of their shops. The tense atmosphere escalated, and just as the emotionally charged crowd was beginning to stir, there appeared an older sour-faced man at the outer edge of the group. With authority, he effectively used his hairy muscular arms to divide the crowd, making a path before him in my direction.

"Are you a Jew?" he asked ominously.

"No, and why do you ask?" I replied.

"What are your religious inclinations?" the man continued.

"Christian," I said, almost without thinking.

The man, clearly respected by his peers, communicated my comment to the agitated throng, some of whom by now were carrying tools and wooden implements. As it turned out, being Christian was slightly more acceptable to them than being Jewish. Grumbling, they slowly dispersed, shooting furtive glances back my way as they filtered into the nooks and crannies of their anonymous quarter. Following that experience, I became acutely aware of how significant matters of faith were, especially in this part of the world.

A new consciousness evolved within me regarding the risk factors in my surroundings, something that has never left me to this day. Few events in this part of the world took place by mere accident. This incident opened my eyes to the possibility of grave and unexpected consequences that could result from my incognizant actions.

I explored this captivating coastal city by day and returned to the youth hostel at night. On the third day, I was ready to telephone Nafisa's family, and I found in my notebooks the phone number she had given me. I was thrilled when Nafisa herself, home from Oregon, answered my call. My friend from Lebanon was ecstatic to hear from me and without the slightest hesitation insisted I wait on the street corner by the pay phone until their car picked me up. Within an hour, a chauffeur driven black limousine pulled to the curb with Nafisa in the backseat! Overjoyed at seeing a familiar face, I quickly climbed in to greet her. The limo surged forward through the busy streets and took us to a lovely part of the city and to the family's high-rise luxury condominium overlooking the sea. From the moment I stepped into the vehicle, it was like a dream.

The elevator brought us to one of the top floors of the building, with the door opening directly into the foyer of the enormous suite. Magnificently appointed with ornate furniture, marble statues and oil paintings, the room provided panoramic views of the ocean. Rich Persian carpets graced polished stone floors and cushioned my every step. There were also several servants, smartly dressed and standing straight. With Middle Eastern music playing in the background, Nafisa introduced me to her family one at a time. Later, after a sufficient amount of pleasantries, she took me to my room. I felt strong emotion upon seeing the private bath, fully realizing I had passed from subsistence living into that of pure luxury within the last hour.

I was embarrassed to inform Nafisa of my concerns regarding the bedbugs I had contracted from the various youth hostels. However, I was troubled about spreading them, and she was gracious in understanding my problem. It soon became a source of humor between us. We agreed not to inform her family at this point but instead made a quick trip to the local pharmacy where the comedy continued. I self-consciously tried to make myself understood to the man behind the counter, by scratching and pointing to different areas of my anatomy. Soon Nafisa came to my rescue and, acting as interpreter, communicated my needs. With the strong powder purchased that day, I rid myself once more of these little devils, liberally fumigating my bug-ridden sleeping bag as well.

There were a number of delicious courses served at dinner where the long polished hardwood table gleamed, hosting about ten family members, including Nafisa's lovely younger sisters. The travel stories fell from my lips as I, the guest of honor, savored each part of the extraordinary evening, regretting to see it end. It had been an extremely interesting experience to make the acquaintance of this gracious foreign exchange student when she was in my country and my family home. How blessed I was to now share her world and meet the influential and prosperous family from which she had come. This amazing young woman handled herself flawlessly in both worlds.

Nafisa's father took care to extend my Lebanese visa for several more days, and then it was time to depart. Once more, I sensed I would never see these lovely people again. Some thirty years later mutual friends told me they had seen her interviewed on television in Saudi Arabia, where she resided and was the owner of a gift shop. I could only assume that she and her family had fled Lebanon just before their terrible war, though I was never able to substantiate this. Their driver dropped me off at a busy taxi pickup spot in the center of town, and we said our farewells. I was alone again, a solitary figure standing on the street corner of a large alien city, a circumstance that was becoming increasingly familiar to me.

Black Mercedes taxis were the preferred mode of transportation used to travel from Beirut into Syria. I positioned myself on the designated street corner where riders who planned to leave for Damascus congregated. When at last the required five people for the trip had gathered, we loaded into the vehicle and our driver followed the road out of town. There were a couple of business types carrying briefcases, a Polish journalist, and one other fellow whom I suspected might be working in the lower echelons of the Syrian government. These were all serious men, thin framed, and dressed in dark and frayed sports coats. Everyone kept their words tightly measured, minimally rationing them out. Aside from the Polish man, I sensed that absolutely no one in this small group would be willing to trust the others any time soon.

The journalist spoke heavily accented English in subdued tones, sharing with me a little history of the area. Positioned in the very heart of the Middle East, Syria and Lebanon had fascinating histories, interwoven together since ancient times with a rich culture and a vibrant trade. The rocky landscapes of the Mediterranean shores to the west gave way to the diversity of olive groves, mountains and valleys we were now beginning to see. We would soon be crossing the Lebanon Mountains, south of Baalbeck, and into the southern extremities of the Bekka Valley.

The difficult road to Damascus first opened for regular commercial travel in the mid-nineteenth century, connecting these two vital trading partners. We continued east, paralleling the south bank of the Beirut River and then up and over low ridges revealing the terraced slopes that faced west. Intermittently, there were tall, massive tracts of dark sandstone looming up before us like enormous sentries guarding the desolate passes.

After an hour of winding our way over the narrow dusty road that led to the Syrian frontier, I began to decode the verbal prompts coming from our experienced driver. The man explained in detail the proper and life-saving conduct to use when crossing this risky border. He cautioned us to remember that the guards would have guns aimed at us at all times, and we should not make any sudden gestures. Nor should we engage in conversation with one another. There was little chance of that, I thought to myself. His final instruction to us was that we focus our eyes straight ahead and let him do all the talking. That sounded fine to me.

The border was now close, and in the distance I could see military vehicles flanked on both sides of the road. Coils of concertina wire marking the boundary stretched out in close spirals, perpendicular to the road and extending from each side of the steel gate. Uniformed soldiers with automatic rifles laid their cold eyes on us as we pulled up to the barrier, coming to an abrupt halt at their command. Once again, tension filled the air, and this time I was feeling my new sense of vulnerability.

Harshly, one of the Syrian soldiers ordered us out of the taxi at gunpoint. The taxi driver led the way, placing his hands on the roof of the taxi and spreading his legs. The guards indicated we should do the same. They groped and frisked us roughly while speaking in emphatic tones to our driver. The officer with the most disagreeable disposition asked us each several questions and then took an extended period to examine our passports. After much delay, they permitted us back into the cab, at which time our taxi slowly rolled away, while our driver cautioned us not to look back. I had no trouble following his instructions to the letter.

Much relieved to be back on the road again, the journalist informed me he had been through this ordeal numerous times. The drama behind us, our conversation turned to Damascus, the capital city we would soon be entering. He told me Damascus was more than 5,000 years old and was one of the world's oldest continuously inhabited cities of record. Located on the banks of the Barada River, the city had survived by promoting manufacturing, trade, and food processing. There were eight ancient city gates, the oldest again dating back to Roman times. Some time later, the old city came into view.

We entered into the main section of old Damascus where the street dissolved into a labyrinth of bazaars and open markets. Everywhere businesses were bustling with activity. There were open-air cafes, a variety of produce stands, and small shops. I was entranced with the graceful domes and arches, attributes of the Islamic architecture that were in evidence all around me. At last, our driver pulled the dark Mercedes over to the side of the road near the heart of the city and let us out.

The driver cautioned me about going out at night as I paid my fare and bid him goodbye. I slung my pack on my back and ambled toward the first fruit and vegetable stand I could find, happy to stretch my long legs again. I walked through the different market places, eating fruit and viewing the dazzling displays of merchandise. There were cases of jewelry and precious metals, textiles, spices, glass, copper work, and even ornate swords and daggers.

Later, my search for a youth hostel unsuccessful, I found an inexpensive and dilapidated hotel where I dropped my gear. After a short rest, I continued to explore the intriguing streets of the Middle Eastern capital well into the evening, discounting the earlier admonitions of the driver.

I noted that a swarthy looking man in an overcoat was tailing me, and regardless of my meanderings, this fellow remained my constant shadow. I surmised he was with the government and had been assigned to follow me. He made little attempt to escape my glances, and my better judgment dictated I should not stay in Damascus too long. After two days in the Syrian capital, I continued south by bus, past the Golan Heights and into Amman, Jordan. Later in the day, I entered the holy city of Jerusalem.

Jerusalem sits on a rock-strewn rise of earth located in the Judean Hills. I had arrived in late February 1967, just four months prior to the Six-Day War between Israel and her Arab neighbors; Jerusalem at this time was still part of Jordan. Throughout history, Jews, Christians, and Muslims have claimed this city a point of great spiritual significance. For Jews, Jerusalem represented the seat of religious and political activities for the duration of the Biblical era. Christians revered this ground for the many holy occasions that transpired here in the life of Jesus. Moreover, the Muslims believed that Muhammad rose to the heavens from this hallowed spot. Shortly after having entered the holy city, I became aware of this powerful amalgamation of spiritual energies.

I stopped some young British travelers in the street; I learned the youth hostel was on the border of "No Mans Land," that dangerous strip of property separating Jordan from Israel. They cautioned me about the bullets that flew over the wall at night. I set off for the hostel with the map they had drawn for me in hand.

Entering the hostel in late afternoon, I found the main living room packed with travelers from many countries. The residents kindly directed me to check in with Sami, the seventeen-year-old Jordanian manager. This likable young man soon presented himself, exuding heaps of goodwill and a natural aptitude for responsibility. After assigning me a cot in one of the back rooms, he invited me to join the group in the living room floor for some story telling and music.

General desultory conversation as well as keen political discourse abounded, while the music of flutes, harmonicas, and guitars reverberated gently off the walls of mortar and stone. Smoke from the wood cook stove curled up the wall, and then danced into nothingness across the ceiling in all directions. While he cooked up a tasty meal, Sami entertained us with anecdotes of his younger years growing up in Jordan. That night the collection of global trekkers from all over the world sat together, trading a wealth of information and stories regarding the routes, costs, and dangers one might encounter on the roads ahead.

In the days that followed I made many sojourns to historic sites, such as Bethlehem, Jericho, the Mount of Olives, the Dome of the Rock, the Wailing Wall, the Church of the Holy Sepulcher, and the Via Dolorosa. I can remember how awed I was when at the Palestine Museum I viewed the displays of Dead Sea Scrolls. These were found in the caves of Qumran, being the rare manuscript fragments of the Old Testament.

One day, I hitchhiked out to the Dead Sea, the lowest point on the earth's surface at 1,365 feet below sea level. I stripped down for a swim in the buoyant salty waters. I placed both hands behind my head and floated on my back with a portion of my body protruding above the waterline. This was a silent and lonely place where the solitary soul could quietly reflect. There was no one in sight as far as I could see and any direction. Naked, I walked barefoot over the warm sands at the water's edge, visually digesting the remote and desolate features. Out here, there was only man, God, and the solitude of the desert. Moved, I suddenly understood how religions had grown from these austere but inspiring surroundings.

One afternoon I came back to the hostel early to find Sami energetically doing his chores. I asked him if the Jordanian people ever ate camel meat. He shared with me that sometimes the poorer members of the community did, and that growing up he had eaten it many times. However, he added, when a camel died of sickness or old age, the meat usually ended up as food for the dogs. Sami assured me that camel meat was available in the markets and further implied he would buy it and cook it for us if we agreed to pay for it. That night I took up a collection for the Great Camel Feast.

Early the next day, Sami rolled out a rough burlap carpet over the large living room floor of the hostel. Refusing any help, he spent the entire afternoon deeply involved with food preparation, working tirelessly over the small stove until all the cooking was finished. Then, he directed the colorful band of vagabond tenants to take their places in a circle on the covered floor. Once seated, Sami surprised us all by sailing large flat unleavened rounds of pita bread around the room to each of us. Next, he brought in several large bowls of yogurt, and evenly spaced them around the circle of guests. Following that, he emerged with a huge sack of steaming cooked rice and poured it out in the middle of the room. It formed a cone-shaped pile on the carpet more than a foot high. Finally, the cooked camel meat came in another bag, and he emptied it over the pile of rice. Great chunks, about half the size of a man's fist, tumbled down the mound of rice like boulders down a mountainside. Pots of tea were set out after the food was in place, and we were ready to feast.

It remained a mystery as to how Sami prepared this large quantity of food, serving in excess of twenty people, from his small wood stove, but he had done it expertly. Cheerfully, he instructed us on how to partake of the delectable meal he had created. We all watched and listened intently as he first took a handful of yogurt from the bowl and clumped it together with the rice held in his other hand, fashioning a round sticky ball. It was a method similar to constructing a snowball. Then, after taking a bite out of the gooey sphere, he followed up by sinking his teeth into a large chunk of the seared and heavily seasoned camel meat. Mesmerized by the process, we mimicked him in every way, anticipating the new flavors that would soon flood our taste buds. The camel was rather tough and wild tasting, making it difficult to develop any kind of a strong craving for the dromedary in the future. The event did spark a superb talent show afterwards, creating an opportunity for the musically inclined residents to carry their impromptu jazz session well into the evening. Those few unforgettable nights spent at the hostel fostered many pleasing memories in the years to follow.

There were many pleasurable days ahead surveying the ancient streets of old Jerusalem on foot. I enjoyed the days of leisurely investigation of this unique vortex in world history. On one particular day, I found myself exploring the connected roofs of the old city with my British friends. We walked a good distance elevated above the streets, jumping from rooftop to rooftop. Occasionally we stopped to take our rest by leaning back on one of the many rounded convex domes that protruded upward through the solid ceilings at our feet. We chatted for hours in the warm sun, enjoying the scenery-packed horizon of Jerusalem.

The larger question of what manner of travel I could use to reach India was always in the back of my mind. On the day that followed the rooftop walk, a spry, energetic and middle-aged man of Italian descent came into the youth hostel and introduced himself. His name was Gino. He brought with him an important proposal at a critical time, providing me with an opportune solution to the question of my journey to the east.

The Treasury of Petra

Pipeline to Baghdad
Chapter Ten

To the desert go prophets and hermits; through deserts go pilgrims and exiles. Here the leaders of the great religions have sought the therapeutic and spiritual values of retreat, not to escape but to find reality. —Paul Shepard

Those familiar yearnings to roam had infected me once again, calling for my return to the road. These longings had gained strength in the days prior to meeting Gino. He appeared suddenly, dropping into my life at precisely the right time to offer an ideal answer to my travel concerns. We were destined to become good friends and stitch together common interests in providing for our mutual gain.

Gino led me out to an aging Mercedes mini-bus that sat in front of the Jerusalem Youth Hostel. The vehicle was cartoon-like in character, with a curved and sagging bumper that resembled a faint smile and a split front windshield reflecting back at me like two large eyes. We sat inside the van to discuss his need for additional riders to share the expenses on an overland road-trip to India.

He mentioned that he carried camping utensils and several tents. Having made the passage to India once before, he was able to estimate accurately that the journey would take four to five weeks. Gino cautioned the passage was not without its elements of discomfort and even danger, most particularly at border crossings. I felt my pulse quicken as he continued to explain his novel proposal. My portion of the fuel costs for the small bus would come to about $50, and I would be responsible for my own food. He added that all the passengers would split evenly the cost of any new tires he might need to purchase along the way. Gino took responsibility for any major repairs to his vehicle.

In addition, Gino declared that he was under contract to deliver two Australian girls from his starting point in London to Madras, on the southeast coast of India, where they would continue by ship to Perth. The girls, in their late twenties, were disgruntled immigrants, returning to their native Australia after two years in England, anxious to get home by the most economical means possible. Traveling overland to India was all they could afford.

I was relieved to find an answer to the problem of reaching the subcontinent and quickly agreed to hitch a ride with him as far as New Delhi. I slept remarkably well that night, knowing my transportation requirements for the next month or more were firmly in place. Gino hung around the hostel for the rest of the day, also signing up Morgan, who had just arrived from Egypt, for the ride to India.

Before leaving for Baghdad, Gino offered to take some of us from the hostel on a side trip to Petra, the Nabataean capital built in the fourth century BC, in the desert of southern Jordan. This was a city carved into the stone side-walls of a monumental gash in the earth. Petra had been lost to human history for many centuries and then rediscovered in the summer of 1812 by a Swiss explorer traveling overland from Damascus to Cairo. An exceedingly dangerous region for a European at the time, he disguised himself as a Muslim sheikh to prevent detection. It helped that he was fluent in Arabic. My curiosity blossomed as I accumulated more historical details regarding this hidden city in the wilderness. Each additional fragment of information fueled my desire to investigate it even further.

We set out over a dusty barren track in a southerly direction from Jerusalem, towards the Gulf of Aqaba. The road led us through a long shallow basin within sight of a range of mountains that formed the eastern edge of the Wadi Araba. While he drove, Gino was good enough to fill us in on some of fascinating history he had learned from a previous visit to the lost city.

Petra had become a hub of archaeological research in the Middle East since first detected by the modern world in the early nineteenth century. Oddly enough, few tourists had ever heard of this secluded and remote site. In 1967, this remarkable location remained relatively unexplored, even though the legends of its exceptional appeal had long preceded its discovery by the public. We felt fortunate to have this unique chance to experience it.

As Gino expertly transported us over long stretches of dirt road, our merry group came alive, singing what popular songs we could remember, helping the hours on the road to slide by quickly. Finally, we reached our destination, climbing out of the van to immerse ourselves for the rest of the day in the ancient city of Petra.

The point of entry was a narrow chasm called the *Siq*, which snaked through a geologic fissure in the sandstone, piercing the eastern side of the range. From the floor of the gorge, I could see a slim band of sky beyond the top of the vertical walls, whose sides climbed for several hundred feet. The sedimentary stone layers reflected soft hues of orange, with some fading into a stunning pinkish purple. The colors blended by degrees, as does a rainbow, gradually crossing the spectrum from one to another. The lengthy path narrowed before opening out into a stunning array of classical facades, astonishingly chiseled into the vertical walls of stone. The group stood in silence, absorbing the view and listening to the multi-pitched groans of the wind whistling through the constricted canyon. They called to us like mournful spirit voices from the past.

The ancient city of Petra, mentioned in the Dead Sea Scrolls, controlled most of the caravan trade leading west to Gaza. Its inhabitants were Aramaic-speaking Semites who lived in the fortress city, encircled by the towering cliffs that protected them from outside assaults. The year-round streams inside the city created an artificial oasis and provided the inhabitants with life-giving water. They efficiently managed the menace of flash flooding by implementing an intelligent system of cisterns, aqueducts, and dams.

The first antiquity to greet us upon entering the city was "The Treasury." This striking façade, hewn from stone, instantly brought to mind many questions. How was such a building even fashioned? How had it lasted all these years, remaining in such splendid shape? What was its true purpose? We continued walking, coming upon a great massif from which were carved the structures referred to as "The Tombs." Again, there were detailed architectural faces created out of a stone slope known as the "King's Wall." Our little posse of adventurers was quiet now, mesmerized by these exceptional displays recessed in sandstone relief. Farther on, we came to the massive outdoor theater area. From here, I could view the heart of the old city, and continued to explore on foot "The Monastery" and "The Temple of the Winged Lions."

I followed walkways paved in cut stones and lined with traditional Roman columns, the remnants of their several hundred years of control, beginning in 106 AD. I made my way over to a sidewall and ascended the sheer stone face using hand and footholds to reach an isolated ledge that I had spotted. I sat there in stillness, pondering the magnificence of this ancient wonder, while trying to capture its essence in my journal.

Late in the afternoon, we congregated back at the entrance to begin our reluctant departure from the secluded city. This extraordinary jewel was once aptly referred to by John William Burgon in his prize-winning sonnet, as "the rose-red city half as old as time." During our ride back to Jerusalem, I delighted in reviewing in my mind's eye the extraordinary images of that rose-red city.

Back at the hostel, Gino prepared us for the trip to Baghdad. He spoke of a long, straight road through an arid wasteland, paralleling an oil pipeline extending from Jordan to Iraq. There would now be four of us embarking to the east besides Gino. There were the two Australian girls, Lynn and Charlotte, Morgan, the young Englishman whom I had met previously in Alexandria, and myself. We prepared to depart the following morning.

Our first stop was Amman, Jordan, where we picked up fuel for the mini-bus and topped off the supplemental fuel tanks on the back bumper. I stocked my pack with flat bread, cheese, oranges, and jam. I was hoping that these reliable stores would protect me from the debilitating and dreaded stomach afflictions that had plagued me since Egypt. Amman was a clean Jordanian city that seemed to function well, and I had faith that the food I had purchased would not cause me any further intestinal problems.

Leaving Amman, we found ourselves trailing a continuous stream of heavily loaded freight trucks rumbling east on a poorly paved road. They were part of a continuous conduit of goods, hauled from the Middle East to the major population centers of Baghdad, Kuwait City, and Bahrain. The long convoy stretched out into the horizon ahead. Passing them was not a satisfactory option, as another truck would merely replace the lumbering obstacle we had just overtaken. The plume of road dust kicked up by the trucks mixed with the toxic clouds of diesel exhaust to limit our visibility and hamper our breathing. It was nearly impossible to avoid the deep ruts in the road that suddenly materialized before us as we moved along. The long line of rolling stock sandwiched us in for hours. From Jerusalem, it was approximately 210 miles to Ar Rutbah, the first Iraqi village beyond the Jordanian-Iraqi border.

We passed the time by sharing our stories. The Australian girls lamented over their short and disappointing stay as immigrants in England and yearned to be home in the "outback" as soon as possible and without incident. Our British passenger, Morgan, was expecting to find a new life in Ceylon with his bother in the tea business. Gino was originally from Italy and told the story of immigrating to Australia through one of their programs designed to encourage population growth. From there he had shuffled back and forth between England, Europe, and Australia concerning himself with various ventures, the specifics of which were vague. I enjoyed the conversational exchanges as it took my mind off the cramped conditions in the van. In time, each of us found our favorite reclining positions and slipped in and out of wakefulness while progressing steadily toward the Iraqi frontier.

A sudden loss of momentum awoke me with a start. The truck traffic had now thinned out, and we were on an isolated stretch of road. There, standing about 100 yards ahead, was a lone Iraqi soldier in his drab military garb, dusty and disheveled, aiming his rifle directly at our windshield. He gestured with authority for us to pull over, then without so much as a word, climbed in and took a seat. After casting a cold stare around the interior of our van, he nodded to Gino to continue down the road. This was the first in a series of uninvited hitchhikers we would encounter; their heavy-handed techniques would leave us all unnerved. We let off our surly and unshaven rider a little farther down the road, whereupon he slung his rifle carelessly over his shoulder and ambled toward a complex of mud-walled dwellings. Then he looked back one last time, leaving us with an intimidating smirk.

Much discussion followed. We were now close to the border crossing, and Gino spoke at length in the same vein as had the Beirut-Damascus taxi driver. The primary rules to remember were to let Gino do all the talking and not to make any sudden movements.

As we came to the Jordanian-Iraqi border, large men with challenging eyes and armed with automatic weapons motioned us off the main road to a designated pullout. Barking commands at Gino until he came to a stop, a stern officer reached into the van for our passports. Then he pointed to some rather primitive-looking earthen huts, much like those we had seen along the road earlier. After confiscating our travel gear at the checkpoint, they allowed Gino to park off the road then took his keys. We followed the soldiers as they marched us each to a separate hut. Mine was composed of a bare room with a tamped dirt floor and a wicker-type cot made from palm fronds. There was a small rectangular opening in the hardened mud wall, which served as a window. It was much too small for an escape.

Someone resembling an officer, wearing a frayed uniform lacking any military adornments, followed me into my hut. He began to question me at length in a thick accent, his meaning difficult to decipher. My rising indignation peaked when he instructed me to remove my clothes. I protested this gross mistreatment and violation of my privacy, but to no avail. The next thing I knew I was standing before the thuggish soldier in my skivvies! He promptly packed up all my personal belongings, including my clothes and backpack, and exited the small room, locking the crude plank door behind him from the outside. It was sobering to find myself in more or less a prison cell with no rational explanation as to why. This was only one of the many times on the trip that I accepted events, as if paying tribute to fate, only in the hopes the true reason for what had happened might come to light in the future.

I passed that evening and most of the next day alone with my thoughts. This stint in solitary confinement gave me pause to reflect on the progress of my trip up to now. My mind replayed the proceedings of the past year like an old movie. Eventually, I had to deal with the realization that I had lost my freedom, an unpleasant revelation. Late in the afternoon of the second day, without explanation, the guard opened the door, handed me my things and walked away without a word. I quickly dressed and burst out into the sunlight, extricating myself from the dungeon, grateful for my liberation. I touched lightly on this experience in a letter home.

(Posted from) Tehran, Iran   *March 7, 1967*

The pipeline runs alongside the road in places but the majority of it is underground. For the most part sandstone, gravel, and desolate desert were all we could see. Military men all along the way came out of nowhere, stopped us, asked for passports, and then climbed in. Finally, we realized they were just hitching a ride with us to the next outpost. We came to the Iraq border in the late evening. It was very spooky. Sloppy soldiers with automatic weapons forced us out of the van and then kept us locked up separately for the good part of two days. They went through all our things before releasing us to continue down the road.

I eagerly joined the other members of our entourage who were already at the van. We headed down the road, exchanging stories, all wanting to speak at once. Fortunately, there were no reports of physical violations, and it appeared we were merely the victims of a good scare. It was obvious that the soldiers had looked through my journals, as certain papers between the pages were not where I had left them. Gino was at a loss, saying he had not been through anything like this before, but added things change all the time in this part of the world. He was only too was glad to be on the road again.

My history courses at the university had referred to this region as the Cradle of Civilization, and I was keenly aware of the significance of Mesopotamia. This area, perfectly suited for growing food, was located in a sometimes-marshy plain and flanked by the Tigris and Euphrates Rivers. Neolithic tribes had migrated and settled here from the north after the last Ice Age, more than 10,000 years ago. Many think the roots of civilization sprouted from this region, spreading quickly from these humble beginnings.

Hanging Gardens of Babylon

Gino added that this geographically favorable area encompassed part of a larger region known as the Fertile Crescent. Here under ideal living conditions different societies melded together, sharing their ideas and discoveries. The Tigris and Euphrates offered exceptional opportunities for inland transportation, and there was an abundance of fish and waterfowl, providing a plentiful supply of protein-rich foods. The fruit of the date palm yielded another valuable food stable for the populace. Melting mountain snows unleashed unpredictable flooding on the Babylonian plain, laying down the extremely enriched and fertile soils. The conditions existing between the two rivers allowed for highly structured systems of irrigation canals, constructed as far back as 5,000 years ago.

Small towns were beginning to appear, and Gino let us know Baghdad would be coming up soon. Our route passed through Habbaniyah and then Fallujah, until we at last approached the outskirts of Baghdad. Parking near the center of the city, we dashed across the dusty, busy streets to step up onto the raised sidewalks that passed under the numerous arched alcoves. This walk led to numerous small business establishments tucked away in hidden corners and alleyways. Tired looking men draped in long shirts guided their pushcarts burdened with wares down the dirt streets. The same streets were cluttered with military vehicles, frolicking children, and stray dogs. Everywhere I turned there were inquiring onlookers, who returned my glances with curiosity and wonder. Absent was any evidence of other Westerners, which left us to be the star attractions.

Begging children followed me to a small bank where I was unsuccessful in cashing a traveler's check. Brown-eyed clerks directed me down the street where I found a larger bank and was able to obtain some local currency, though not the U.S. dollars as I had wished. The poverty was worse than I had seen in Cairo. There were signs of political instability, with tanks guarding the radio station and troops with rifles directing traffic. We stopped at a police station and registered. They gave us directions to a campground at the edge of the city for foreigners passing through. They informed Gino before leaving the station that we should not try to visit Babylon. We wondered how they had read our minds, as this was our next planned destination. After setting up camp, Gino entertained us with more of Iraq's intriguing history.

The official British Mandate in Iraq had ended in 1932. The next twenty-five years brought the discovery of oil, the founding of the Arab League, and the overthrow of the Hashimite monarchy. The newly created government then proclaimed Iraq a republic, and there followed a period of significant instability and changes in leadership. The resulting coups that took place ceded the reins of power to the Ba'ath Party. We happened to be making our transit across the country during these tumultuous times.

We ignored the warnings of the local constabulary and left the campground early the next morning, bearing due south, intent on seeing one of the Seven Ancient Wonders of the World. The road to Babylon followed the Euphrates River in the general direction of Al Hillah. Gino's overriding confidence quelled the chorus of doubt that had been mounting among some of the passengers. Soon there was a consensus that the real crime here would be to find ourselves this close to such a timeless and historic landmark and fail to explore it. Though many mysteries still surrounded the exact location of the antiquity, we continued on to what appeared to be the authentic and official site.

Gino lectured us in depth on the stories and legends associated with Babylon while we all absorbed this information attentively. He shed light on "the paternal healer," or Hammurabi, the first king of the Babylonian Empire. He established Babylon's complete dominance over the vast Mesopotamian region and its peoples around 1800 BC. One of his well-known contributions to history was a collection of edicts, written on a six-foot tall stone tablet referred to as Hammurabi's Code. In due course, this code became the foundational law for nearly all of the Semites, which included the Babylonians, Assyrians, Chaldeans, and Hebrews. The empire fell into gradual decline after his enlightened reign ended.

Much later, King Nebuchadnezzar II constructed the Hanging Gardens of Babylon during his forty-three-year rule, beginning in 605 BC. The alleged purpose for this monumental project was to remind his homesick wife Amyitis of her cool green native home of Media, located in the mountainous valleys of Iran. Writers chronicle that Babylon's splendor far surpassed anything known in the world at that time. The inside walls were fortress-like, protecting the exquisite temples and palaces, some containing immense statues of solid gold. The famed Tower of Babel, a temple to the god Marduk, looked down upon the city from what seemed like the heavens.

Some writers tell us the hanging gardens themselves were 400 feet in width and breadth and rose to a height of 80 feet. Other historical accounts indicate they rose 320 feet above the Euphrates River. Overhanging cascades of plants and flowers flourished from the irrigation systems that brought water to the different rooftops, terraces, and balconies. These layered vaults, filled with soil deep enough to permit the growth of large trees and vines, extended across the elevated walls. The displays formed a lush covering for this artificial mountain that rose from the flat Mesopotamian terrain. Unfortunately, only a mound or "tell" had survived the eons since its magnificence. Gino told us the skeletal mud-brick remains of vast foundations were really all the visitor could view of these ancient dreamscapes. We pulled into the site and parked.

There had been significant efforts made in extracting the earth, which had covered the ancient structures over time. There was evidence of the careful process of soil removal in every direction I looked. Loose piles of earth lay heaped at the perimeter of this historical dig. The effort seemed entirely the result of hand labor. I watched dedicated men hovering over their implements, consumed in the noble effort to unearth the treasured relics of a Babylonian past.

There had been mud-brick walls unearthed, and they protruded vertically from out of the excavation area. I saw lion-like figures, glazed in ornamental relief on the face of the brick panels as I meandered through the site, carefully stepping over the extracted soil. I had to admit, with the exception of the occasional piece of equipment lying about, there was no real confirmation that a highly prized professional operation was at hand.

The lack of security was apparent, and I was amazed at the informality of it all. It would have been easy for anyone to pack off one of the bricks. Maybe this explained why the police in Baghdad had implored us not to proceed to Babylon. It was an inspiring day, and we drove away in the late afternoon entertaining visions of how the Hanging Gardens might have actually appeared.

After several more days in the Baghdad area, we moved in a northeasterly direction towards Jalawlah and closer to the Iranian border. We passed through groves of date palms near lazy rivers and viewed thick patches of marsh reeds that pushed themselves up along the water's edge. I reflected on the rich and unique history spawned from this geographical area and felt exceedingly fortunate to have touched a small part of it.

Tehran

The Caspian Sea
Chapter Eleven

Ah, make the most of what yet we may spend,
Before we too into dust descend.
—Omar Khayyam

Small rural Iraqi villages materialized before us and then faded quickly to our rear as we progressed toward the belt of foothills that extended to the Zagros Mountains. This impressive range rose in the distance ahead, just beyond the Iranian border. As we left the Mesopotamian lowlands, linear ridges began to form, occasionally giving way to the lightly forested broader valleys. This would be our last night in Iraq. With no available police station to consult, Gino pulled the mini-bus onto a heavily rutted side road and carefully motored towards a grove of nearby trees in search of an adequate campsite.

Soon we came upon a location where fallen logs had formed an almost perfect half circle, the ideal setting for our needs. We parked the van and unloaded our gear, still within sight of the main road. Morgan and I went on a short expedition in search of firewood while Gino pitched camp and set up the tent for the Aussie girls. Some blankets thrown over the logs gave us a place to sit while we ate dinner.

The temperature began to drop soon after sundown, signaling it was time to break out our ground cloths and sleeping bags. The fire had diminished to a glowing bed of hot coals and now radiated a steady soothing heat. I had always enjoyed the aroma of a campfire, and the smoke brought back fond memories of camping experiences as a youth. I threw a couple more chunks on the fire and then climbed into my down bag for the night, or so I thought. I reclined while looking directly up into a blue-black sky peppered with bright stars. The camp was quiet except for the snapping and popping from the fire, and I began to drift off, falling into a deep and abiding slumber.

Some time later, I was startled into consciousness by the loud sounds of a heavy vehicle and men yelling down on the main road. A large troop lorry had come to a halt near our turnoff. Pausing for a moment, the truck then repositioned itself, and ominously turned our way, pushing forward slowly down the side road in the direction of our camp. A shot of adrenalin exploded through my body, and I was instantly wide-awake, alerting the group in a muted voice of this latest menace.

A dozen or more Iraqi soldiers poured out from the back of the drab-colored army truck and, rifles in hand, quickly encircled our small camp in military fashion. An officer slowly approached us, requesting first in Iraqi, then in broken English, to see identification or our passports. He carefully studied each of the documents we had given him and then, displaying a troubled expression, began to speak.

"Why are you here?" he asked. Gino, who spoke bits and pieces of Iraqi, made an effort to explain our presence. Shortly after that, the officer barked commands to his uniformed subordinates and several of them immediately charged into the woods with their flashlights to gather additional fuel for the fire. The sharp sounds of breaking branches followed, with the soldiers soon returning to camp bearing great armloads of firewood. At once, our dwindling campfire transformed itself into a conflagration of dancing flames, generating vast amounts of heat and sending a column of sparks high into the night air.

We understood from the troubled Iraqi officer that camping here exposed us to danger from the rebel Kurds who frequently came down from the northeast to cause problems in the area. He conveyed that the bonfire acted like a beacon, indicating heavy activity to any would-be attackers, and this would provide us greater safety. The thought did cross my mind that all this business about the Kurds could well be just a story imparted to gain our confidence.

Exhausted from these new stresses, we all retreated into the warm confines of our sleeping bags once again, trusting the Iraqis were friendly and telling the truth. The soldiers obediently stayed at their posts guarding our camp throughout the night. Then, at daybreak, without a word, they climbed into their truck and moved on down the road. The mechanical whine from the low gears of the lorry slowly diminished into silence, leaving me with another interesting story for a future time.

As we progressed northeast, through the river valley of the Nahr Dyiala and on to the Iranian border, I paused to reflect on the precariousness of my situation. The mini-dramas such as with the soldiers were becoming an accepted ingredient of my life, unfolding almost daily. Knowing this, I was becoming aware of a certain equanimity that was developing within me, a quality that surfaced just as I needed it. An overall acceptance of occurrences as inevitable continued to grow, as I increasingly found myself immersed in uncertain, even dangerous circumstances far beyond my control. Due to the element of unpredictability in these countries, my fate was truly out of my hands. For peace of mind, it simply became easier to view it that way, and in time taking it a step further, having a faith that someone was watching over me.

Crossing into Iran brought some favorable changes, the first being the ease of dealing with the border authorities. The political climate seemed much more relaxed, similar to what I had experienced in Europe. In addition, the Iranian roads seemed in far better condition, which made our ride more comfortable. The topography, which formed a natural barrier between the two countries, changed radically to one of mountains and high gravel basins. We pushed the little mini-bus ever higher, covering long distances without seeing any foliage. In this arid desolation, a village would appear here and there, at the edge of an oasis, tucked away at the base of one of the many rock ravines. In time we came to our first major city in western Iran, that of Kermanshah.

This ancient provincial capital, which sat elevated in the fertile Karkheh River Valley, was a commercial center for grains, sugar beets, fruits, and vegetables. Textile production was also prominent, and we passed many shops displaying the eye-catching Persian carpets produced in the area. Due to its location on the old caravan route to Baghdad, now some 235 miles behind us, Kermanshah had been a key market center as far back as the fourth century. The streets were clean, and there was enterprising activity going on all around us. The Iranian people seemed delighted to meet us, regardless of where our curious wanderings took us. The majority of the population was of Kurdish extraction. It was here we spent our first night in Iran, with plans to pull out at dawn.

Our next major destination was Tehran, 354 miles to the northeast in the direction of the Caspian Sea. We spent hours threading our way through mountain passes where gusts of cold air caused us to shiver and reach for our sweaters. As we crossed the flat plains, the temperature would rise; the terrain was better able to catch the rays of the sun. Some geographical areas of this country seemed barren, with only great slopes of scree and falling stone visible. Our route would then open abruptly out onto a fertile basin, populated and thriving. We camped for the next night on the western edge of the city of Hamadan, the morning finding us back on the road.

It was early March 1967 when we pulled into Tehran. We were road weary, having traveled over 2,200 miles in the ten days since Jerusalem. There was a high backdrop of snowy mountains rising from the northern edge of the city. The name "Tehran" came from the combination of two Persian words, "Tah" meaning "end or bottom" and "Ran" meaning "mountain slope." This was a fitting name indeed, considering the prominent edge of the Alborz range we could now see. This imposing set of mountains stretched its spine from the Caucasus in the west to the southern flanks of Turkmenistan, a republic of the Soviet Union, in the east. It separated the Iranian metropolis from the watery expanses of the Caspian Sea, directly to the north.

Wisely, Gino checked in with the local police again, and found them to be extremely accommodating. They directed our group of five to a temporarily vacated dancing school in the suburbs of Tehran, allowing us to use it as our base camp for the next several days. We met the school security guard at the front gate, and after entering the building, he opened one of the classrooms for us with a well-used skeleton key. We made our beds in the aisles between the desks and were able to take much-needed showers, luxuriating in the first hot water we had enjoyed on the journey. This delighted us all, especially the Australian girls, who were ecstatic over the shower and toilet facilities.

Our little band of travelers percolated with excitement as we began to explore this newfound city. Food was of paramount interest to all of us! Long-grained Caspian rice with lamb kabob was one of the local favorites, available on any major street corner from the vendors for just a few cents. Shish kabob, or skewered meat, appeared to be a ubiquitous and tasty staple for the Iranians. There were also platters of saffron rice, supplemented with spinach and bean dishes. The inhabitants were affable, smiling and greeting us with, "*Salaam*," a salutation meaning "peace be upon you." Several times, gracious strangers in the street extended invitations for us to visit their homes and share dinner with them.

We enthusiastically accepted two of these invitations, experiencing extraordinary evenings with our warm and hospitable hosts. The families appeared large and extended, with people coming and going at will. The women wore traditional *chadors*, colorful full-length fabrics thrown over the head and held shut in the front. The apartment interiors were modest, appointed with a few special heirlooms, particularly carpets and nicely framed paintings on the walls. For the most part the rooms were spare, but there was the occasional piece of ornate furniture, passed down from a previous generation. We took our meal at a low table, near the floor. Some sat on cushions while others sat directly on the Persian carpets. After dinner, we listened to the emotionally captivating scores of Iranian music over the family radio. The conversations drifted in and out of politics.

The Shah of Iran, Reza Pahlevi, the last of a continuous monarchy lasting for over 2,500 years, was still on the Peacock Throne at that time. The original throne, created for the Mughal Shah of Jahan in India in the seventeenth century, fell into Persian hands in 1739. Encrusted with precious gemstones and formed primarily of gold, it supposedly held the largest diamond in the world at the time, the *Koh-i-noor*, or "The Mountain of Light." Legend foretold the diamond brought misfortune and death to all males who wore it. The fate of the original Peacock Throne fades from history shortly after that.

The diamond eventually ended up in the Crown Jewels of the United Kingdom, the latest in a series of historical transfers as a spoil of war. It was here that I viewed the incredible stone in the summer of 1962. Then, I asked my Iranian hosts about life under the Shah.

Although there was some mention of censorship and the questionable methods employed by SAVAK, the Shah's secret police, generally people we spoke to expressed satisfaction with how things were going. Many Iranians enthusiastically recounted they had relatives living in the United States, and they often inquired if I had traveled to a specific state with which they were familiar.

Historically speaking, Tehran had a tradition of dissension among its populace, probably stemming from tensions between the different mountain tribes who had once dwelled there. However, in these modern times, this sentiment was not detectable. The city was decidedly cosmopolitan and Westernized, with the residents of Tehran well-educated and acutely aware of their unique place in the world, past and present.

Persian carpet shops lined the streets and attracted buyers from many parts of the globe. These customers had much in common with the traders of old, who brought not only their money, but also their various influences into the region. I was told a carpet purchased in Tehran for around $1,500 could be sold back home in the U.S. for at least $15,000! When I considered my current net worth of roughly $200, I concluded these business opportunities were well beyond my reach. In addition, I was skeptical of these claims, as it was usually a rug merchant imparting them.

Some historians have surmised that Iran, or Persia, was a significant enough force in civilization to postulate that the study of history itself began here. Ancient cultures of the Iranian Plateau existed even before those evolving from Mesopotamia. The name

Iran, meaning "the land of the Aryans," is synonymous with an empire that once extended from the Euphrates in the west to the Indus in the east. It offered enormous contributions to human history, from the cultural remains of Paleolithic Neanderthals in the Zagros Mountains, to the enduring legacies from leaders like Cyrus the Great and Darius. The messages from Iranian history still speak to us today.

The Cyrus Cylinder created the first formal declaration of human rights, and has been said to have influenced the framing of the U.S. Constitution. The Nile-Suez Canal, coinage, and road systems produced by the visionary King Darius were the forerunners of later achievements in Western civilization. The King's revisions in the legal system lent credence to his acquired name, "Darius the upholder of the good." The Persian Empire was the first global superpower, fashioned from and represented by a position of tolerance and respect for other cultures and religions. The legendary Silk Road injected new influences into China as well as brought new ideas back to Persia, connecting the different arteries of thought and trade for the benefit of all. Much of this information we learned from our Iranian hosts.

Feeling the need to press on, we followed one of these ancient routes north, away from the city, climbing up into the higher elevations of the Alborz range. This course led us through phenomenal gorges carved from stone by the perennial melting snows. Cutting across the backbone of this major range, the road at times penetrated deeply into the mountains' granite core. Relentlessly winding up and over nature's climatic barrier, we left the arid and desert-like central Iranian plateau behind. There were peaks on all sides of us now, their Jurassic shoulders of limestone dressed in forest steppe and bonsai-like Juniper shrubs. The higher margins exposed permanent snowfields, while a white powder of frost dusted those levels below. The temperature plummeted in the mountains, and feeling the cold, we were happy to begin the descent down the northern side of the Alborz crescent, following the road that led us through the impressive Chalus River Valley. Our path parted vast forests before taking us down to the vacant sandy shores of the Caspian Sea.

The vast breadth of this inland sea reached out before me, extending beyond the limits of my sight. Gino had told us this was the largest enclosed body of water on earth. Gazing out across the flat expanse, I beheld the slightly arched horizon line that was a distinct division between the dominions of sea and sky. Landlocked and below sea level, this great "endorheic basin" swallowed up the large rivers that poured into it, among them the Volga and the Ural. Although three hundred miles wide and seven hundred fifty miles long, this massive accumulation of salty water, that rested at the bottom of a closed basin, was somehow not subject to tides. This great sea had a lower level of salinity than those of the oceans and was the well-stocked repository for freshwater as well as saltwater fish.

The Caspian Sea and its rivers were the prolific breeding waters of the prehistoric looking sturgeon. With its extended snout, rigid looking body, and pronounced bony protrusions, it was distinctly different from other fish. Some lived to be 100 years old and could achieve a length of up to 30 feet. The unfertilized mature female produces much sought after caviar. Many of the local inhabitants here fished, harvesting the roe, or fish eggs, a lucrative bounty extracted from expired sturgeon in the small processing plants located on the southern Caspian shoreline.

Colorful cans packed with the rich black *beluga* originating from this region were transported the world over to satisfy a runaway epicurean appetite for this fishy delicacy. Russia also played a large role in this industry, procuring their product on the northern shores of the lake as well. Only a small percentage of the sturgeon harvested yielded the priceless roe and, as a result, future populations of the great fish were certain to dwindle.

We had passed into the Mazandaran province, thick with vegetation and lush woods. The area appeared untamed and sparsely populated. It was evening, and we were heading east, with the vast glassy sea to our left and the sun directly to our rear. It appeared as a great orange marble sinking slowly behind the distant western edge of the mountains. Gino pulled our van over to a secluded beach to settle in for the night. All in our little group had agreed it was far too cold to sleep outside on the ground that night. As usual, the temperature had fallen dramatically after sunset.

Extolling the virtues of my down sleeping bag to everyone who would listen, I accepted a dare and, against Gino's advice, decided to sleep on the frozen sandy shore outside. Stretching my long legs while sleeping outside was always preferable to sleeping in the fetal position in the back of the van. Early evening brought an ever-increasing chill before I realized the high probability I had made a mistake. My pride would not allow me to move back into the van, so I just snuggled down deeper into the warm darkness of the bag, covering my head with my trusty wool sweater, breathing in just enough of the frosty air to survive. The night progressed slowly, and I finally fell asleep to the howls of the frigid wind from off the Caspian.

I awoke to the voices of my travel-mates calling loudly from the vehicle's windows. Peeking out, I was shocked to see them flailing their arms and pointing. By some fluke of nature my bag had been encrusted in a cocoon of ice that had formed while I slept, leaving me encapsulated in a frozen chrysalis! We all got a good laugh over that one, and I nursed a bad sore throat for the next few days.

We exited the Caspian region in the morning, following roads over the desolate and arid strip of northeastern Iran, tracing the mountainous boundary south of Turkmenistan. Topographical uplifts on both sides of us had left a natural passage some fifty miles wide cradled between two mountain ranges. Again, windswept and forgotten villages came into our field of vision, and then quickly disappeared into the horizon to our rear. We moved across desert plains of gravel, dotted with the occasional ruins of ancient mud-brick forts and time-withered communities like Bojnurd and Quchan. Then we journeyed through the Kashaf River Valley, which led us to the city of Mashhad.

This metropolitan Iranian outpost was the second largest city in the country, the picturesque and primary destination of Islamic pilgrimages. It was significant in our pilgrimage, as it was the last major Iranian city we needed to negotiate before reaching the border of Afghanistan. The name Mashhad conveys the meaning a "place of martyrdom," as evidenced by the elegant Imam Reza Shrine, the resting place since 818 AD for the revered Imam. The strikingly handsome golden dome above his grave demanded the absolute attention of all who had caught a glimpse of it. Two glittering minaret prayer towers of like material reached skyward in radiant architectural splendor over the sacred complex below. The Imam Reza Shrine was sprawling, dominating the city square with various chambers and passageways, some displaying the vividly colorful and intricate tile mosaics. With so much to see, we made the decision to spend an extra day here before continuing eastward to the frontier.

This Muslim city flourished with an economic activity level resulting from ages of providing for pilgrims who were omnipresent in the streets. Daily, the numerous transportation junctures into this holy site attracted thousands of new consumers to view the vendor's wares in the shops and outdoor marketplaces. The region also had a reputation for spawning great Persian poets and acquiring some tolerance for intellectual pursuits of a more secular nature. The venerable poet, mathematician, philosopher and astronomer, Omar Khayyam, creator of *The Rubaiyat*, came from this intellectually fertile area. I could visualize how within these landscapes, illuminated by a clear yellow light of the sun, gifted men might well be inspired to produce great works.

Filled with the energy around us, it was difficult to plan for departure. We parked the van on a secluded side street that night, where we slept until early morning when the Muslim call to prayer woke us for another interesting day of exploration.

Destiny beckoned for us to leave yet one more intermittent destination, as we recommitted to the route east. Our troop of travelers expressed some regret at leaving Mashhad, but a sunny morning found us rolling out of town to the southeast in the direction of the Afghan border. It gave me immense pleasure to realize that I had tasted this rich culture for just a moment in time and that I would be able to savor the unique flavors found here for many years to come.

Greece to India
Route

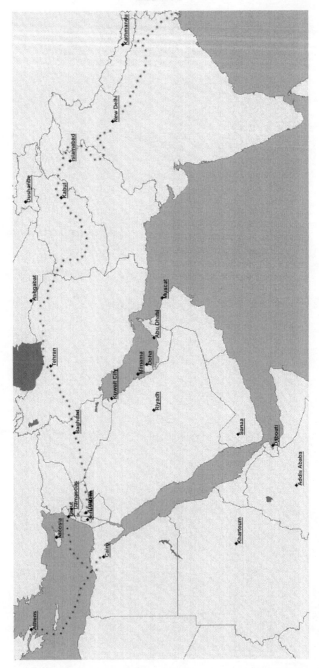

Alas Afghanistan
Chapter Twelve

Journeys, like artists, are born and not made. A thousand differing circumstances contribute to them, few of them willed or determined by the will—whatever we may think. —Lawrence Durrell

Not until years later would I begin to comprehend the degree of misery woven into the war-torn history of Afghanistan. The dictionary defines the word *alas* as "an exclamation of sorrow or pity." These were my feelings when crossing into the unusual land where time had stood still and storms in the hearts of tribal men still raged against the scourge of unwanted intruders. Since my visit, this resistance has continued, and there is no good reason to believe it will ever cease, for it is the natural consequence of a fierce and proud people.

Our passage across Afghanistan was a difficult trudge through the stubborn wintry chill that remained in mid-March. The biting cold from the previous night resided in the rocky soil all day, and I could feel its icy breath when I walked across the ground. The overcast skies covered us like a giant shroud. The high alluvial plains and the dry creek beds that divided them were devoid of noticeable plant growth. Aside from the occasional sighting of a solitary shepherd, tending his flock in the distance, there was nothing to distinguish these expanses from the barren surfaces of the moon.

Coming into archaic Afghanistan from Iran, where the vast achievements of Persian and Zoroastrian culture had been evident, presented a remarkable study in contrasts. My curiosity continued to be piqued, as I sensed our total immersion into a culture that was quite different, fostering new questions about this lonely land and its people.

Gino tried to convey to us the nature and character of those who inhabited these forlorn regions of the world. Centuries of hardship and bitter struggles had honed their survival instincts, leaving a tough and resilient populace. The rule of warlord society, brutal and barbaric, embraced the basic maxims of power and influence. A "survival of the fittest" mentality blended easily with the prevailing traditional views of family and religious ideals. Harsh conditions had always existed and led to intense competition between tribes unless, of course, they were fighting a common foe from the outside world.

Here, they practiced the dictates of fair dealing selectively. The Machiavellian proverb "the ends justify the means" existed in these mountain passes long before such concepts were taught in Western universities. Treaties and agreements, both in war and peace, were inconsistently honored and adhered to, much to the dismay of the naïve intruder looking to strike a deal. No one understood this fact better than the British, after their fatal retreat from Kabul in January 1842. Here they suffered their worst defeat ever in the First Afghan War, losing 16,000 soldiers and *aids de camp* in a brutal massacre that transpired *after* a negotiated truce.

The relatively short drive into Herat from the border of Iran led us through several primitive villages. Eslam Qal'eh presented us with our first typical glimpse of the ancient world we were about to enter. Small drainage ditches, not much more than open sewers, ran parallel on each side of the dirt streets. This meager water supply appeared to be the single such resource for the entire village. One person would be washing his body in this roadside trickle while ten feet away a woman kneeling down in her burka would be washing the vegetables for dinner. Further down the line I saw children urinating in the same ditch. I wondered just how long it would be before the next wave of dysentery hit us.

Pushtu and Dari (Farsi) were the official languages spoken here. Gino knew a touch of Pushtu, which added enormously to our options. Our route led us into the Harirud Valley on the way to Herat, passing several farms and the occasional village. Gino informed us the agriculture of the region was primarily grain, cotton, fruit, and other seasonal crops. These fertile regions, irrigated by the Harirud

River that surged down from the Central Highlands, supported a population that followed the agriculture and food supply. Herat was the crucial economic center for all of western Afghanistan, as it was the main crossroads for trade and a primary artery for transportation. It was late afternoon when we drove our dusty van into the city.

The hotel in Herat was three stories tall and composed of wooden beams, dried mud and straw, fashioned from the time-honored methods of nomad construction. Our little group of five came into the hotel eager for a substantial meal and a warm bed. After checking in with the young boy standing behind the crudely constructed counter, we deposited our gear in what you might call the lobby and walked into the restaurant on the main floor.

This was a dark, dingy, and smoke-filled room with a dirt floor. There were low tables and the customers sat on carpets laid over the tamped soil. Some were leaning back casually against the outside walls of the room while drinking their tea. The place was quite crowded, full of lean Islamic men with black beards, some wearing sheepskin garments and others in long robes. Many packed swords or daggers, and wore their turbans neatly coiled on their heads. The scent of the heavily spiced mutton stew simmering from iron caldrons in the kitchen wafted through the dining room. I looked back towards the lobby after sitting down and saw older boys making repetitive trips up the plank staircase with large water jugs on their shoulders. Later I discovered this was to fill the cistern on the roof, which supplied the gravity fed water system for our cold-water showers.

Protecting our ravaged intestines was a clear priority, and we were cautious in ordering, choosing white rice and cooked vegetables that we deemed safe. Refrigeration was for the most part nonexistent, and it was customary for the cooks to season the meats heavily, masking the rancid flavor of the near-spoiled animal flesh. It was anybody's guess how long the fare may have been hanging in the open-air street markets, coated with flies, prior to preparation. There were not many choices on the menu, and reading it was like making a futile effort in deciphering hieroglyphics.

After dinner, we sought out the young English journalist who had been sitting in the lobby. He was on assignment in Herat, sent to report on the progress of the mammoth road projects initiated by the Americans and the Russians. He informed us the Russians were using road designs proven impervious to the perils of flash flooding, allowing water to rush over the road and not under it as with bridges. Experiences in Siberia with near arctic temperatures had taught them how to better solve the problems of buckling and surface degeneration due to freezing. The American sections were testaments to how not to build a road, with bridges and complicated viaducts leading to vast canal networks constructed to carry away the excess floodwater. These road surfaces were decomposing, and the water systems were showing ominous signs of filling up with silt. He also told us the Russians were building their road segments to military tank strength, possibly with a future eye on invasion. This did become a reality only eleven short years later, in 1978.

We spoke for hours with the Englishman about the stern, independent, and foreboding temperament of the Afghan people in this land "civilization left behind." The Afghans would view it much differently, saying they lived this way by their own choice. The journalist captured our interest for the rest of the evening with his personal discoveries regarding these extraordinary people. Their mere name translated from the older Persian to mean, "Noisy, unruly, or less than sedate."

He remarked it was no wonder the very long list of invaders, beginning with Alexander the Great, followed by Genghis Khan and his Mongol hordes, Tamerlane, Babur, and in modern times the British had never once caused the Afghan people to acknowledge their defeat. Throughout history, the least attempt by outsiders to subdue this inhospitable region and its peoples invariably met with catastrophe.

The more successful of Afghan defenses were due, in part, to the expert use of *jazails*, that smoothbore, long-barreled muzzleloader accurately fired from great distances by the Afghan tribesmen. They perched virtually unseen on the rocky mountainous promontories well above their hapless opponents. Setting the Afghan version of the Kentucky Rifle carefully in a forked rest, they fired fitted lead balls, ignited by powder kept dry in pouches made from camel scrotums!

The common wish held by all the would-be conquerors was to control the Crossroads of Asia, and to use Afghanistan either as a buffer for protection from a surly neighbor or as a gateway into other countries. Each in his own time discovered how simple it was to make the thrust into Afghanistan, and correspondingly how much more difficult it was to make the retreat back out. In the end, none of these uninvited guests came to control any part of this wild country.

Hiking the dirt-packed streets of Herat the next morning, I was impressed with their great width, built to accommodate the extensive bazaars that bordered them. Bartering merchants offered leather goods, metal work, and different kinds of fabrics. There were hats of tightly napped wool made from the skins of young lambs. Bulky hand-knit sweaters of rough spun yarn hung on outdoor racks in the wind, exuding the strong scent of natural lanolin into the air. Camels and horses carrying their riders trod through the streets in a ceaseless parade of random activity. Cold winds off the Hindu Kush blew fine dust everywhere. Cloaked women shopped the marketplaces in their screened burkas, which covered them from head to foot.

I saw an ancient citadel built for the city's defense against the territorial claims of the Persians, who had once challenged them from the west. The protection of the city was a timeless and fundamental concern. Herat was also the home of a fifteenth-century mosque, and we walked the scattered ruins of its elegantly ornamented minarets. The occasional fakir with his opium pipe sat in the shadows that fell between the earthen walls of the street shops. It was all here and had been for centuries. This ancient trade route constantly exhibited its great treasures, and invariably, there was something here for everybody.

I spoke to some of the travelers who had journeyed here from the West and were hanging out in the streets and cafes, most here for some aspect of the drug trade. There were no real laws to hamper this, with raw opium and hashish being easily obtainable by the international smugglers who visited Herat. It was here I spied the Smith Brothers again, those suspicious characters who had left the Greek island on the ferry with Darlene. She did not appear to be with them.

Rumors abounded of great fields of opium poppies grown in the warmer months not far from town. Local men approached us several times in the streets; these were hard individuals with vacant eyes, wishing to sell such items. Their bodyguards viewed us suspiciously from the background, with hands tightly gripped on the hilts of their daggers. There was a lawless element of intrigue in Herat, probably not unlike our Old West, and we were constantly in anticipation of the danger that was in the air.

The van was fueled and our packs filled with flatbread, oranges, and other items we deemed safe to eat. Increasingly, we continued to suffer from the ravages of intestinal bugs that kept us in a weakened condition. About the time we got used to the organisms in the water of one locality, it was time to move on to another. Of course bottled water had not yet come upon the scene. We were continually experimenting with different foods in an effort to find anything that was more favorable to our digestion.

Moving toward the southwest plateau on a Russian-built section of the Herat-to-Kandahar road, we braced ourselves for a ten-hour journey over 400 miles of dirt road towards the town of Farah. After a couple of hours, we could see the snow-capped fingers of the Hindu Kush Mountains reaching out towards us. They called these the Central Highlands.

Well into the journey we started to encounter heavy snow, making it impossible in some stretches to determine where the road was in front of us. Gino asked me to take the point, which required walking out in front of the mini-bus to probe the snow with a stick, in search of the road. I was wearing the only footwear I had, heavy wool socks and the sandals made for me by the Greek leather worker in the *Plaka*, near the Acropolis. It was not long before the numbing cold was climbing up my legs.

On the Russian section of road in the Afghanistan outback, we came upon a mysterious apparition, one that gradually grew out of the horizon as we came closer. Upon approach, it appeared as a mirage, something we had seen before when traversing the deserts of Iraq. They were small and indistinguishable at first, later growing into a more sophisticated shimmering and ethereal presence. As we drew closer to this current ambiguity, the outline of a manmade structure appeared. Was that the derelict remains of a Grand Hotel? Closing in on the anomaly, we could plainly see we were correct, and the damage to the building complex from weather and pilgrim alike was obvious.

No landscaping could be detected. There were only the sand dunes that had drifted up against the exterior walls of the hotel, inclined at a sharp angle. We drove up under the covered entrance of the dilapidated and ghostly hotel, designed for valet parking. As we piled out, I could easily imagine a uniformed doorman standing there.

Upon entering, we saw the vacated remnants of the main desk, with a counter partially dismantled, I assumed for firewood. There were no hotel employees and rooms were apparently free, which only added to the surreal nature of the situation. We crossed the threshold of the main lobby to find nomads squatting in a circle, roasting kabobs over small fires kindled directly on the tile floors. It was obvious there was no power and no running water. Windows were broken, and sand was everywhere. Someone indicated with hand gestures that we were welcome to take a room, which we did, finding nice bathtubs without the water. The Australian girls were intent on taking a bath, instructing the young nomad boys to bring buckets of water from the well out back and to fill their tubs with the cold water. Oddly enough, the boys agreed and the bucket brigade was born. The hotel was woefully out of place, as useless as a movie set dropped in from another civilization, from another time.

We later learned the Russians had built the hotel with the backing of international investors as part of the terms in their highway agreement. We could only surmise at this point that it was another casualty of different cultures meeting in the middle of nowhere. The Afghans certainly did not need such a hotel, and it continued to present a scene difficult to grasp.

The winds howled mournfully that night. We sat around a small fire one of the "guests" had built on the floor of the lobby, talking to a young man from Europe who had appeared out of the wasteland from behind the hotel. His English was good enough to tell us he lived in his desert camp adjacent to a band of nomads who tended their flocks. This explained the bleating and bells we had heard earlier. He was just a short distance out, still having access to the hotel well. He claimed these people were prone to violent behavior and would kill a stranger for a quick move or questionable look. In the months he had been there, this small group of Afghan nomads had just recently allowed him to camp close to them, but it was clear he was not to enter their camp. He warned us not to make sudden moves if they approached.

Word came to us after reaching Kabul a few days later that there was a European man shot to death in this area, presumably by the nomads. We assumed it was the fellow camped near our hotel. These kinds of happenings went unpunished in this part of the world, and it would not be the last time we caught wind of such things. Again, in Kabul, we heard about a young European girl who was stoned to death in one of the parks for not wearing a *burka* to cover her. This story absolutely unnerved the Australian girls, who were traveling uncovered.

We left early in the morning on the last stretch of road to Kandahar. The ride took us most of the day. At last the ancient city came into view, and so too did the thick walls of hardened mud that surrounded it. We entered the town and stopped on a side street. Small caravans of several camels each plodded slowly through the streets. Herds of goats trailed them. Shy and subdued women wearing long shawls lurked at the corners of primitive houses. Typical of the oasis towns here, there were bazaars and mosques, the one here claiming the tomb of the first emir of Afghanistan, Ahmad Shah.

Legends say Alexander the Great founded this southern Afghan city, and its colorful history grew from those early beginnings. Not far away were the ruins of the original city destroyed by a Turkmen ruler in 1738. Sparsely populated, Kandahar was located approximately 3,450 feet above sea level on a rich irrigated plain with evidence of fruit and grain production. The wool textile mills and fruit processing plants provided jobs for the inhabitants of this fertile region.

This stretch began the proposed improvements of the American sections of the Afghan road called the Kandahar-Kabul highway. The next 670 miles would take us over sixteen hours of very hard driving, over frozen dirt track with snow and ice. A greater visual presence was now emerging of the Hindu Kush range. These snow-crested mountains were the western extensions of the Himalayas, running across this landlocked country from east to west.

It was bitter cold regardless of what the small heater in the mini-van pumped out. This remote and desolate country spoke to us in wails sung by the frigid winds that poured down on us from the rugged central mountains. Confining our driving to the daylight hours, we took two more days to reach Kabul. On the rare occasions we saw other vehicles, they were usually trucks.

Kabul had endured centuries of upheaval, brutal wars, and international intrigues. This ancient capital city, situated on the banks of the Kabul River at 5,900 feet elevation, had resisted the grip of unwanted conquerors from the outside throughout Afghan history. These people had dominated the dramatic narrow mountain passes to the north, south and east for 3,500 years. The most celebrated of these were the Khyber Pass and the Kotal-e Lataband Pass, both found on the road from Kabul into Pakistan.

The city conveyed the vibrant energy of a south-central Asian capital and, once again, there were the characteristic ditches running parallel to the dirt streets. Reinforced concrete stem-wall construction had been used for the multi-storied buildings. The time-tested hardened mud-walled houses with sloping roofs spread out at the base of them in all directions. Tarps and tents prevailed in the majority of the bazaar areas.

The enduring tribal loyalties that had made unifying this country of warlords impossible were unmistakably visible. As we walked through the smoky shops we saw small bands of bearded and dark-eyed Afghans sitting close together, talking and drinking *chai*. The men were clannish and similar in appearance, as if they had come from the same compressed genetics offered from one isolated valley. The clothes they were wearing looked cut from the same bolt of primitive cloth.

After finding the Khyber Restaurant, the international traveler's sanctuary, we had something to eat and later secured rooms in a nearby hotel. A long walk to stretch our tired legs from the many cramped days in the van was in order. Proceeding slowly and always with caution through the hardpan streets of this foreign world, we felt ourselves viewed with cool suspicion by the locals. They were curious but respectful and generally left us to our own devices. However, angry mobs could quickly form and Gino implored us not to provoke the local devotees, regardless of the circumstances.

The road construction project of the Americans was apparent, and one day I decided to seek out the project supervisor about a job. My funds were running low, and I thought this would be an interesting place to settle down for a while. They were looking for heavy equipment operators, a job with which I was familiar. I spoke with the foreman who asked me to come back and talk to him again in a couple of days.

I spent the next day exploring Kabul on my own. I stopped for lunch, recklessly eating an unknown meat dish, heavily spiced and served with flatbread. As I exited the dirt floor restaurant, I suddenly felt light-headed. Soon after that, completely overcome with severe stomach cramps, I began to sweat and my steps became unsteady. Within thirty minutes, I collapsed, finding myself dizzy, vomiting, and unable to stand. The thought occurred to me I had been poisoned! Miraculously, some British Overseas Service volunteers saw me from the balcony of their apartment and rushed to my aid.

These folks were the equivalent of our Peace Corps volunteers. They proved to be extraordinary people, and two of them carried me back to their room where I lapsed into unconsciousness for the next two days, delirious with fever. They said I spoke aloud of my childhood, turned a shade of gray, and lost control of my bowels. On the third day, I started to come around. My body felt stiff and sore, like the day after the first high school football practice of the season. In addition, I was terribly dehydrated. They nursed me back from the edge with tea and toast. This did not help with my problem of continuing weight loss, and I was very much aware of how loose my clothes were becoming.

The volunteers informed me this was a local bug and that it could take me weeks to recover. They also explained that utensils were absent among the common people and that in this part of the world people used their right hand for eating and food preparation and their left hand was for matters of personal hygiene. It was easy to get the hands mixed up! As a result, there were many nasty germs in and around the food. This especially affected travelers adversely, as they had very little immunity to the local bugs. I told them I was familiar with this system of using the hands, as I had not seen toilet paper since Europe, only a can of water.

The British Overseas Service friends contacted Gino at the hotel and informed him of my illness, and he immediately delayed the departure from Kabul. Everyone waited for my recovery as several days passed. Finally they could wait no longer and asked me if I were well enough to travel. My enthusiasm for the job prospect on the Afghan road had now dimmed as I realized I was in no shape for heavy labor. Concluding I would continue to Pakistan with our group in the van, I prepared to say goodbye to my new British friends. I mentioned to them that I had been accepted into the American Peace Corp but due to the knee problem had not been able to undertake my assignment in Malaysia.

Along the way, I asked different people I had met to contribute to my reading list by recommending a book. This provided them an opportunity to share something with me that had influenced their lives. These new friends introduced me to the author Herman Hesse, placing a copy of *Siddhartha* in my hands on my way out the door.

Through the ages, the Kabul River had efficiently carved passes through the mountains east of the city. Travelers in the Khyber Restaurant coming from that direction had showered us with descriptive accounts of this tall meandering gorge in the earth's crust. Following this narrow conduit away from Kabul, we were soon amazed at the spectacular ravine that began to envelop us. It masked the bright day, making it appear as if we were looking at the sky from the floor of a well. It soon swallowed our mini-bus completely.

Khyber Pass

Khyber Pass
Chapter Thirteen

And there fled on the wings of the gathering dusk
A savour of camels and carpets and musk,
A murmur of voices, a reek of smoke,
To tell us the trade of the Khyber woke.
—Rudyard Kipling

The road leading into the sunrise took us away from Kabul and cut across the eastern edge of Afghanistan. We moved steadily through scenic mountainous territory in the direction of the Pakistani border. Gino maneuvered the mini-bus forward over the dirt road that formed the contour line running parallel to the river. The steep and barren gorges made the path ahead oftentimes appear impassable. Great talus slopes of broken rock seemed to shore up the mountains around us while erratic boulders formed immoveable bulkheads at their base. The country was treeless, harsh, and desolate, and with each mile we traveled, the emptiness was more apparent. Here, these extreme and unforgiving regions had shaped the lives and traditions of a sturdy tribe of residents known as the Pushtuns.

The Afghan roads had been demanding, and maintenance stations were virtually non-existent. Each transient took his turn in forming the road, gradually breaking down the once coarse stones to gravel in their passing. Forced to slow down countless times for the deep ruts, Gino was a master at maneuvering around the many rocks that had fallen on the road from the towering mountain ledges above. This was a wild country, as untamed as were its people.

Gradually, the topography changed as we drove farther east and closer to the Afghan town of Jalalabad. The arid rocky ground began to give way to vast irrigated plains that spread out in all directions before us. It was a more fertile land around us now, one that drank from the pure rivers flowing out from the majestic Hindu Kush range. Pushtun farmers here produced large quantities of fruits and nuts, permitted by the warmer temperatures. Rice and other grains were cultivated in the fields. We had stumbled upon a hidden climatic utopia where everything flourished. This was in stark contrast to the cold and lifeless high plateaus we had passed over in the long journey across the country.

A most esteemed Mogul Emperor of India, Akbar the Great, first frequented this paradise nestled on the banks of the Kabul River around 1560. Later in history, Jalalabad came to be the winter capital of the old Afghan royal families, drawn to the area by the benefits of mild conditions and available food. It was an exotic name, befitting such a place, the last major town to encounter before making our approach into the historic Khyber Pass. We stopped here to fill up on fuel and check our well-worn tires before proceeding.

Throughout history, the Khyber Pass had been an important focal point of political geography in this part of the world. In Aramaic, Khyber means "across the river" or a "divide." The pass slices through the Safed Koh Mountains and forms the easiest land passage across this natural geologic barrier, one thirty miles long and fifty feet wide.

Our course traced the same timeless narrow tracts toward the Indian subcontinent that multitudes of adventurous traders, pilgrims, and conquerors had taken before us. Gino told us that the Macedonian conqueror, Alexander the Great, used this route to invade the fertile plains of the Indus Valley in 326 BC. For centuries, this caravan route was the road used by smugglers and men of commerce, as well as the bandits who trailed close behind them. Adventurers from many different periods in history followed this path to fame, fortune, and in some cases, failure, famine, and death.

In the third Anglo-Afghan War of 1919, the British and the Afghans engaged in ferocious action at Khyber Pass. A multitude of tombstones marked the sites of fallen warriors on both sides, who died from the monumental conflicts that occurred within this strategic juncture. As we rode along, viewing the graveyards at the roadsides, I felt an uneasy shiver run up my spine. I wondered if these were in some way a warning. Great battles came to life in my imagination, and I could almost hear the cries of the wounded and smell the scent of gunpowder in the air. This mountain pass linking Afghanistan with Pakistan stood as silent witness to the glories and tragedies born out of the historic events that transpired here. There had been much bloodshed in the confines of these steep and narrow canyon walls.

In modern times, fleeing refugees used the pass to move their families and belongings to safer locations, depending on the direction of the conflicts. I could not help feeling exposed as I scanned the ridges towering above, wondering if modern day snipers with their *jezail* rifles might be lying in wait. Cautiously we threaded our way along the river and around the sharp bends of the rough road. In due time, we put the stony ravines of the Khyber Pass behind us in our slow and steady migration east.

Now we were entering into a new valley, one that held the frontier town of Peshawar, our first stop inside the Pakistani border. I wondered how we would find this new country and if it would be as primitive as Afghanistan. We crossed the frontier without incident, moving towards the next town.

Driving into the busy village, we were somewhat shocked to see men armed with pistols and daggers, standing in doorways on each side of the road. Others swaggered across the dirt streets like the gunslingers of our Old West, dressed in baggy trousers, vests and loose shirts that hung down over their waists. Conditions in Peshawar were as dramatic as they were curious to me. In a letter home, I recorded some of my impressions.

(Mailed from) New Delhi   *March 27, 1967*

...we came into the first city in Pakistan traveling east. It was Peshawar, a wild place! Swarthy, bearded men wearing turbans were everywhere, some walking the dirt streets casting threatening stares, others squatting low on their haunches at the street corners, as compressed and efficient human forms. It seemed they were all

waiting for something to happen, the next violent act or maybe just for their kabobs to cook on the open fires over which they hovered. This was a smugglers' town, and everything had its price, even people. I got lost at night wandering down the dark alleys where the children followed me throwing stones. I startled a man in the shadows, and, seeing I was a Westerner, he instantly pulled a knife, forcing my quick retreat into a dirt-floored teahouse where I again shocked them all by my arrival. I sensed I should not have been there...

Our little band of nomads from the West decided to try one of the small local restaurants. There were intimidating looks on the faces of the locals, possibly unhappy with the uncovered heads of our two Australian women. The story of the European girl who had been stoned to death in Kabul for the same indiscretion was fresh in our minds. We entered a little shop and took a pillow, sitting cross-legged on the earthen floor. It was plain there was only one kind of tea available, as it came quickly without our having ordered it. We all requested the curried lamb, the dish stewing in a pot hanging over the wood fire at the other end of the smoky room. A barefoot waiter brought the bowls to our table, a fixture barely off the ground. He seemed completely fixated on our presence. Like some of the dangerous places visited before, we felt on display with all dark eyes upon us as we consumed the rancid tasting mutton. As expected, several of us came down with a bad case of dysentery later.

Delighted to be free of the smoke and the scrutiny, we exited the restaurant and hurried back to our van, with many inquiring children following in our wake. With no hotels in sight, we parked on a secluded side street and decided to sleep in the mini-bus. The lack of restroom facilities when we were sick was a problem with which we were now familiar, but still one not easily solved.

The primary consolation of being in the group was the opportunity for discussing the degree of misery each was experiencing. These pity-pot sessions were not without their humor. Listening to the constant litany of complaints and protests was somewhat therapeutic, but over time it was also something I found increasingly difficult to tolerate. I had to remind myself this was all part of the trying experience of traveling with a group overland to India in a small van.

Peshawar was unsettling; hostile glances from the men of the town reminded me of the time I walked into a biker bar on First Street in San Jose, said the wrong thing, and had a fight on my hands. However, here we were apparently the only Westerners in a town of tough men toting knives and guns. Having all agreed we had seen enough of the sights, we left Peshawar the next morning, anxious to find a less explosive location where we did not feel so isolated and vulnerable.

Our next major city, 100 miles down the road, was the provincial capital of Rawalpindi. Apart from the wide main street, the city was a chaotic tangle of crowded streets, bazaars, and military installations. It was the center of power and politics for the country, with coups and assassinations being common occurrences in Pakistan's short history. Through time, this geographical region had been a strong trading hub for the Punjab and Kashmir regions. We continued moving.

Six hours later, we rolled into Lahore, road-weary and desperately in need of baths and provisions. In addition, we had pushed the Mercedes van long and hard and it was ready for an oil change and a service. Having left Jerusalem, Jordan, on February 25, it was now March 22, and we had been on the road for nearly a month. Living out of the confined quarters of the mini-bus had frayed our nerves past all reasonable limits. I was eagerly anticipating our arrival in New Delhi and the time when I could take leave of the group and strike out on my own. The girls were planning to stay with Gino as far as Madras.

Pakistan did not feel like a safe place to me, and everything I read about it at the time confirmed my feelings. For the most part, this country had known turbulent and chaotic times since its creation and independence in 1947. This was one result from the partitioning of India by Britain's last viceroy, Lord Mountbatten. There were still great underlying strains between the Muslim and Hindu factions, especially over the incorporation of Kashmir into India. Pakistan had not yet achieved a working democracy and continued to be ruled by military dictatorships. Gino had warned us to stay out of trouble here, to keep a low profile and not make waves, especially in the streets with the vendors. "It does not take much for the mob mentally to break out here," he said. His words would turn out to be indisputably and regrettably prophetic.

After a prolonged scavenger hunt, we finally found ourselves in front of the Lahore police station. Gino climbed the stone stairs and entered the building to register us as "visitors in transit." He was excellent at finding relatively safe places for us to spend the night. We waited patiently in the mini-bus as a crowd made up of young and restless teens gathered outside the van. The Australian girls opened the windows and began talking to them, something Gino had cautioned us not to do. They first inquired, "Where are you from?" Then the inevitable follow-up question, which we had heard many times before, "Are you Muslim?" At this point, the girls carefully shut the window with a smile; an eternity passing before Gino emerged from the station. He pushed his way through the crowd that had gained in size and climbed into the van, promptly driving us away, careful not to run over anybody. He brought with him the directions to a youth hostel where we had permission to layover for the night.

We made our camp in the walled yard of the state-run traveler's hostel located on the outskirts of the city. There were showers and restrooms, something we now considered great luxuries. Several other overlanders from Europe were staying there as well, this being a welcomed arrangement for the local police who were concerned for our safety. After cleaning up, I washed some clothes and hung them out to dry in the late afternoon sun. Later, we cooked the last of our food on the portable camp stove. The compounding of different stresses over the last few weeks had left us emotionally drained, so we turned in early for the night.

The next morning, sufficiently rested, Morgan and I accompanied Gino into town. The girls stayed behind to relax some before the tenuous Indian border crossing that was to come. After making several inquiries, we found a place to service the Mercedes bus. Gino decided to wait with the van while Morgan and I chose to disappear into the congested back alleys and side streets to look around. It was apparent early on that all eyes were upon us as we negotiated our way farther into the labyrinths of the small businesses and cottage industries. Morgan exuded the air of an upper-class Englishman, irascible and even haughty at times. This did not play well with former colonial subjects and more than once on the trip we pulled him from troublesome encounters. We finished our walk, and then caught a ride with Gino back to the hostel.

My letters home painted just a glimpse of the life in Lahore, something alien to anything I had previously encountered before the trip. However, I was increasingly familiar with these scenes as they became more commonplace.

(Mailed from) New Delhi   *March 27, 1967*

...the dusty and chaotic streets were crowded with rickshaws, colorfully decorated freight trucks, men on bicycles, and people walking among sheep marked for ceremonial slaughter. There was obviously a religious and venerable respect for the cows that ate from the merchants' stands with impunity; fresh cow manure was scooped up with bare hands as quickly as it was expelled, then expertly patted against the walls of buildings where it stuck, drying in the sun, becoming a future source of fuel...

A day in the markets of Lahore was an experience in itself and we spent hours in search of supplies like toilet paper, matches, stove fuel, and food. We had some free time that evening to lounge about, tell some stories, and listen to the local music on the small record player we found at the hostel.

In the evening, after dinner, Gino put forth an amazing amount of information about our next major destination, the Golden Temple of the Sikhs in Amritsar, Punjab province, India. He expounded on this most revered religious center of Sikhism, a religion I would learn more of in the days to come. Established in the late fifteen hundreds, the temple was a marvel to behold. A stone tank lined with marble steps, constructed to support a quarter-million-square-foot artificial lake, was the centerpiece of the Golden Temple.

He also spoke of a white marble bridge that led out to the golden prayer room in the middle of the sacred lake where readings of the Holy Scriptures occurred daily. The outside perimeter of the walkway around the lake was walled with buildings several stories in height. Gino revealed to us that much of the inside temple was covered with gilded sheets of gold. He unveiled just enough information that night to set fire to our imaginations. We were anxious to learn more about the Sikhs and their fascinating religion after our upcoming arrival in Amritsar.

Tensions were high at the Indian-Pakistani border in the spring of 1967. The route between these two antagonistic countries had been closed from time to time as we had made our way overland from Jerusalem. To our good fortune, the border was now temporarily open, and we did not want to miss the opportunity to pass into India. Gino thought it best we not delay by staying in Lahore any longer than necessary. We did not want to take the chance that the border would close again, isolating us in a difficult part of the world. Therefore, we decided to leave for Amritsar the following morning.

Sleep came effortlessly that night, with each of us looking forward to the border crossing the next day. We sensed passing over this frontier was an appropriate climax to the investment of time and energy we had expended. We had paid our dues, making the journey to India, not by jet plane or ocean liner, but by the more difficult overland route. It had been an extreme rite of passage we were all proud of, and soon we would collect our reward, experiencing Mother India and her countless, timeless treasures.

Golden Temple of the Sikhs

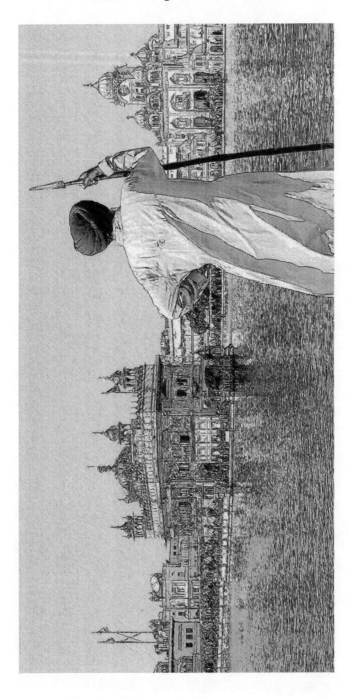

The Golden Temple
Chapter Fourteen

Life is a pilgrimage. The wise man does not rest by the roadside inns. He marches direct to the illimitable domain of eternal bliss, his ultimate destination. —Swami Sivananda

The level of tension within the country we were preparing to leave was easy to sense but difficult to describe. Increasingly, we felt the existence of some unseen threat, requiring a constant state of vigilance. It was like standing on the slope of a volcano that could erupt at any time, to spew molten lava from its many vents. In Lahore, I felt isolated in a population decidedly homogeneous in appearance and belief. The restless spirit infecting the inhabitants seemed born of emotion more than reason, and it was present throughout the day in our dealings with the local people. Whether this feeling was a product of our weary minds or actually one reflecting the truth made little difference. The exhausting effect on our psyche remained the same. The consensus was that we exit Pakistan as soon as possible, before anything unpleasant could develop.

It was early morning when we broke camp at the youth hostel, loaded our gear into the van, and rolled down the road towards the Indian border. As the teeming city of Lahore faded into the distance behind us, we took pleasure in looking ahead to Amritsar and the Golden Temple of the Sikhs. Our spirits lifted at the thought of experiencing a new country, knowing the personal goal of each of us to reach India was now within grasp.

The drive into the Punjab region was not without apprehension, as India and Pakistan had been warring enemies for years, specifically over Kashmir. The idea of crossing the frontier between these two large antagonists was very worrisome. As we closed in on the border outpost, Gino reminded us to stay relaxed and not create any unnecessary commotion. Stopping, we were required to register inside the compound, where we soon found ourselves answering endless questions and filling out numerous forms. We expected these delays, but they still tried our patience. We were at the mercy of suspicious border bureaucrats for more than an hour, before at last being set free. We were grateful to be back on the road.

Soon we encountered the first Indian village, where Morgan and I decided to take a walk through the marketplace in search of sugar cookies. These had become a great staple for us, as they were one of the few foods we could count on to not give us dysentery. Others were oranges and eggs, when we could find them. Cookies were much more plentiful, usually found in most of markets of the villages along the way. They had become "legal tender" on our mini-bus, with much bartering and trading going on among us, especially in times when one or the other of us had exhausted their cookie supply.

Morgan and I left the van together on the cookie expedition, moving steadily through the crowded streets where we eventually found ourselves separated. After making my purchase, I began to look for him. I scanned the boiling sea of human beings that filled my field of vision. Then I heard loud voices coming from the far end of the bazaar. I hurried over to find Morgan arguing loudly with one of the vendors over the price of cookies. The tenor of both the men's voices rose to an uncomfortable level, attracting much attention. Embroiled in a heated discussion of whether to pay one cent or two per cookie, Morgan's face had now turned deep red. It all seemed quite absurd to me.

The rather ominous collection of inquisitive villagers that had begun to surround him had me concerned. I stepped up and put my hand firmly on his shoulder. "Morgan," I said, "it is time to go." Caught up in the hard bargaining and emotion of the moment, he resisted my suggestion, shrugging me off.

The situation escalated. The shopkeeper was bedrock firm on the amount quoted and Morgan just as committed to the price he insisted he had heard. I forcefully said to him again, "Look around you Morgan. It is time to forget the cookies!" By now, several hundred curious onlookers had congregated around us. I felt squeezed by the warm bodies of the scrutinizing villagers who pushed their way closer to view the commotion. Finally, Morgan realized the gravity of the circumstances and together we carefully backed away from the gathering crowds. Morgan had calmed down by the time we got back to the van, though he remained resolute in his belief that the shopkeeper had misquoted him in some way. Maybe he was right, and I pondered several times after that why I bothered to rescue him.

We drove eastward away from the village, following a narrow raised dirt road that was the top surface of an elevated levee. Lush green farmland gave way to evenly terraced rice paddies that flanked the road on both sides. These sectioned and tailored flooded fields acted as large reflection ponds, corralling the captured images of the cloudy skies across their mirrored surfaces. The contrast in scenery from the hard and dusty ground of Pakistan to the verdant fields now before us was vividly apparent. I assumed this was due to a more plentiful water supply, a greater fertility in the soil, and the more sophisticated use of irrigation techniques.

I had heard that in this part of the world, a man's most prized possession was not his wife or his house as one might think, but instead it was his water buffalo. For the Indian farmer this equated to owning a top-of-the-line John Deere tractor back home. These beasts of burden, domesticated over thousands of years from the wild oxen that once roamed the countryside, remained the most useful of all the farm animals. The huge bovines, blue-black in color, stood five to six feet high with large, wide, curved horns. Without their presence, rice farming in India would be nearly impossible.

A man with a buffalo could plow his own fields, plow those of his neighbors, haul goods to market, and even raise the roof of his new house. The manure made excellent fertilizer for the fields and was a useful source of household fuel after it was dried. Should the animal happen to expire, there would be plenty of meat to consume or sell, and the hide was tough and thick, well-suited for leather products that lasted a lifetime.

Gino had cautioned us regarding some of the dangers of this rural farm area, with the Asian water buffalo coming at the top of the list. Not because these animals were a danger in and of themselves, as the much-feared and unpredictable Cape Buffalo of Africa, but simply because of the valued relationship between these draft animals and their owners. It was important to stay clear of them on the narrow roads, as absolutely nothing excited the farming people more than a threat posed to their animals. This certainly must have been in the forefront of Gino's mind as we slowly came upon the bullock cart loaded high with agrarian goods on the road ahead. I could see there was a single water buffalo pulling it.

Astonishingly, for reasons we would later learn, the mini-bus did not respond when Gino first applied the brakes. His careful and systematic pumping gave way to a desperate stamping of the pedals on the floorboard. The mini-van simply continued its forward momentum, unimpeded. Confused, we all watched helplessly as we nosed ever closer to the back of the heavily loaded oxcart ahead. When it was obvious that stopping was unlikely, we all braced for the collision. Our worst nightmare was about to come true, affecting all of us adversely by adding a new and potentially lethal dimension to the day.

With a shudder the van hit the bullock cart, driving it forward with a sudden jolt far enough to throw the water buffalo off balance. The beast went down with a loud bellow, spread eagled in the road with all four legs splayed out in different directions like a compass. We were horrified! It did not look promising. Surely, some of the animal's legs must have been broken, if not all of them. The sprightly operator had flown off the seat, landing in the dirt about ten feet in front of the cart. Apparently unhurt, he picked himself up and walked over to survey the damage. He was an older man, frightfully thin, with skin like dark tanned leather.

Our leader stepped out of the bus, but instantly found it difficult to stand. The recent light rain had caused the fine natural clay surface of the flat roadbed to glaze over, rendering it slick as glass. Our tires had no chance of gripping the slippery road. The mystery solved, we now had to face the problem this peculiarity in circumstances had created.

Gino approached the driver, penetrating the language barrier as best he could, showing a sincere effort to extend his apologies to the man. Ignoring him, the angry fellow rattled off a clutch of words, alien to us and then briskly walked over to the edge of the road. He called aloud, with his hands cupped to his mouth, signaling to the multitude of workers in the field. Then, he walked over to the opposite edge of the levee bank and did the same thing. Upon hearing his call, the fieldworkers began to rally to his defense. They immediately ceased what they were doing and came quickly in our direction, bringing their handheld implements with them.

Meanwhile, the pathetic and prostrate buffalo had not missed one mournful note. A more pitiful sound I have never heard. The oxen's wild eyes were now rolling uncontrollably in its head and drool was slithering down over its lower lip into the puddle forming on the ground under its quivering chin. I had gotten out to help Gino negotiate but we both could see the situation was about to turn nasty.

About this time, Gino produced his wallet in what proved to be a futile effort to offer the injured party financial restitution. Intrigued with his attempt to consummate such a transaction, I hardly noticed when the first stone hit the van. I became galvanized by the danger, however, when I saw the hundreds of field workers walking steadily towards us begin to pick up the pace. I hollered to Gino that trouble was coming our way, fast. He acknowledged me out of the corner of his eye as he continued with his stressful rounds of unilateral negotiation. More stones were hitting us now, one cracking a side window of our mini-bus.

The early arrivals came up close to the van, delivering threatening stares while yelling loudly and shaking their fists. Obviously all the pains taken to compensate the man for his loss had failed. Acknowledging this, Gino stuffed a large wad of paper money into the driver's hands, then turned and quickly came back to the van. By this time, our new friends were trying as best they could to roll us over. The Aussie girls were close to hysterical. Surrounded by very unhappy people, we frantically secured the door locks while Gino started the rig up and prepared to depart. The angry crowd seemed to freeze for one crucial instant.

Gino honked the horn repeatedly and carefully started maneuvering our bus around the bullock cart. He was aware of how serious the situation was and mindful not to make it worse by running over anyone at this crucial time. Then, he edged the Mercedes between the abrupt shoulder of the levee road and the outstretched legs of the injured animal. Moving past the scene of the accident was critical. We all knew there would be dire consequences should the animal be abused any further. The crowd had pulled back now but the road remained slippery, and I could hear the high-pitched whine of our tires spinning on the clay when Gino over-accelerated. At last, we began to pick up speed, leaving the unfortunate situation behind us. Mutual feelings of relief streamed forth as we realized we were out of immediate danger.

Initially, there was silence in the bus, and we continued to hightail it out of there as fast as we could. Looking back through the rear window, I could see a great crowd of workers milling over the scene of the accident like ants crawling over a dead grasshopper. As they disappeared in the distance, we let out a collective sigh of relief. The anxiety levels began to subside, and we were absorbed in the fact we had just escaped another very unpredictable situation. This sequence of events could well have been the end of the journey for us all.

Our arrival in Amritsar that evening was a fitting culmination to a very long day. The back streets to the temple were crowded with pilgrims streaming in the direction of the main gate. Fatigue from the many stresses of the day consumed us but had not diminished our eagerness to see this place of great renown. We parked on a side street and followed the human flow of devotees. I marveled at the entry gates of the Golden Temple now before us. Humbly we entered the holy site, pleased to learn that one of the main tenets of Sikhism was to provide accommodations to the inbound wayfarer. All newcomers were equal in their eyes, and the Sikhs assumed by our mere presence that we had come to Amritsar for worship. We were pilgrims!

The chants and devotional poems filled the hallways, pleasantly enveloping us. They emanated from the marble, gold-enshrined temple that sat as an island, centered in the holy lake. A lake named, the "sacred pool of ambrosial nectar." The calming sounds of the readings continued to permeate the chambers as we walked along. Tall, well-spoken men with tightly trussed beards and neatly wrapped turbans covering their long hair greeted us courteously and graciously. They were impressive individuals, wearing ceremonial clothes with their traditional long swords at their sides, fastened by a waistband. We signed in and were led to our rooms, small and simple enclosures with no furniture, spare but adequate. I had long since learned to sleep on stone floors. The Sikhs gave us tea and rice, the rice served on a shiny green banana leaf, something I would see more of in the future.

We learned that the holy devotions began in the early morning and lasted long past sunset, many times with the accompaniment of flutes, drums, and stringed instruments. Echoing across the serene lake, the music induced a trance among the pilgrims walking the marble concourse that encircled the water. After we got settled in our rooms I went out for a walk. It was an enchanting stroll with the moonlight reflecting off the water and the reading of the evening prayers.

Throughout our stay, we observed pilgrims immersing themselves in the sacred lake, the body of water fed by an underground spring. This represented a ceremonial cleansing and purification of the soul rather than merely the taking of a bath. The bathing was symbolic of something like a formal confession done in the West, undertaken to dispense with the ills and wreckage of the past, while making room for new and positive growth in the future.

The temple complex incorporated dormitories to house the travelers and included a large hall where people dined without charge. People of all religions and races were welcome and invited to share in the glories of this venerable site. One day, an older Sikh took me aside to shed more light on the history of the complex and his religion. These elders made themselves available to the visiting pilgrims for counsel and peacefully walked the grounds with some of the visitors during the day.

The Sikh spoke of a primary figure in early Sikhism, Nanak, who lived in the last part of the fifteenth century and early sixteenth century. Nanak had a great curiosity for religions. His thoughts centered on ideas to refine and reform, much like Martin Luther was doing at about the same time in Europe. The Punjab region of northwestern India where he lived gave him great opportunities to study both the Islam and Hindu religions. He questioned many aspects of their traditions.

Nanak preached a new message that spoke of one universal God and a society that would bring Muslims and all the castes of Hindus together. Nanak's followers gave themselves the name Sikhs, derived from the Sanskrit meaning *disciple*. Much persecution was to come later for the Sikhs who would gain the reputation of honorable and fierce warriors, only after picking up the sword in the name of self-defense.

Originally, Amritsar was the name of the ancient lake in the region, later becoming the name associated with the Sikh complex. Finally, the city itself became Amritsar. Those who have researched the origins of the word find it translates as "a drink from the gods." This was a drink supposed to elicit certain states of euphoria and raised states of consciousness while introducing an enduring enlightenment of the human spirit.

Every aspect of the Amritsar encounter was positive. It brought our band of travelers to a soothing and safe sanctuary, for a much needed rest. We discovered that we ourselves had become as pilgrims, absorbing the energies and noble character that we found in this most holy of places. We shared food with our warm, intelligent, and honorable hosts. In the years since my memorable visit, I have made many return journeys to the Golden Temple, as often as my imagination would allow.

Streets of Old Delhi

Delhi Delights
Chapter Fifteen

A journey does not need reasons. Before long, it proves to be reason enough in itself. One thinks that one is going to make a journey, yet soon it is the journey that makes or unmakes you.
—Nicolas Bouvier

A drive of one day took us through a series of small villages situated along the road leading south from Amritsar to New Delhi. This poorly maintained thoroughfare was the preferred route of wandering feral peacocks, overloaded oxcarts, and the occasional domestic elephant pulling a log. We carefully dodged the washouts in the road, carved by outflow from torrential rains in the Himalayan foothills nearby. Arriving on the outskirts of New Delhi, on March 27, 1967, I posted in my journal that we had now been traveling in the mini-bus for a full month, covering roughly 3,000 miles of twists, turns, and adventures since Jerusalem.

Delhi was a major Indian capital with all the associated trappings of chaos, poverty, and overpopulation that go with a large Asian city. However, there were also many architectural wonders on display here, and it was more precisely two cities blended into one. There was Old Delhi, built during the Mughal Empires that ruled India (1556–1857), and then there was New Delhi, fashioned and influenced by the British during their rule (1858–1947). I was immediately aware of the more modern of these sophisticated lineages as we motored slowly through the suburbs that led us to the grand avenues encircling the radial hub of Connaught Place. Not since Europe had I seen such broad tree-lined boulevards, with their impressive rows of government buildings. It was obvious that much forethought and planning had gone into the layout of New Delhi.

There were constables standing on elevated platforms, dressed in their bright, white, neatly pressed uniforms. They directed the traffic like maestros of distinction would conduct a great symphony. With a curious mixture of authority and compassion, they took command of the chaotic and unruly intersections. Somehow, there was even time for them to deal with the occasional anomaly or misfit that caused delay in the river of mayhem that passed. Their presentation represented the perfect application of the "golden thread of communication," that ideal of the British Bobbies, as put forth by Robert Peale, their founder and namesake.

After a brief drive though the urban district, Gino took us to the boys' senior secondary school located near Old Delhi, away from the main arteries of activity. He had secured accommodations here on his previous visit to India, the school doubling as a youth hostel in the summer months. Gino had spoken fondly of the presiding headmaster and had been looking forward to seeing him again. A big smile broke out across our tired driver's face as we pulled onto the shady grounds and followed the driveway up to the multi-storied brick building. Great trees stretched their full branches over the carpet of green lawn that surrounded us.

Inside we met the man Gino had told us so much about. We extended our greetings to him while some of the more curious students struck up conversations. Inundated with questions about our journey, it was only a short time before they were treating us like returning heroes from a foreign war. The students begged to hear more of our travel experiences.

This was a fine collection of well-disciplined youths. They were intelligent, alert, and smartly dressed in their school attire. Our new patron explained that the school year was still in session and the youth hostel was not yet in operation. However, before we had time to feel the jolt of disappointment, he promptly added that we were welcome to stay, partaking of free room and board for the next few days. His one request was that we make time to speak to his students about our journey from the Middle East, possibly in the evenings after their classes. We wholeheartedly agreed.

After taking much-needed showers, we drove into the city to explore some of the sights. Soon we lost ourselves in the beguiling charm of the rich cultural history this metropolis reflected. The evidence of its vibrant past, the architectural diversity in the Persian and Indian styles, and the mood cast from the ancient forts, temples, and mosques overwhelmed our small group. My favorites were the market places and bazaars where the artisans presented their wares in the open-air vistas under a skyline of ancient stone spires and domes. The impressive list of historic sites and monuments within this capital of India was long. Gino took us into the old city, where we parked the mini-bus and carefully maneuvered through the marketplaces on foot.

Monumental traffic jams intermittently plugged the streets as we navigated the packed sidewalks adjacent to them. Amid the incessant honking, thin men on bicycles jockeyed to fill the slim gaps in the traffic. There were others on motor scooters, their women hanging off the back. Next to them, the rickshaw taxis pursued their madcap dash to penetrate the wall of congestion. Hordes of people, some dressed in business suits and others donning the traditional *dhoti kurta* pajamas, closed in on us from every direction. Occasionally a half-naked sinewy man with a look of urgency on his weathered and leathery face would run past us barefooted. The block of ice he carried over his shoulder in a gunnysack would end up in one of the washtubs full of water and bobbing Coca-Cola bottles, tended by a sidewalk vendor.

The vehicles moved dangerously close to one another in a chaotic yet controlled flow. There were no traffic lights and intersections became a confluence of the different directional streams. Nowhere did I see anger or road rage, a testament to the Hindu religion. The occasional bullock cart of goods drawn by a lumbering water buffalo passed by, causing even more delays. Dilapidated rickshaw taxis squeezed between and around the maze of obstacles in front of them. This scene unfolded amidst clouds of dust and flies, in crushing heat and humidity. I sensed this to be the timeless saga in the streets of Old Delhi.

We stopped at the famous *Lal Quila*, or Red Fort. Built on the banks of the Yamuna River, this imposing sandstone palace was another of the many accomplishments bestowed upon the world by Shah Jahan. The Red Fort, built between the years 1638–1648, represented a complex of splendid marble and red sandstone creations housing the great halls of the Emperor's government from the times preceding British rule. It was a challenge to both my mind and that of the casual viewer to accept the massive exterior walls, so enormous and imposing were they in height and breadth. In fact, some towered skyward for over a hundred feet while bastions and towers, positioned strategically, clung to their walls. The outside rampart walls extended for over a mile around the fort. We entered the citadel through the Lahore Gate.

Inside, weathered buildings of marble, topped with copper domes, gave way to secluded gardens and a multitude of arched arcades. Known as the Meena Bazaar, these partitions once housed the great goldsmiths, weavers, and carpet makers of Delhi. Backdrops rich in detail, along with ornate facades sculpted from the trademark red rock of Agra, reached out to tantalize our senses.

The bazaars of Old Delhi completely captivated my spirit. I could not know then that these impressions would draw me back some forty years later for another look. They were kinetic oceans of human expression, sweeping over me in waves of wonder and delight. The unique smells, sights, and sounds surrounded me, enticing me to go deeper into their hidden corners for discovery. I felt the strong call to leave the group, cut the cord that bound me, and to roam free.

Reason ruled, and I returned to the school with the group, noting my room and board remained conveniently arranged and that Gino was taking us to Embassy Row the next day. There were visas I needed to obtain for the future. I ignored the tempting summons this time, but not for long. Within days, the bazaars would lure me back into the flourishing confines of narrow streets, stalls, and vendors. I would come back to Old Delhi, to rent a room and explore its world. "What other wonders must be out there?" I asked myself.

That night, back at the school, we had a pleasant dinner with the young students in the cafeteria. The boys were polite and in conversation presented themselves as intellectually astute, seeming light years ahead of our students back home with regard to maturity and academics. After dinner, several of our group sat at a table in one of the classrooms and shared travel stories with them. Their eyes opened wide with enthusiasm, and they hung on our every word. It was plain to see their curious minds were on fire, and they were nearly unanimous in their expressed desire to see the world someday.

The next morning we went to Embassy Row, seeing once again the result of the superior city planning used to lay out the governmental sections of New Delhi. Most of the embassies were located in the same general area, which facilitated the application process in obtaining my visas for Burma, Thailand, and Malaysia. Some visas only required waiting a short time, while others necessitated leaving my passport for a day or two, something that always gave me cause for worry.

The headmaster had provided us with more historical information about Delhi the previous evening at dinner. He told us that both the new and the old cities were strewn with the reminders of different converging influences from a complicated past. The history of Delhi dated back nearly five millennia to the Pandavas who had founded the city. In the olden days, Delhi dominated the ancient trade routes, gleaning wealth from the course of commerce that once extended from India's northwest corner eastward past the great plains of the Ganges basin. This perplexing land of wonders was bursting with a multi-faceted cultural heritage, sometimes difficult to categorize and comprehend.

The imperial power of the Mughals ruled most of the subcontinent before the British arrived. They were incredible builders as evidenced by the enduring mark left on the land and culture. Their reign fell into decline primarily due to wars of succession and wars of expansion. Islamic law and taxes imposed on the non-Muslim members of the citizenry caused resentment. The powerful control imposed by a rigid orthodoxy created a climate of rebellion, which sparked periodic agrarian quarrels and new revolts among the people. The era of the Mughals ended with the arrival of the British in the mid-nineteenth century.

Some of the refreshing vestiges of order I had seen came from the British, an enduring legacy of their colonial rule that I had noticed to a lesser degree in Egypt. I again made the personal observation in my journal that countries or colonies that were once part of the British Empire seem to have retained a well-lubricated system of government for tending the affairs of state. Shortly after Delhi came under British charge, the new rulers installed their own city administrators. In 1911, the city was made the capital of India. It was then that the planners decided to rebuild the city in a grand imperial style, assuming it would be a colony of England forever.

During our sojourns into the city, I marveled at the vast number of imperial leftovers, in the form of architectural treasures, from these two great imposing forces in Indian history. The strong and enduring strength of Mother India, combined with the foundational influences of Hinduism, had evolved from these two imperial heritages. Indians had known great periods of change and had survived by adapting and absorbing the outside influences, which over time had become their own.

On a personal note, I was feeling gratified in satisfying the great longing of my youth, that of learning more about our world. I too was absorbing outside influences and processing fresh information that was slowly becoming part of me. The one constant element most easily identifiable by all of us from our travels so far was change. As we had moved across the different countries in a short span of time, we had become more skilled in accepting the enormous challenges presented by our confining and stressful conditions. The pressures of change, both from without and within, had affected us sociologically on a daily basis. On the road, we were compelled to continue perfecting the art of "give and take," and "live and let live," among ourselves. Small pressures had often mushroomed when dealing with issues like personal hygiene, driving schedules, flatulence, and mood swings. These areas of conflict had been discussed at the informal "steering committee meetings" called by Gino along the way.

This short study in interpersonal relations had taught us all that to survive we needed to cooperate and practice tolerance. Even with that, our patience with each other had drawn very thin, and by the time we reached New Delhi I was eager to follow through with my original plan of striking out on my own. That time was now drawing near.

Two days later, I bid my travel-mates farewell at the school, grabbed my backpack, and began the long walk back to the colorful streets of Old Delhi. My first order of business was to secure a room. I searched the streets in vain for some clue as to where a hotel might be. It was late afternoon when I rented a tiny space over a small restaurant at the top of two flights of stairs. The room was off a narrow side street of the old city, and the smells of curry and incense permeated the confines of the narrow staircase. A padlock was an important item carried by the backpackers of the world, used to secure the lockers sometimes provided at the youth hostels. I placed my padlock in the hasp on the door of my new room and went out, spending the rest of the day exploring.

I was pleased with my newfound independence, and the small room quickly became home. Rent was eighty cents a day or ten Indian rupees. There was a small nightstand, a thick woven mat on the floor for a bed, and a bare light bulb to illuminate the patched dark blue walls. Perched on one of those walls, frozen in stillness next to the bulb, was a large Tokey Gecko lizard about eight inches in length. He ignored my entrance into the room and all movements thereafter, appearing content in the light that drew the flying insects he so desired. In that regard, I was grateful for small favors. We accepted each other's presence in the spirit of mutual coexistence. Four days later, when I left the room, he was still on the wall by the bulb.

I liked being in India, and it dawned on me how pleasant it was to occasionally hear English spoken, a very high caliber of English at that. It was just one more little benefit that took away some of the sting of being totally immersed in a foreign land. The next morning I wandered through Old Delhi, coming upon the enormous Jama Masjid (Friday Mosque), a seventeenth century contribution by Shah Jahan. Its vast interior courtyard was capable of holding 25,000 worshippers at one time.

For hours each day I walked the bazaars, fascinated with the methods of dealing between the different traders and vendors. The buyers and sellers conducted their negotiations in a courteous manner, firm but without argument. The bargainers on both sides were determined and shrewd.

From the heart of the market area it was difficult for me to see where one section ended and another began, though they each had their specialty. The herb and spice stalls radiated brilliant colors with mounds of saffron and turmeric sitting in great sacks next to the chilies and tea. The fresh fruits and vegetables were artistically stacked and displayed to attract passing prospects. Proprietors sat patiently within the booths of these linear supermarkets, like spiders waiting in a web. When darkness descended, the booths transformed into habitats where the owner and his family could sleep for the night.

One morning, after taking breakfast at one of the stalls, I felt a slight tug at my sleeve. I looked down into an angelic face reflecting the deep dark eyes and bright white teeth of a young boy of eight or nine. He beckoned me to come with him and dashed off into the sea of people. Curious, I followed him. He moved fast through the crowded market, looking back occasionally to confirm I was still behind him. I could barely keep up as he dodged and weaved through the many towns-people out for their morning shopping. At times I lost sight of him completely, only to find him suddenly at my side, taking my hand and continuing to drag me through the labyrinth of street shops and makeshift shelters.

I vaguely remembered taking this route a day earlier. We suddenly cut under some silk cloth on a line, and after sidestepping around a canvas alcove, we came to a cubical of a room with a Persian carpet on the floor. A rotund, distinguished looking man with a shaved head and long black handlebar mustache sat in the middle of the carpet.

From the charisma he projected I mused he could well have been the Mughal Shah Jahan himself. The man nodded at the boy and one of his servants in attendance handed him some rupees whereupon the young boy vanished behind a filigreed curtain of silk.

Curiosity had the best of me. The man offered me a seat on a brightly colored silk pillow, and his servants brought us tea. We talked. He asked where I had come from and how I had arrived in India. After a short but cordial visit, much to my amazement, he expressed an interest in the pale yellow, wash-and-wear shirt I was wearing, something I had purchased at a department store before leaving the U.S. Wash-and-wear had just come into popularity, and this fellow, being a merchant, obviously knew of its valuable qualities. The bargaining then began for the shirt off my back! He was a portly man, gracefully carrying the badge of opulence in his protruding stomach. I could not imagine my shirt fitting him by any stretch. We finally settled on a price of thirty rupees, enough to cover my rent for the next three days. The merchant tried on the shirt. With a big smile, he buttoned it down to his round belly, leaving the bottom three or four buttons undone. We shook hands, and I found my way back to my room, shirtless in Old Delhi.

After several additional adventures in this captivating Indian capital, it came time to take my leave. I walked to the train station with my pack and made ready for the railway journey to Agra, the home of yet another of Shah Jahan's wondrous gifts to humanity, the Taj Mahal.

Taj Mahal

Source of the Ganges
Chapter Sixteen

I am part of all that I have met;
Yet all experience is an arch wherethro'
Gleams that untravell'd world, whose margin fades
For ever and for ever when I move.
How dull it is to pause, to make an end,
To rust unburnish'd, not to shine in use!
—Alfred, Lord Tennyson
from Ulysses

Waters from the melting layers of compacted ice and snow trickle down over the high contours of the Himalayas, following gravity's incessant draw. Vast networks of descending brooks and streams converge, becoming rivers that push their meandering channels forward to feed the Ganges, India's longest river. It is a holy river that, as Hindu legend would have it, flows through heaven itself and retains all the purifying attributes. Retracing these venerable waters to distinguish that first seeping source has been the dream of many an inquisitive adventurer and spiritual seeker alike, to find the source of the Ganges.

One great river that nourishes the Ganges is the Yamuna. It flanks the ancient Indian city of Agra, where I had now come by train. Disembarking the passenger car, I walked through the crowds of people on the platform and found a small travelers' retreat at the edge of town, where I took a room. There was a bed with a nightstand, and a carpet of matted hemp. The windows were dressed in wood shutters only, and there was a ceiling fan. It was here I spent the remainder of the day.

The antiquated bicycle rickshaw I chose the next morning to deliver me from Agra to the Taj Mahal had been in service long past its prime. In a near effortless motion, a small-framed Indian man with incredible muscle definition magically propelled the wobbly three-wheeled vehicle forward over the bumpy road that led out of town. His two dark-stemmed legs of iron churned in front of me as the contraption rolled on through the village suburbs. I had never ridden in a bicycle rickshaw before and felt a touch of embarrassment sitting there comfortably while he labored away.

The feeling of guilt was gaining strength in the realization that this operator, half my size, was transporting me down the crowded road of many hazards. I could no longer ignore this and, with a sense of urgency, commanded him to stop. I requested we trade places, that he should ride and I should peddle. The man was flabbergasted and responded with an intense, if not ferocious, resistance. I had already resolved in my mind that things would be this way and refused to allow him to persuade me otherwise. Reluctantly the skinny little fellow placed his muscular body into the well-worn passenger seat while I mounted the bike portion of the taxi and began to pump.

We continued down the road, our roles reversed. The oncoming rickshaw operators were unified in their contempt for our new arrangement. Fists were in the air, and their surprised faces revealed revulsion difficult to describe. Discontent consumed my passenger who continued to protest emphatically. He tried to convey to me that I was breaching some sacred commandment of the *Rickshaw Owner-Operators Bylaws* that could well cast him forever into infamy among his peers. I surmised this was more about tradition and face-saving than any violation of a municipal code. It was not long before my Western guilt had sufficiently subsided and my legs had become amply exhausted that we were able to stop, change positions, and then continue our journey in the original configuration. Peace returned to the rickshaw.

Moving down a dusty road that divided desolate patches of farmland, I pondered on just how difficult it would be to acknowledge that your lot in life, immoveable and permanent, would be operating a rickshaw day-in and day-out. I began to understand why the major emphasis of the Hindu religion focused more on the acceptance of spiritual values rather than the material ones. I reflected on some of the tedious and repetitive jobs of my past. I had swept sidewalks as a boy for the merchants of Ashland after school. When I was a little older, I mowed lawns. Then there was the summer I worked for room and board on a farm and bucked bales of hay and milked cows every day. Other summers I had loaded boxcars with lumber. These were all difficult jobs, yet I took some solace in knowing they would eventually come to an end.

Had I been born in India, I well could have been the man now peddling me down the road, forced to dutifully accept this position as one of the limited choices in the life of a laborer. Were I to now temporarily take his job for a few months in a naïve experiment to understand his plight, I would certainly fail in reaching my goal. Regardless of the Westerner's efforts to go native and try to experience the life and true consciousness of the people, it can never really happen. There are just too many safety nets in place for the outsider. For example, birth-nation alone gives the visitor certain powerful advantages. Just a short walk to the embassy of one's homeland is a powerful ace-in-the-hole to play, and invariably can provide some satisfactory arrangement for a ticket home. Contrary to my driver's situation, there will always be some way for the foreigner to escape the circumstances. Ultimately, to fully understand the rickshaw driver's existence was impossible for a guest in transit as myself. All that was really visible to me was a life of hopelessness, only made tolerable by his religion. I suspected he felt much different about it.

At last, we pulled up to the arch-shaped main gate of the great compound of the Taj Mahal, parking near the multitude of rickshaws that had delivered other visitors descending upon Agra from different corners of the world. My driver was grinning and, I assumed, happy that I had finally taken my rightful place as a passenger. I paid him a few extra rupees, which made him even happier. I proceeded through the main gate with great expectation. Now, I could see the exquisite grounds, a reflection pool leading to the mausoleum, and the manicured side gardens where teams of monkeys played like energetic undersized acrobats.

The Taj Mahal towered gracefully into the air like a polished gem radiating its ethereal symmetry in all directions. The gleaming architectural wonder in white marble found a place in my mind from the instant I first set eyes on it and has been a resident there ever since. The red sandstone platform provided an impressive base for the "White Jewel." The Taj Mahal, built over an extended period of years (1629–1650), by the Emperor Shah Jahan was a tomb in memory of his favorite wife. It represented a memorial to the great love between a man and the woman who bore him fourteen children. They interred the Shah himself in the mausoleum after his death. The gorgeous dome, flanked by four substantial but slender minaret prayer towers at the corners of the base, appeared as a floating onion-shaped cap. It hovered gracefully, covering the ornate walls of inlaid design that housed the vast number of carved alabaster screens below.

As I explored the glorious grounds of the shrine, I felt as if I had entered into another world, harmonious and whole, where the culmination of brilliant talents had come together to yield perfection. The greatest artisans of the time came to Agra to be a part of this monumental project. They used the labor of more than a thousand elephants just to haul the materials to the site. This magnificent example of Mughal art was the faultless triumph of Persian architecture and design, successfully bridging the ideal with reality.

In addition, I saw it as a timeless treasure connecting the past to the future. At the same time, it reflected an essence of excellence to generations of visitors well into the future. I felt blessed to absorb its radiance on that day and found it difficult to leave. My departure for points east by train was planned for the next morning, so I went back to my sultry little room and collapsed under the fan, savoring my thoughts of the day and making entries into my travel journal.

I made my way to the station at dawn, enchanted by the sounds of the exotic songbirds as I walked along. It was fun watching as the village came to life and it was obvious the villagers enjoyed watching me as well. Small children, curious and friendly, trailed me regardless of where I went. The depot was now in sight. I figured my chances of getting a seat on the crowded train were much better if I arrived early. I stepped up to the platform and made my way to the nearest passenger car, then swung my backpack aboard and stepped in. The Indian Railway System once again revealed to me that odd combination of chaos and efficiency that allows it to serve the multitudes so well. However, there was always a certain atmosphere of desperation present as the passengers maneuvered for position and scrambled for seats.

I spied a foreigner sitting tranquilly on a second-class bench by himself. He was wearing a dark three-piece suit and a white dress shirt with a tie. His shoes were immaculately shined. The man sat in a rigid pose on the edge of his seat, as if anticipating some unpleasant medical examination. His hands were resting, one on top of the other, over the brass handle of an ebony walking stick. The derby that balanced precariously on his head betrayed sprouts and tufts of thinning white hair that tumbled out from under the brim. In general, he was a good-looking fellow for his age, and much too well-dressed for an Indian train.

Seeing the car was filling up fast, I leaned in his direction and asked if I might join him. He nodded in the affirmative and after stowing my backpack, I sat down next to him. I was delighted to find a comfortable spot on the train, especially with a Westerner. He seemed fixated on the crowd outside, a condensed horde of bodies now covering the loading platform from which I had just come. My travel companion had a serene manner about him.

With a sudden jerk, the carriage bolted and slowly we began our forward motion. A mesmerizing cadence, punctuated by the resonance of the steel wheels spanning the rail-seams in the track sections, invaded the cabin. After we were underway, I turned to the man and introduced myself. We chatted a bit, but finding that the conversation soon died without my repeated infusions, I became content to sit and look out the window, just as he was doing.

The Yamuna River meanders downstream past Agra and through a long flat plain before reaching its confluence with the mighty Ganges near Allahabad. Our rail route would take us through the Indian cities of Kanpur, Allahabad, and Lucknow before reaching my destination of Varanasi, "the holy city of light." Located on the venerated shores of the Ganges, this was the most important city in all of India for Hindus. I updated my world map as the train rolled through the outskirts of Agra.

The locomotive moved us through a theater of Indian life, one sequence after another. There were scenes of poverty and destitution exemplified by the makeshift hovels and shanties that bordered the tracks. Next, we raced through the fenced industrial yards of rusty and derelict equipment, the remnants of civilization's discarded bits and pieces. Finally, we moved into the lush green farmlands serviced by dikes and small irrigation canals that traced the perimeters of the neatly laid out fields. This was the land of the water buffalo, that beast of burden seen pulling the crude wooden plows through the fields. Seeing India from the window of a moving train was becoming a pleasurable pastime that would leave me with many lasting impressions.

At last, my new friend began to speak. He was gracious and humble and, oddly enough, his soft voice projected clearly above the various sounds coming from the train. Early on, we exchanged accounts of how we each had come to be in India. Later, the conversation took a turn, and he began to address deeper and more philosophical issues, those regarding destiny and our existence. He spoke as one who had known life's extremes, tasting both the sweet and the bitter fruits encountered on man's mysterious journey. He seemed one confident of his presence in a country overwhelmingly foreign in so many ways. Intrigued, I plied him with more questions about his life.

He was an Australian. This was his third trip to India and, he said with assurance, "his last." He related his story in a clear and calm voice, speaking precisely and using an economy of words. His first trip to India had been as a young man in the service of his country, a surveyor on loan to the Indian government. He had hiked a great deal of the subcontinent from north to south, mapping and laying out benchmarks, charting the geology and posting his various measurements as he went. The numerous years in India, had left him yearning to return home. When his commission was up he willingly went back to his family's Western Australia sheep station.

Long after his return to Australia, the enchanting visions of the lovely Indian countryside and its people remained in his mind, often visiting him in his dreams. Over time, his passion for another visit to India grew strong in his heart. He formulated plans and saved his money, hoping that the day would come when he could return. His wife thought him mad to want to leave his home for the excessive heat and humidity that he so often had spoken about. However, in time she passed away and a door of opportunity then opened for his return to *Hindustan*, as he preferred to call it. As a result of these circumstances he had the chance to walk in the land of his dreams again and to embrace a great love.

Plagued with hereditary heart trouble beginning in his forties, he had a major heart attack while on this second visit. He had no choice but to return to Australia for convalescence and medical care, though his mind and heart remained in India. Now his unfinished love affair would have to wait, while he proceeded through a long and slow rehabilitation program. He conditioned himself, following closely the instructions of his physical therapist, while at the same time focusing on his return to India. He studied more of the country's history and culture and immersed himself in the Hindu religion. Later, much to his disappointment, the word came from his doctors that his heart had sustained permanent damage. The prognosis was not favorable.

At this point, he concluded he would travel to India for a third and final time, to live out his last days in the country he had come to love. He was now fifty-five years of age, and it was his wish to seek out the Source of the Ganges. The idea of finding those elusive headwaters had been in his mind since his early days of surveying. He realized it could well be an endless or even mythical quest, as there were multitudes of tributaries to be explored, a task that could easily take the lifetime of a young man. He was now making a pilgrimage to the Ghats of Varanasi to meditate at the holy site before embarking on this singular mission.

I asked my new friend, an avid student of Hinduism, to refer a few books for me to read. He promptly recited some fifteen titles and authors, which he had on the tip of his tongue. I wrote them down, and in the next month read two of them. His love of India had caused him to seek out Eastern solutions to his health problems, something the rest of the world was just starting be aware of about this time. The Australian was a remarkable man in so many ways, and I felt honored to have met him. We exchanged our warm farewells to each other and then walked our separate ways.

I got off the train in Varanasi and found a small room in a cheap hotel near the shores of the Ganges, the river that cast such a wide influence over the country. It was hot and muggy, and I was grateful for the squeaky overhead fan that steadily churned the air in my room. I leaned my gear against the wall and went out for a look around.

It was not long before I came to the Ghats, a stone stair-stepped terrace down to the water where the religious pilgrims came to bathe and spiritually purify themselves. Not far away, I was shocked to see the funeral pyres of sandalwood and straw ablaze, cradling bodies of the dead draped in ceremonial saris and robes. Their burning flesh expelled a black and oily smoke. Great vultures circled above, scanning for morsels as the packs of wild dogs darted in and out of the ashes snapping at the appendages of the burning corpses. For the small children and babies who had died, it was a tradition to submerge them in the holy river with rocks placed on their lifeless bodies. Vendors shaved the heads of male relatives in mourning, save for one small pigtail at the back of their head, said to be their "pull-strap" to heaven. I walked these shores, viewing the ongoing religious ceremonies for hours.

After stopping for some curry and rice at a small stand on the street, I retired back to my room. My head was spinning with all I had taken in during my afternoon of exploration. The evidence of poverty and starvation was everywhere. It was impossible to compare what I had just seen with anything on the journey so far, and I felt a degree of sensory overload. I opened the shutters and let the evening breeze flow into the room through the arms of the great banyan tree standing outside.

Several hours later, I heard a faint knock at the door. I opened it to find a small boy standing in front of me, speaking in words

I could not understand. He was trying to sell me something wrapped up in newspaper. I assumed the hotel people had sent him. Curious, I opened the paper to see what looked to be a brownish vegetable material that I first assumed was some kind of herb or tea. I sent him away with a few rupees, only to realize later they were buds of *ganja*, the Indian version of cannabis, used by some of the people in a medicinal way to temporarily take away the misery of their living conditions. "An interesting service for a hotel," I thought.

That evening I went out for a walk, following the sights and sounds of the night. I came to the top of the stone stairway leading down to the Ghats, revisiting the vast ceremonial gathering place from earlier in the day. Right away, my eyes locked on an elderly man with a long white beard sitting in the center of a small hexagonal raft. He was wearing a white garment and his legs were folded up in the lotus position like a jackknife. There was an oversized book spread across his lap. The patriarch had been reading to the small group of seated disciples that surrounded him. Candles burned around the perimeter of the small boat, casting them all in a pale yellow light. Large brass incense burners hung from chains, fastened to the ornately carved roof that covered the sitting area. A mat of loosely scattered flower petals adorned the carpet on which they sat. The men were wearing garlands of marigolds, flowers of significance. One of the devotional students was playing a sitar while another was on the tabla drums. Although this may have been a typical setting for Varanasi, it was new to me and I had to make sure I was not dreaming.

The teacher looked up and acknowledged my presence at the top of the stone stairs. His inviting gaze was unwavering. As he continued to focus on me, I sensed peace and clarity penetrate my soul. Then he brought his hand up and beckoned me to come aboard the raft. Trusting my intuition that he was not some malevolent *svengali*, I made my way down to the river's edge and carefully walked the narrow plank that spanned from shore to the small vessel. The disciples nodded and made more room for me; then they passed over a large pillow. The elder read from the ancient scriptures while one of the men reeled in the lines that tethered us to the bank.

Soon the raft was set adrift, to pinwheel freely into the evening on the waters of the "great river of life." The events were out of my control, and I relaxed, trying not to concern myself with our destination. The Ganges was the great artery passing through the very heart of India, and I accepted I was now floating along on its subtle currents. Through the night, the teacher in the white beard read from his great book, and his students periodically recited ceremonial incantations. After several hours, I began to reposition myself, trying to avoid the painful leg cramps that had begun to set in. I am sure my boat-mates sensed I was close to reaching my limit. More time continued to pass.

Dawn was now beginning to break, and the bright orange ball that was the sun burst through the river mist. The melodic calls of India's birds resounded over the surface of the river from both banks. Observing I was uncomfortable, two of my new friends began to paddle us closer to shore. They waved to a man sitting near the bank in a canoe, a local river taxi. The canoe came along side and after sufficient bows and *namastes*, I transferred my stiff angular body to the smaller craft. My voyage had been part of a long religious pilgrimage that would take the devotees even farther down the river in the days to come. I was grateful and honored to have been a part of it. As I looked back over my shoulder, the older man gestured with a blessing.

Happily stepping out of the canoe onto shore, I paid the river taxi operator and asked him about the location of Varanasi. I tried to calculate just how far down river we had drifted, but then realized it did not really matter.

I had survived yet another extraordinary and spontaneous Indian experience. While I walked upstream, I reflected on the significance this sacred river held for the Hindu people. Its waters had lapped up against the many holy locations along its banks, repeatedly cleansing documented places of pilgrimage for more than 5,000 years. All forms of nourishment came to them from the currents surging through the tentacles of this living body.

Hour after hour, village after village, I walked up river in the direction of "the city of light." When I was tired, I would rest. When

I was hungry, I would eat. When it was too hot, I would sit under a tree. When I got lost, I followed the river, always the river.

In my mind's eye, I spied its humble fountainhead, in the crisp thin air of the Himalayas, a babbling spring from out of the mountains, narrow enough to step across. I thought of its massive width where I was now, barely able to see across the water in the morning mist. The river had been my patient and comforting provider throughout the long night and for one brief moment, I too yearned to commence a search for its illusive source.

Suddenly, I was standing at the junction of a major road and there I soon picked up a ride offered by the driver of a freight truck. He was on his way to Varanasi. I slept most of the way, and we arrived late in the hot afternoon.

After a few more days in this city of wonders, I paid for my room, packed up my things and prepared for a new adventure. This one would take me to the Himalayan foothills and the Indian-Nepalese border on my trek to Kathmandu, Nepal.

The Varanasi Ghats

The Three Madonnas
Chapter Seventeen

He travels safe, and not unpleasantly, who is guarded by poverty and guided by love. —Sir P. Sidney

Varanasi had been as mystifying as it was exhausting. Exposure to the hard edge of Hindu life as it existed within this cultural and religious center had left me with a myriad of impressions to sort out. I found it emotionally draining as I continued to accept ever-greater doses of the foreign reality around me. However, I did have to admit that I was becoming somewhat desensitized from the new visual incursions that I was processing daily. One of the redeeming benefits of repeatedly being subjected to unfamiliar conditions was that it did provide some degree of immunization against what was to come in the future. As I drew more accustomed to the different aspects of Indian life, there evolved within me a greater understanding. However, these unusual experiences did pull me, incrementally, farther away from the land of my birth, a land that was now but a distant memory. I felt India was becoming my new home and I was feeling less and less a stranger in an unfamiliar land.

The long walk through the narrow dusty streets of Varanasi had brought me to the train station. The surroundings reminded me of Old Delhi, the streets oozing with a stirring collage of activity. I was finding the cities of India were now all beginning to look alike. I stood on the platform where it was already unbearably hot, and the annoying flies circled my head incessantly, looking to extract a nano-droplet of moisture from my brow. I boarded the packed train designated for Patna, a population center farther downriver.

I found the cars completely occupied, with some passengers sitting on each other's laps. Nevertheless, I continued to walk up and down the crowded aisles, dragging my pack and looking for a place to sit. In the end, I found nothing. Exiting the car, I hurried down the tracks in search of an empty boxcar as the train whistle blew, signaling departure. I threw my pack in the open door of a freight wagon and hoisted myself in just as the train was starting to move. I was relieved to have boarded successfully.

On the platform I had eaten a banana and a leaf full of white rice for the price of a few pennies. The beggars had besieged me. I had gone some time without food, and the rice took away the pangs of hunger that had been building during the walk to the depot. Clean water was not available and dysentery continued to be a problem, subduing my appetite. I drank the water where I could find it regardless of the posted warning signs.

The uncomfortably hot temperatures subsided as a slight breeze streamed in through the door of the boxcar from the outside. The countryside passed by in an obscure smear as we alternately passed through villages and farmland. Occasionally we stopped, and then backed up to switch out different freight cars for their routing to other lines. During these long periods it seemed for sure we were progressing backwards as much as forwards. Other times we would pull off on a siding, waiting an eternity for the oncoming train to first appear in the distance, and then streak past us in a roar, the horn shrieking, the sounds distorted by the violent movement of the passing cars.

My tired mind attempted to match the squeaks and rattles of the train's percussion with some musical score I had once cherished. Snapshots of Indian life continued to flash by as I sat quietly on the floor propped up against my backpack reading *The Hindu Way of Life*, one of the books on the list given me by the Australian surveyor. I had found it in an old bookstore off the main street in Varanasi. I was coming to understand more the basic tenets of this most important religion of India.

I was discovering that this complex body of ideas, deeply ingrained in the psyche of the believers, brought with it a powerful and corresponding social system. Vedic writings laid out four classes, or castes, of people: *Brahman* (priests and scholars), *kshatriyas* (warriors and rulers), *vaisyas* (trades people and farmers), and *sudras* (servants and ordinary workers). At the time of the Aryan Period (1500 BC) a fifth group emerged, a kind of a non-caste sort who took on tasks too low for even the *sudras* to deal with. These were the *untouchables*, and they had little contact with Hindu society in general, as it was their lot to perform the least desirable tasks. Mahatma Gandhi, credited with leading his country to independence through nonviolence, desired to free these untouchables from their sad and hopeless circumstances. His influence on India was far-reaching.

Unlike Christianity, Hinduism is a polytheistic religion having many gods and goddesses. Three of the most important of these are *Brahma*, the creator, *Vishnu*, the preserver, and *Shiva*, the destroyer. In his spiritual journey to become a good Hindu, the disciple learns to cherish the role of each and to call on them respectively in worship as needed. Though foreign concepts to most Westerners, I found that I was able to comprehend these basic ideas, and hoped they would help me to understand the Indian people in a more enlightened way.

Further reading exposed me to the three elements that are basic to Hinduism, *Dharma*, *Karma*, and *Reincarnation*. These are in many ways interdependent. *Dharma* is the idea that one must carry out the moral duties of life in accordance with personal position or station. *Karma* is what we might call natural law. Hindus postulate that for everything a person does in his life there is a consequence, and that virtuous deeds yield rewards. The converse is true as well; the sins of the individual will bring about punishment. The belief of *reincarnation*, or rebirth, states that each person will live multiple lives before achieving a final supreme goal. This occurs when we at last overcome all evils and earthly desires. It then follows that a person's misery or happiness either in this life or in a future life depends on both the good and bad deeds he has committed.

I found the complexity of these foreign doctrines sometimes confusing, yet in other ways quite logical and congruent to my moderate Christian upbringing. The little volume I was now reading helped me to understand some of the religious traditions of India, but I had to remember that Hinduism was not the only religion practiced within the borders of India. There were others like Jainism, Buddhism, Islam, and Sikhism that I felt obligated to research and make an effort to comprehend. These great religions had intermingled throughout history, borrowing from and blending with each other for centuries. I continued to reflect on the Australian surveyor. I was beginning to understand why he had devoted such a vast amount of time to study in preparing for his final visit to India.

The average Indian citizen struggling with existence knew little of the rest of the world's material advantages and opportunities. I was not sure if it would have made a big difference if they were aware of this. It seemed the man-in-the-street had no detectable plans for escape lingering in his subconscious mind. To the contrary, there was almost a blind acceptance of life's duties and expectations in the present. Recognition of this life as "meant to be" without discussion, argument, or even rebellion was the rule. Life was here and now, and that was all there was, until a future reincarnation. Hinduism played a large role in the tradition of compliance, yielding a stoic and nearly blissful detachment from the daily pains and sufferings. I had begun to cultivate a similar outlook, if only as a matter of self-preservation.

We were now well over halfway through the journey to Patna, and I was again hungry. My eating habits had changed drastically during this trip. Growing up I had been a persnickety eater, but traveling had quickly cured me of that, extending the perimeters of my fussy tastes to much wider margins of acceptance. Now I exposed myself to the hot and spicy curries offered by the street vendors. Though some dishes had proved adverse to my system, the majority of them stuck with me. I had gained a new respect for food, and in liberating myself from my childhood dislikes, I ate what and when I could, for I never knew just how long I might be without. On several occasions, I had gone for as long as four days without eating, usually those times when I was ill. It was only on rare occasions I saw someone overweight in India, one being the portly merchant to whom I had sold my shirt in Old Delhi.

I disembarked the train at Patna to take a one-hour horse and cart ride to the river. Next, I boarded a small steamer and slowly motored up the Ganges for two hours. Finally, I located the other train that was to deliver me in approximately twelve hours by rail to the Indian village of Raxaul, the stepping off place to the isolated mountain kingdom of Nepal.

The many arms hanging out the train windows were a strong indicator of my tardy arrival. Plainly visible were the destitute faces of the people peering from the train, while other souls were clinging to the external ladders. There were even riders on the top of the passenger cars, appearing as insects that had just lighted on some giant beast. Inside, I found first- and second-class to be jammed with a mass of humanity. I quickly exited the car and shuffled down the tracks with my gear as before, looking desperately for my reliable option, a vacant boxcar. Many cars down the line, far from the platform and its chaos, I found one holding only a few people.

I heaved my backpack high onto the floor of the boxcar and after some trouble finding a foothold, climbed aboard my new home. I was hungry and depleted, my clothes covered with the soot cast off by the engine from the earlier rail journey. There had been no time or opportunity to get food, but I still had a few sugar cookies left, my emergency backup. Consumed with weariness, I secured my spot inside the boxcar, spread out my sleeping bag and lay myself down for a much-needed rest.

I felt exhaustion creeping though my body and realized that once again I had pushed myself beyond my limits. Lack of sleep and food had caught up with me, and I felt the victim of loneliness that serenades the solitary traveler in times like these. I mused to myself what a difficult chore it would be to explain this current situation to anyone back home. The contrasts were too immense, the perceptions too perplexing, the task too great. People would not understand. Little did I know then these experiences would eventually become the guarded private memories held in a chamber of silence for years after my return home. I would find it better not to speak of them. Putting my thoughts to rest, I relaxed and let the gentle hypnotic swaying of the train lull me into a deep sleep.

Many hours passed before I awoke to find my movements almost totally restricted. I was confused for an instant, then realized the boxcar had completely filled with people from the different stops while I had been sleeping. To my utter shock and amazement, I realized I had actually become a human bench! Two slight Indian men were sitting on me. People began to move as I rolled over and brought myself to the sitting position. Every eye in the car was on me, and I was stunned to the core by what I saw next.

Three Indian women turned my way and kneeled directly in front of me. Their straight black hair fell to the middle of their backs and their piercing dark brown eyes effortlessly penetrated my blue ones. Each of the women had a small cosmetic beauty mark on her forehead, an auspicious symbol of the third eye called a *bindi* or *pottu*. At second glance I noticed they all held babies wrapped in small blankets. The women acted in unison as together they called out the beggars' mantra, "*Backshish, backshish, backshish.*" Each one of them raised their hand, and then pressed their fingers to their mouths, indicating a sincere desire for nourishment. They were radiant, and this unexpected wave of feminine energy nearly paralyzed me with fascination.

Their simple body movements appeared unconsciously synchronized at this unique and fateful moment in time. With grace and applied determination their humble gestures, hand to mouth, continued unabated while I searched the recesses of my mind on how to meet this unexpected situation appropriately. I looked around the boxcar at the rest of my audience. A hundred sets of eyes were bearing down on me, scrutinizing my next move.

Knowing I had very little to give I searched my pants pockets, pulling them inside out, to illustrate my own near destitution. Aside from the few dollars I had put away to sustain me while in Nepal and the pre-purchased airline ticket to be used to fly from Calcutta to Bangkok, I was broke. This gesture had little effect on these women or their supporters, for regardless of my current circumstances, I was obviously someone from the West. My mind raced as I continued to search for a solution. Then I suddenly remembered the sugar cookies. The pressure from the intense stares mounted as I opened my pack and pulled out a small paper sack. Opening it, I found four sugar cookies stashed in the bottom. I pulled them out and carefully placed one in the hands of each of the three women. I took the last cookie for myself, which they all seemed to understand.

As if choreographed, the women each took a bite of their cookies and began to chew. I thought to myself, "But what about their babies?" Then, as if in immediate response to my mental query, all three of the mothers carefully leaned down as if to kiss their babies, but instead transferred the chewed up cookies, mouth to mouth. As mother birds feeding their hungry chicks, these women had resourcefully made the baby food that satisfied their maternal instincts, leaving me with one more touching story to share.

All eyes went back to looking out the boxcar door. The women nodded to me in gratitude and with tender smiles turned to face in other directions, as if nothing had ever happened. I was pleased with the way this had all unfolded. Not only with the graceful way in which the three women had handled the feeding but also in how the solution had presented itself to me. We had all been a part of a beautiful event, and the end result was perfect and complete. No more, no less. I had earned my acceptance among the passengers, and I lay my head on my pack and went to sleep. I was vaguely aware of dreams, delightful dreams, vivid and unforgettable, of riding in a boxcar somewhere in northern India, with the three Madonnas.

Holy Man

Kathmandu
Chapter Eighteen

If you think you're free, there's no escape possible. —Ram Dass

The train delivered me north, to the Indian border community of Raxaul, where I continued on by horse and cart for about an hour to the Nepalese border. It was here that the long meandering mountain road up through the Himalayan foothills began, eventually leading into the Kathmandu Valley of Nepal.

After several inquiries, I learned that the operators of the ornately decorated freight trucks, which convoyed daily into the Himalayan Kingdom, occasionally took on riders. Seeing a half-dozen of the loaded trucks lined up, I questioned one of the bearded drivers waiting in his rig for a freight inspection. Pointing straight up, he affirmed in a pleasant singsong English that I could make the journey with him if I was willing to ride in the small luggage rack positioned over his cab. He indicated it would take us about twenty-four hours to cover the 145-mile distance. I quickly climbed up the sideboards of the truck and settled into my open-air perch above, making ready for another extraordinary excursion.

A short distance out of town the road became much steeper, snaking up over the densely wooded ridges that were thick with magnolia forests, pipal trees, and giant rhododendrons, some reaching heights in excess of thirty-five feet. There were banyan trees as well, with their great rolling convoluted trunks spreading over the ground. Their stringy root vines hung from massive overhead branches that were dressed in elliptical leaves. Intermittently, the radiant displays of foliage formed splendid flowering arches over the road, at times nearly blocking out the sun. I felt I was traveling through an enchanted land as we continually passed under the fragrant canopies.

Throughout history, solitary ascetics and spiritual aspirants of the Eastern faiths had come to live in these alluring forests.

We climbed steadily higher into the mountains, the truck laboring hard in the lower gears throughout the afternoon and into the night. I was constantly jarred back and forth, as we negotiated the many large ruts and potholes, the result of unbridled erosion that had etched deeply into the narrow unpaved road. Many times head-on traffic compelled us to retrace, backing up until reaching a turnout in an effort to make a way for the oncoming trucks. They edged down from the higher elevations while nursing their smelly, squealing brakes. I made ready to bail off several times when my driver maneuvered the rear dual wheels dangerously close to the edge of a sheer drop-off, hundreds of feet straight down.

We stopped occasionally at small roadside shanties, cobbled together with a multitude of building materials. Here my driver, who was eager to converse with others about the weather and road conditions, got something to eat and took his tea. The Nepalese women inside these roadhouses prepared *chapattis*, those flat circles of tasty unleavened bread. These were fashioned on an iron grill that spanned an open fire of burning twigs, with the two ends resting on well-positioned rocks. Steamed rice, the curry dish of the day, and scrambled eggs were also available.

The women of this country accepted responsibility for the food preparation. They had become masters at creating sufficient amounts of heat by skillfully feeding sticks into the flickering flames. I watched as they efficiently placed each small segment of a broken limb or an assortment of twigs onto the tiny fire. They were following a technique most likely taught them by their mothers and grandmothers. There was a scarcity of firewood in this region, and it was essential that people utilized the fuel in a most resourceful way. This was, quite simply, a matter of survival.

Later in the evening, during one of the stops when I remained on the truck, a "Holy Man," or *saddhu*, stepped out from the dark recesses of the thick jungle that flanked us on each side. Catching my eye, he approached. The man's long white beard and flowing gown were iridescent in the moonlight. His presence somewhat stunned me, and I concentrated intently on his face as he parted his lips to speak.

"Where do you go?" he asked in accented English.

"To Kathmandu," I replied.

I sensed that should I dismount the rig, at that precise moment and disappear into the foliage with him, for better or worse, the experience would transform my life forever. Stories of Westerners finding their gurus in this part of the world were commonplace. The clarity of his gaze called me, as if he were saying he was now prepared to take on a new disciple. Retaining my independence, I stayed aboard the truck, resolute in continuing my journey to Kathmandu. Smiling, he brought his hands up slowly, pressing them together near his heart in a traditional manner, while at the same time bowing gracefully. "*Namaste,*" he whispered. I respectfully followed his lead, mirroring his words and actions with the same gesticulation. Then he simply vanished, into the depths of the forest from which he had come.

The driver returned to the truck, and as we rolled away into the darkness, I pondered the interaction that had just taken place. I had previously learned that *Namaste* represented both a spoken communication and a gesture of friendship, signifying the oneness of the universe. In addition, it means to adorn, honor, celebrate, or anoint. I have never forgotten the aura of calmness and assurance that surrounded this ascetic on that special night. In general, the West was just now becoming familiar with certain Eastern disciplines, such as meditation and yoga, and their far-reaching potentials in an increasingly stressful world.

The luggage rack had a floor area just large enough for me to sit, making it impossible to stretch out my long legs. The travel fatigue came in successive waves. It had been several days now since leaving Varanasi. It was mid-April, and I was looking forward to settling in one place for a while. The dysentery that had been with me off and on since Afghanistan was wearing me down, and my weight had continued to plummet. My Levis were now ridiculously loose, and they billowed about my thin waist and bony legs like pantaloons. My travel fund had now diminished to less than $100, and Australia was still a great distance away. My passionate determination to reach the exotic capital of Kathmandu had kept me focused, possibly beyond reason, and I was due for a long rest.

The next afternoon the freight truck passed through a string of outlying villages that would lead me to the Nepalese capital. Bands of barefoot children trailed the truck, waving their little hands, while women carrying great jugs of water on their heads walked with an enchanting sway along the edge of the road. Old men, blind from years of unprotected exposure to the high-altitude ultraviolet rays, meditated in doorways framed with ancient hand-hewed timbers. I sensed they might be waiting patiently for the next life to come or possibly praying for a merciful reincarnation. The driver carefully guided the old truck through the constricted and dusty arteries that eventually brought us to the center of the city, one that over the centuries had spread out from the banks of the Bagmati River.

Out of the corner of my eye, I caught a glimpse of a young Western woman among the people milling in the streets. The truck came to a stop in one of the small village squares near a cluster of canvas covered open-air shops. I climbed down from my lookout over the cab and expressed my gratitude to the driver, handing him a few rupees. With a wide grin and a twinkle in his eye, he twirled the exceedingly long mustache that extended completely across his deeply pocked face.

My joints ached from sitting such a long time in one place. Happy to be walking, I swung my backpack up to one shoulder and moved out into the undulating sea of people, elated over my arrival. Soon, I spotted the blue-eyed blonde girl I had seen from the top of the truck. I walked up to her as she was engaged in bargaining with a vendor at one of the small yogurt shops. Not having communicated with another Westerner since the Australian man on the train, I quickly introduced myself. Tears of joy filled my eyes when I found out she was an American.

Her name was Annett, an athletic girl who had departed from Europe for India after participating in the Olympic swimming trials in Germany. Like me, she had been enchanted with stories of traveling overland to the mysterious East in hopes of exploring "foreign and unfamiliar worlds." The romantic inclinations of her vagabond heart had led her to Nepal. In the days to come, Annett became an invaluable source of information, quite willing to share the helpful tips she had learned while living in the valley. Before we parted, she gave me directions to the Blue Tibetan, where I could find reasonable lodging, among other things.

She also suggested we meet soon for a walk to the Swayanabath, the so-called Monkey Temple, which we would do later in the week. Unfortunately, Annett left Nepal shortly after that when her visa expired, becoming just another friendship casualty of a lifestyle where people were constantly on the move.

The Blue Tibetan was a combination restaurant and inn, colonized by a small and constantly changing contingent of hearty world travelers. I spoke with the proprietor, a Tibetan refugee who had brought his family over the elevated mountain passes from Lhasa, fleeing the Chinese occupation of his homeland. He had set up a thriving little business, as had many of his compatriots who were now residing in Nepal. Well received, the Tibetans, who were Buddhists, lived in peace and harmony with the Nepalese, who were Hindu. I soon secured a small room upstairs for ten cents a day. The "rooms" were more like cubicles in a communal dormitory, floor spaces slightly larger than it would take to lie down, and separated by hanging blankets as walls. Due to the price, no one ever seemed to complain.

In the days that followed, I exposed myself to the many tasty dishes served up at the Blue Tibetan Restaurant. The most common of these offerings was a large pancake made from crudely milled grains, served with butter churned from the milk of the yak. These were appetizing and filling, costing only a few pennies. They became a mainstay for those travelers who had come to the end of their financial rope.

Yogurt was also available, brought to the table in small disposable earthen pottery bowls. A thin skin of coagulated crust sat atop the curdled yak milk providing an adequate protection from the multitude of flies that continually circled. It was important for the consumer to extract this natural lid before partaking of this sour and fermented dish. There were also rice concoctions like *dal bhat* and *chuira*. This restaurant was primarily vegetarian, but a platter of water buffalo steak and rice, covered with a variety of steaming vegetables, was available at an eating establishment just down the street for about a dime. For the most part, I ordered from the vegetarian menu, but I did reward myself with the other delightful infusion of protein on several memorable occasions.

They served an abundance of hot tea in all of the restaurants in the city. Of course, it was of primary importance to boil water thoroughly before drinking and taking tea was a pleasant and safe way to stay hydrated. To order, one simply called out, *"Yuk Chai,"* or one tea.

The communal tables at the Blue Tibetan exhibited at any one time a diverse population of charming characters from all over the world. These were the progenitors of a budding subculture that, unbeknownst to us at the time, was about to revolutionize modern world history. A generation of dope-smoking, peace-loving, anti-establishment, rucksack wanderers was just beginning to take hold, and Kathmandu was destined to become their Mecca. Hashish was plentiful and cheap, sold at the "government store," and the word on the street was that the Nepalese officials looked the other way if they discovered someone using it. All the signposts were in place, and the "Darma Bums" as Jack Kerouac once called them, would soon be multiplying simultaneously on nearly every continent as this worldwide movement commenced to evolve.

My arrival in Kathmandu only slightly preceded the advent of that broad and sometimes perplexing name tag of "hippie" that would come out of San Francisco during the city's 1967 "Summer of Love." One could not deny that at this time the longer hair and unkempt nature of the transients on the road were far more the rule than the exception. The youths I encountered were traveling cheaply from country to country, where the comforts of home such as hot water, fresh towels, washers and dryers were simply not available. This, combined with a certain rebellious attitude towards traditional values and appearances definitely contributed to the untidy lifestyle of some.

The variety of tongues spoken around the café tables during the day presented no apparent problem for anyone. The common denominator that truly bonded the group together was not necessarily the language, but instead the actual journey to Nepal itself. The hardships involved in traveling overland to Kathmandu proved a natural screening process, the result of a choice made deep within the soul of only the most ardent international traveler. An atmosphere of mutual respect prevailed, and it was evident to all of those who had entered this holy and isolated Kingdom.

I say holy because of the ancient religions sequestered within the region, existing relatively undisturbed through time. This was a country distinctly isolated from the invasions of armies and ideas spawned by the outside world. Protected by the great mountain ranges, Nepal had remained separated since man's early history from the prevailing evolutionary social and industrial progressions experienced by the West, and some of her neighboring dominions. This unique background and location, much like that of Tibet, fanned the fires of idealism and drew utopian and spiritual seekers from different corners of the earth.

The city was awash with Hindu temples. There were also many Buddhist *stupas*, those holy hemispherical mounds, crowned with pagoda-style roofs, housing sacred relics and emanating peace. The narrow dirt streets of the city wound through an eclectic maze of scenes. The exploring pilgrim walked in the shadows of ancient multi-storied buildings, complemented with timeworn wooden balconies and shutters. Durbar Square was just one of the historical locations amidst this old part of town where well-placed and detailed religious carvings and sculptures of Hindu deities presented themselves. The two major religious influences of Hinduism and Buddhism continued to survive comfortably and compatibly. I had heard that there was some kind of religious holiday every single day in Kathmandu, clogging the streets with parades of celebration, musical processions and other spiritual festivities. To this, I bore witness.

From time to time, I observed an exceptionally appealing young girl who came to the restaurant. She could usually be seen sitting quietly in a corner of the Blue Tibetan, writing in her journal. I had learned from Philip, one of the young men who seemed to know her, that she kept to herself and was of a highly sensitive and independent nature. She was of medium height, demure, with two long, blonde braids that fell to her small waist. This young woman was lean, with the exception of her voluptuous breasts, and was clothed in an attractive and simple gown of natural muslin cloth. Like me, she always wore sandals. Sometimes she came to the restaurant with her guitar, shyly singing to us in a soft and sad emotional voice. The music haunted the hearts of all who heard it. Her name was Sofia, and she had come all the way from Copenhagen.

I was smitten at first glance and planned my day around visiting places where she might appear. The wall of nervous anticipation that repeatedly blocked my efforts in meeting her finally dissolved, and on one special day I introduced myself. She spoke excellent English and after a short conversation I asked her if she would care to join me in a walk down by the river. With a gracious smile, she politely accepted my offer. It was not long before I felt very comfortable around her and sensed the presence of an old soul in a young body, like someone I had known for a lifetime. We spoke of many things as we strolled through streets so alien to our respective homelands. She enjoyed hearing my stories of growing up in a small Oregon town, and I was captivated with the detailed accounts of her childhood in Denmark.

Later in the afternoon, Sofia looked over to meet my smile with a rare, penetrating eye. Frozen in silence, we stood facing each other as she searched my face for some inkling of assurance. Then after professing her trust, she slowly began to unveil a sordid tale of sorrow and endurance like none I had ever heard before. It was a story that would be impossible to forget, for as long as I lived.

At sixteen, this adventurous spirit had left Denmark to see the world. Sofia followed one of the more common routes to the east, a risky trek for a woman by herself that took her through Turkey. Her youth and radiance drew men close, regardless of where she traveled.

Naïve and alone, it was not long before careless associations shuffled her into the custody of white slave traders. She alluded to many unpleasant ordeals that took place before her captors finally sold her into a harem in one of the Arab countries. In the months that passed, she plotted her escape, waiting patiently for fate to open the door just wide enough for her to pass. When the opportunity presented itself, she was able to flee, though not without some violence of which she refused to give the details. Able to hitchhike once again, some friendly European travelers had given her a lift as far as India in their Volkswagen bus, and from there she had made it to Nepal. She was now eighteen and planned to return to Denmark, when the opportunity arose.

The heavenly days passed much too quickly, as we continued to explore the marvels of this fascinating city together. One day she timidly confided to me, that since her traumatic experiences while in captivity, she had been unable to be physically intimate with a man. This explained her rather delicate demeanor and confirmed the message that I had heard circulating around the Blue Tibetan regarding her vows of chastity. We continued to enjoy each other's company, and I immersed myself deeper into our platonic friendship, one ascending away from the carnal passions that she so aroused in me. We agreed to build our friendship on a higher and more spiritual plane.

We discussed the prospect of taking a much longer walk, a trek of several days duration. Two days later, we walked out of Kathmandu at dawn, heading for a remote village at the edge of the foothills. We moved at a steady pace through most of the morning, steering clear of the packs of wild and sometime rabid dogs that roamed the countryside. In time, we began to climb, endlessly it seemed, up over the multitude of terraces used for centuries to farm the slopes of the Kathmandu Valley. Level agricultural land was at a premium here, and since time began, people had been carving these hillsides into utilitarian and picturesque contours.

We scrambled ever higher over the stepped landscape that formed the natural tapered walls of the valley. In the late afternoon, we came to a waterfall that cascaded down through an eroded break in the overhanging hillside. Much to my surprise Sofia proved uninhibited, and with unconscious poise disrobed and slowly pressed her creamy nakedness into the cool water that dropped down from overhead. I could not resist the primordial callings and found myself tracing the profile of her shapely form with my eyes. My heartbeat amplified, and soon I stepped into the falling water to join her.

I watched as the water trickled over the perfect curvature of her youthful bosoms, around her taut waist, and then randomly followed her long tapered legs to the ground. That I could not be closer only increased my desire, a desire nearly impossible to quell.

After drying off in the sun we found a narrow well-used path at the top of the terraces and continued with our trekking, following the ridge line ever higher. The next two days bought us in contact with the Nepalese mountain farmers. We stayed in the same trekker huts they rented to those climbers going to Namchebazar, en route to base camp of Mount Everest. These primitive shelters only cost a few pennies a night. The relationship between Sofia and I remained restricted as she wished, but we slept close to each other at night, the bond of trust growing ever stronger.

Early in the morning after our second night, we awoke to the sound of someone knocking on the plank door of our hut. It was one of the farmer's sons. Stepping out into the dawn, we could see our gain in elevation from the hiking in the days before. It had brought us high atop a narrow crown that offered an expansive view. On the horizon, we could see the encroaching ocean of clouds that cloaked the Himalayan peaks, evidence that the monsoon season was nearly upon us. Suddenly, as if commanded by our wishes alone, the winds parted the thick vaporous veil. The sun projected a bright pink and yellow *alpenglow* across the jagged skyline in the distance. The boy pointed wildly, crying aloud, "*Sagarmatha, Sagarmatha*." We beheld the saw-tooth chain of white mountains, slightly lower than the one icy pyramid positioned near the center. It was the grand prominence of Mount Everest!

Our fingers touched lightly during those precious moments and overall, that morning topped all the extraordinary occurrences I had experienced on the journey so far. The scene seared itself into my mind, remaining as clear today as it was forty years ago. The pain and suffering I had endured was but a petty tribute to have paid for such a splendid reward. I took pleasure in knowing I was continuing to quench my enormous thirst for seeing and experiencing the wonders of the world.

Later in life, I developed a passion for mountaineering and acquired a large collection of books pertaining to Mount Everest for my personal library. I have taken great pleasure in rereading them from time to time, turning back the pages of my memory to those glorious moments long ago when Sofia and I stood on that lonesome ridge in a faraway land to lay our eyes on the highest point on earth.

Later, we started the long hike back to Kathmandu, covering the downhill trail in much faster time. Entering back into the city we acknowledged our gratitude to each other in sharing such a unique experience. Then we parted for a few days as we each had matters to attend to. I continued to process in my mind all I had experienced on that incredible trek into the mountains.

Sadly, the next time I saw Sofia, she informed me of her plans to go back into India. I felt my heart sink. She only had two dollars left and her destination was Bombay. She had heard European girls were making a good living there, as starlets in the budding movie industry. It all sounded a bit ominous to me but she was intent on following this plan through.

She was leaving Kathmandu as she had come in, a solitary traveler hitching a ride on one of the freight trucks. On her back was a traditional Nepalese basket, holding her personal items. Sofia wore the support strap for the basket stretched across her forehead, exactly as the Nepalese women did when transporting their great bundles of firewood for long distances.

As a parting gift, she handed me one of her most treasured possessions, the simple green blanket that was her bed. She told me it had originally come from an Indian hotel. For one sublime moment, our eyes met warmly to exchange unspoken volumes, then after a light embrace she nodded goodbye and climbed aboard the ornamented truck leaving for the Indian border. It would be seven long months before I again heard of her. I would still be traveling.

I too was extremely short of funds, and one day made the decision to sell my last valuable possession, the down sleeping bag I had purchased from the Berkeley outdoor store before leaving the country. I walked to Durbar Square and sat down cross-legged in the market place next to the other vendors, and displayed my wares. The nights had become far too warm to sleep inside the bag, so I had been lying on top of it for the last month. Now, with the blanket Sofia had given me, I would be able to sell the down bag, raising some much-needed money. Several of the Nepalese men were very interested in it, and a small crowd of the curious immediately surrounded me. The bargaining soon began and, to my delight, I quickly sold it to a Nepalese Sherpa for twenty-two dollars, a large amount of money in Nepal.

With the assistance of one of the onlookers who acted as interpreter, I learned my buyer was a veteran of Everest expeditions. In addition to my bag, which he was now purchasing, he was in possession of another one quite similar. My bag would allow his brother to sign on as a porter for the Everest climbs, insuring him future employment for many years to come. The Sherpa invited me home to meet his family while he retrieved his money.

I ducked under a smoke-stained timber and stepped inside the dark dirt-floored room that was the main part of his residence. The ceilings were exceedingly low and Hindu icons graced the walls. Through the haze of incense that filled the air I could see his other down bag hanging on the wall. It was green and had a satin nylon finish, matching my blue bag in every way except for the color. For him these bags were valuable and indispensable tools of his trade. He disappeared into the next room but soon returned with a smudged and well-worn $20 bill, American money, which he handled to me with a smile, making up the difference in Nepalese rupees. For me, this $22 deposit into my travel fund would provide the necessary funds to complete the crossing of India, to Calcutta. He bowed, and with praying hands uttered, "*Namaste.*"

After a month in Nepal, I came down with a serious infection in both of my eyes. I suspected the cause of this malady stemmed from the excrement of cows, pulverized into the streets for centuries and eventually becoming a fine toxic dust that hung in the air. I was not alone with this ailment. In time, the condition disappeared on its own, though only after I had experienced many miserable mornings, awaking to find my eyes glued shut from the dried mucus that had formed on my eyelids during the night. This problem caused me to delay my departure and visit the Royal Palace for a visa extension.

Reflecting on my six-week visit to the Kingdom of Nepal, I concluded that the perseverance involved in reaching this goal had become increasingly important to me as I had made my way east. The destination had provided a clear purpose to bolster me in times of great sickness, financial insecurity, and discouragement. There were occasions when I nearly gave up the dream, but I always returned to my stated objective of walking the streets of this ancient capital. This journey had been well worth all the discomforts and uncertainties associated with it.

Before I left this extraordinary little country, there was yet another interesting story that was to develop, one involving some highly unusual men who called themselves "mercenaries."

Stupa at Swayanabath (Monkey Temple)

The Mercenary
Chapter Nineteen

A journey is like marriage. The certain way to be wrong is to think you control it. —John Steinbeck

Swarms of flies occupied the airspace just above the narrow dusty streets of Kathmandu. Nearly every quarter of this Nepalese capital city hummed with the sounds of their beating wings. I was shocked when the untouchables, lowest of Hindu castes, came to extract the sewage from the various establishments, and the flies covered them like a thin suit of black wool. The buzzing sound of these airborne menaces heralded the approach of the potty wagons and the beleaguered, downtrodden, and hopeless souls that tended them. These powerful sights and sounds left indelible images, steeling me in preparation for those to come.

Try as they might, the workers of the Blue Tibetan Restaurant were unable to prevent flies from entering their establishment. The winged devils would simply follow in the wake of new customers stepping through the front door. These annoying insects would pause to harass those of us sitting around the dining room, and then make their way back to the kitchen, sometimes ending up in the pancake batter. It was not surprising to find their expired bodies served up in this house specialty. Those of us who knew of this problem scanned the cakes thoroughly for the telltale "dark spots," surgically removing them before consumption. Flies or no flies, the pancakes continued to be an inexpensive culinary delight for the budget travelers who frequented the restaurant.

One afternoon the front door of the Blue Tibetan Restaurant swung open to accommodate the usual cloud of pests that had been circling lazily outside. With them came five rough-looking men, all over six feet tall, tanned and well muscled. As they stepped across the threshold one at a time, I could see that each had a holstered sidearm and a large hunting knife in a leather sheath on his belt. They entered with confident swaggers, laughing loudly and creating excessive pandemonium before approaching one of the larger tables. The men knocked chairs about as they roughhoused and jousted with each other over who would sit where. It was apparent these were a much coarser breed of travelers than I had previously encountered.

The warm and cheerful mood that existed in the restaurant before their intrusion now began to chill. A wave of tension washed across the faces of the small group of international customers who sat at the adjoining tables. In a very short time some of the patrons began to remove themselves, paying their bill and walking outside, eager to change the "vibe." The customers who remained, which included me, watched with curious interest, trying to discern what surprises this new situation might bring.

Unabashedly, the men told us they were soldiers-for-hire, independent mercenaries who roamed the world at will, moving from one conflict to another. They worked for the highest bidder. One of them went on to say they took *what* they wanted—food, women, and whiskey—*when* they wanted. At this the other members of their little group laughed. It shocked all who listened when the brigands continued to brag about pillaging everywhere they had been, leaving a trail of destruction behind as they stayed one step ahead of the authorities. One of the men boasted they had recently been "up in China, blowing up bridges!" My curiosity aroused, I began conversing with the apparent leader of the contingent. He was an American, and his name was Kevin.

"Call me 'Mercenary,'" he said, flashing his cold gray eyes. We talked long enough for me to find out that he originally hailed from Kansas. After a stint in the armed forces he had struck out on his own, first working as a bodyguard and then gravitating to other types of employment that were clearly under the radar of legitimacy. He revealed that, in addition to him, the group had enlisted a French-Algerian, a Belgian, a Scot and another Frenchman, all of whom were sitting at the table. They had been traveling together for a number of months, engaged in completing some "odd jobs" here and there for different governments. Kevin continued to relate shocking details of their exploits to several of us who had now gathered to listen. As he continued to speak, coolness descended over me, as I sensed him to be lawless, with a lack of boundaries and, from the sound of things, without conscience.

What initial set of circumstances and conditions had led this man to step outside the norms of civilization, I could only guess. Those sacred social compacts that have held most ordinary men in check seemed not to be in place for him. The more we talked the greater was my awareness that he had walked unrestrained in the world of the mercenary long enough for it to have become a habit, an ingrained way of life. From the tales he told I surmised his path would, in all likelihood, someday be the end of him, and I told him so. He gave me a crazy grin, and then agreed.

In distinct contrast to the drama developing around the table of the mercenaries was the quiet and unceasing display of humble service by the Tibetan owner of the restaurant. The older man dutifully delivered one steaming dish after another from the small kitchen at the back of his restaurant. He moved lightly on his feet from table to table, smiling and nodding greetings to his faithful cliental. He was an industrious man, one who had survived many hardships and injustices before immigrating to his adopted homeland of Nepal. I could see his quiet strength in the map of character lines that ran across his face. His eyes scanned the room periodically, alerting himself to any new and unforeseen danger that might threaten his business or the welfare of his customers.

With much fanfare and bantering, the mercenaries finally placed a large food order, supplementing main dishes with many add-ons. A young waiter filled his order pad with a list several pages in length, written in the artistic character-like Tibetan script. It had been confirmed soon after my arrival that he was the owner's son, a younger and fresher version of the older man. After the orders of the mercenaries had been taken, the young waiter disappeared into the kitchen to help his father prepare the food.

Sometime later they both returned, bearing hot platters of appetizing food that filled the dining room with enticing aromas. They placed a number of delectable dishes in front of the mercenaries, as if bringing tribute to kings. It appeared that nearly everything on the menu was coming out of the tiny kitchen. A massive feast of gargantuan proportions commenced as the reprobates, still displaying their rowdy behavior, began to devour their bounty. The banquet took nearly an hour, the mercenaries consuming pricy selections I had never dared to order.

Afterwards it was time to pay. The proprietor presented the bill, laying it on the table near Kevin. He picked it up and scrutinized the bill at length, while the other members of his entourage began to snicker. Then the mercenary gestured his satisfaction with a nod and calmly reached for the over-sized biker billfold stuffed in his back pocket and secured by a chain. From this Kevin produced a thick fold of cash money and, without counting it, placed the wad into the Tibetan's hand. The gang of five then nonchalantly stood up and began to walk in the direction of the front door. It was precisely at this moment that all hell broke loose, causing the atmosphere in the room to change radically!

Kevin had paid the Tibetan proprietor with worthless Chinese money! This was a multiple insult, as the currency had no intrinsic value in the Kingdom of Nepal, and it had come from the country that now occupied the owner's original homeland. This occupation had resulted in the separation of his family members by ultimately compelling the man, his wife and son to flee Tibet into Nepal. Shaking his head violently, the proprietor tried to hand the currency back to Kevin and his cohorts, who by this time were laughing uncontrollably.

It was now obvious the men had never intended to pay for the lavish meal they had just consumed. An argument ensued, and Kevin reached for his pistol. Seeing this, the older Tibetan swung gracefully to the wall which displayed a Gurkha Sword (*kukri*) and took the wicked looking boomerang-shaped weapon down in both hands. The short stocky man then whirled around in a fluid martial arts movement to face his adversary while firmly gripping the handle of the sword.

With the reactions of a cat, Kevin removed his sidearm from the snapped holster, bringing the pistol up level with the angry face of the proprietor. The room fell silent and all eyes focused intensely on the bizarre event now unfolding in front of us. The two men stood frozen in a passionate and deadly standoff, the Tibetan and the mercenary, the virtuous man and the evil one.

I jumped to my feet from a chair in the corner of the room and, raising my hands, issued a command. I was attempting to defuse the escalating situation where it was plain to see someone was about to get killed.

"Stop," I shouted, "before something happens here that you will both regret." I wondered if this was enough for each man to save his pride. The cold facial expression of the American did not waver as he and his crew took this momentary interruption to begin a slow retreat out of the restaurant, sneering and scoffing as they went. Squadrons of flies hovered in formation outside the door, poised to enter the room. The Tibetan man vented his fury in a tongue quite foreign and incomprehensible. I could only assume it included some kind of demand for immediate payment, this time in Nepalese money.

Finally, Kevin, with his weapon still in his hand, moved into the street, while the proprietor's son rushed to his father's side. We could still hear peals of laughter and the reverberations of their loutish behavior as the perpetrators sauntered on down the street. The honorable defender replaced his sword on the wall, shook his head, and walked back into the kitchen still muttering angrily under his breath.

The normal cordial atmosphere slowly returned to the restaurant, and the volume of chatter around the tables increased dramatically. The stunned customers continued to exchange opinions and comments well into the afternoon. The owner of the Blue Tibetan Restaurant reported the incident to the Nepalese police and to the army that day, but as far as anyone knew, he never received compensation for the great quantities of food prepared and served to the heartless invaders. It was one of those unexpected and miscellaneous costs of doing business.

The next day news circulated around the table at the restaurant that a young Nepalese girl had been accosted and abused, causing thoughts of the mercenaries to surface in all our minds. Crimes of this nature were rare among the local populace. There were additional reports of trouble down by the river at the swimming pool, a philanthropic venture built from foreign investment. It was even rumored that hand grenades had been detonated.

I made my way down to the pool the following day, where I found the mercenaries. They had commandeered the swimming pool and were living the good life, enjoying the facilities intended for the Nepalese children. I sat down next to Kevin and engaged him in conversation. Initially, I informed him that the "word on the street" was the Nepalese army was going to escort the bunch of them out of the country soon. To my amazement, he met my words of caution with callous indifference.

In a different approach, I chose this time to introduce the concept of "karmic debt," an integral component in a philosophy of successful living familiar in this part of the world. The central idea was that a man creates bad Karma when he violates the domain and right of free choice of those around him. This sets up an energy imbalance that yearns for resolution. An injured party usually seeks to "get even." I told him that Karmic debt, generally repaid in kind, can follow a person in this lifetime or, as Hindus believe, into future lifetimes. Surprisingly, he listened.

I furthered explained the theory that this imbalance will continue to exist until the inequity corrects itself and the Karmic energy returns to its original equilibrium. Given this, I mentioned to Kevin that he was most likely destined to receive a large repayment for his misdeeds at some time in the future. He seemed shocked I would speak to him of such matters, and quickly dismissed it as rubbish. I suspected sharing a country of birth and possibly my size, allowed me the license to get away with communicating so frankly. We parted company that day and, as I would be leaving Katmandu soon, I naturally assumed I would never see him again.

I had already extended my visa in Nepal once. Now with it set to expire again in a few days, I decided to take a small Nepalese passenger plane for the very short and economical flight ($7 US), back to Patna, India. I made the rounds and said goodbye to those friends I had made around the tables of the Blue Tibetan, among them, the owner. Then on the day of departure, I made my way to the airfield.

Circling up and out of the Katmandu Valley, I was captivated with the view presented from the window of the small aircraft. The jagged ice-covered peaks of the Himalayas extended out as far as I could see, looking like the terrain one might expect to find on Pluto. Great climbers reacted to this inhospitable and formidable landscape as if it were a gauntlet, thrown down to challenge them, daring an intrusion into these frozen realms. Adventurous souls would always be compelled to answer this call, to seek new routes up sheer and icy exposures. Some of them would succeed in depositing their bodies on the frigid mountaintops, forever frozen in the dry heartless winds of time.

As the drone of the small craft's engines filled my ears, I thought back over my interactions with Kevin the mercenary. How could I know then, that either by accident or divine providence, I would meet him again some ten years into the future, on life's circuitous road? At that time we would have an extended conversation lasting most of an afternoon. I would come away with some degree of closure regarding the extraordinary experience I had with the mercenary, after he told me the rest of his story.

The authorities had finally banished him and his men from Nepal, after which the Nepalese army was escorting them out of the country. The mercenaries overpowered the handful of troops, and left them tied up at the edge of the road. After commandeering their weapons, they continued on to the Indian border in the Nepalese Army jeeps. They made their way back to Europe from there with many more infamous exploits to their discredit.

A tale of death and destruction unfolded after they deployed their services in Africa. His comrades had all died while fighting in the Congo. Some of the captured mercenaries in those campaigns were tortured, and then roasted over fire pits by the opposition, to die slow and horrible deaths. He had managed to escape but the loss of his comrades and the experiences in the Congo had left a devastating mark, causing him to totally re-evaluate his life. Alcohol and drugs were the first to go.

I remained spellbound as he shared his story of an astonishing "spiritual conversion." He told me of finding a "higher power" he called God, and that his main goal in life now was to perform good deeds and to right the many wrongs he had left behind in the self-centered whirlwind that had been his life. I perceived a changed man, humble and quiet, thoughtful and considerate. I could only hope and pray that it would last.

I never saw Kevin again after that chance reunion in 1977. This interesting meeting with him, a decade after my return home, caused me to have a deeper appreciation for the miraculous and wondrous twists that life has to offer. Many times since, I have thought of the American whom I confronted in Kathmandu, the man I knew as "The Mercenary."

Burma to U.S. Route

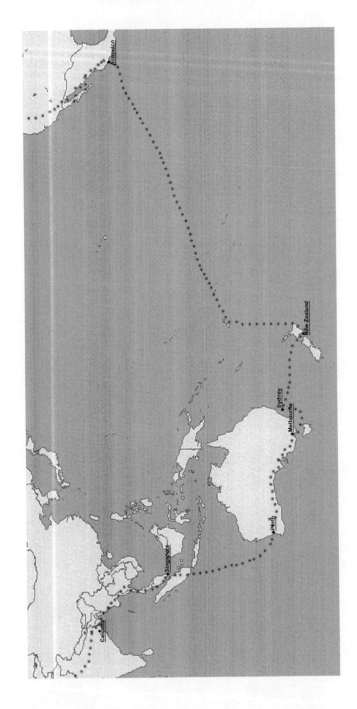

The Burma Connection
Chapter Twenty

If one does not accord the journey the right to destroy us a little bit, one might as well stay at home. —Nicolas Bouvier

Crushing heat enveloped me as I stepped from the door of the plane and descended the portable staircase to the scorching runway below. The flight to Patna seemed to have taken only a few minutes, but the change in humidity from Nepal to India was dramatic. The limited departures of public transportation into town condemned me to park myself on a concrete curb and stew in my own juices for the next couple of hours. Lady Luck smiled and I finally secured a lift into town with a freight truck, driven by a wiry old man wearing a turban and a mischievous grin. I strongly suspected he had sized me up at first glance as someone a bit out of place. We exchanged few words as he focused on the narrow tree-lined road, paralleled on one side by a shallow irrigation canal. The silent Samaritan deposited me on a crowded street in the center of town, pointed me in the direction of the railway station, and then motored away leaving a smoky exhaust trail behind his antique truck.

Placing one foot in front of the other, I threaded my way through the mass of gaunt inhabitants to the train depot. Here I boarded the familiar overloaded Indian passenger train, this one heading east for Calcutta. It was another long journey, this time through the flat and fertile agricultural plains of northeastern India, etched here and there by meandering tributaries, most of which emptied into the Ganges. After awhile I realized that the conductor had failed to collect for my passage. I later came to understand from my inquiries that it was commonplace for foreigners not to pay, though no one ever did cite the reason.

The familiar rhythmic sounds of the steel wheels rolling over the tracks soon lulled me into a deep sleep. The rail excursion extended all day and through that night, with the occasional detour by the engineer to an alternate siding, allowing an oncoming locomotive to blast past us with a long line of cars in tow. We reduced our speed frequently, coming to rest at the numerous stops along the way where the tide of passengers would ebb and flow between train and platform.

Early in the afternoon of the next day the long and repetitious cycle finally wound down when the conductor announced in English and Hindi that we were coming to our destination. It had been twenty-three long hours since I boarded, and I gladly joined the other passengers in preparing to disembark. Most of them were now on their feet, shuffling about and lifting their bundles down from the overhead wrought iron luggage racks. I was eager to get outside and do some walking after all that sitting.

I left the train, embedded in the crowd of exiting passengers that was now pushing out into the Calcutta streets. Our movement was fluid, like a legion of manikins dressed in white kurta pajama suits marching forward to fill every space in the streets ahead. I followed the surging masses up one artery and down another, turning at last onto a side street in my effort to break free and find a room. It was difficult if not impossible to identify the hotels. Frustrated, I wandered door to door, passing a series of business establishments, unable to read the script on their overhead signs.

Though encircled by people, the specter of loneliness loomed up strongly from within. The homesickness that had surfaced periodically took hold of me, and suddenly I did not want to be in India. Instead, the memories of home vividly came to mind. I fantasized about driving down a country road in Oregon with my girlfriend, listening to popular music on the car radio and looking for a place to have a picnic. There was a food basket in the front seat stuffed with fried chicken, homemade rolls, and potato salad with plenty of dill pickles. Then, as I had previously learned to do, I curtailed my dreams to address the problem before me.

The current reality was, I could not find lodging. As a result, I spent the next several nights sleeping in one of the park quadrangles near the center of the city. I had observed in the large metropolitan areas of India that some of the European travelers used these grassy public commons for camping; the grounds were often accented with a number colorful tents. Here in Calcutta, the heat and humidity must have driven them out, for I saw very few travelers.

Calcutta was the one-time capital of British East India, a city of historical prominence that could trace its origins back to the 1690s. As India's largest metropolis, this teeming mass of human activity had spread steadily over the banks of the Hooghly River for the previous three centuries. The river had cut through the delta of alluvial soils upon which the city sat, and eventually became one of the many open mouths that emptied into the Bay of Bengal. Calcutta exuded a certain cosmopolitan ambiance while at the same time leaving one with the sense that things were just a hair's breadth from spinning out of control. The non-violent religious tenet of Hinduism as practiced by the Indian people was the societal glue that I guessed held it all together.

It was now the end of May 1967. Workers in the mailroom at the American embassy had informed me that Calcutta in the current monsoon month was challenging, if not wretched. The insufferable heat and humidity bore down heavily on the novice and initiated alike. My clothes were constantly drenched in an endless deluge of perspiration and there was no relief in sight, day or night. Mother India, lovely in so many fascinating ways, could easily demoralize the Westerner unaccustomed to the strain of Indian travel. Some I had talked to became the victims of a crippling malaise, leading them gradually to a complete submission after only a few weeks under these conditions. After two months in India and Nepal I felt the telltale signs, and realized it was time to take my leave.

Although more the musings of an older man than the ideas entertained by someone my age, I was beginning to understand that the seasons of accelerated learning in my life came after corresponding periods of great trial. My most effective and memorable educational experiences seemed to come about when the boundaries of my personal growth were challenged by added risk or pressure. This was especially true under the conditions of elevated stress like the one I was feeling at this time.

This global odyssey had caused me to see my existence, more or less, as a series of passages. Initially these passages were merely physical transitions from one country to another. Later, as I became more seasoned, I could see how these changing events, in fact, altered my perceptions. I had progressed from an idealistic youth out to see the world, to a more serious individual, one now concerned primarily with surviving the realities brought on by the quest itself. There were times I felt the journey had educated me past my abilities to absorb the lessons. The one overriding thought in which I continued to hold an abiding faith was the idea that I would emerge from this great contest a stronger individual than when I had begun. I continued to believe without question, that fate would not give me more than I could handle.

One of the few assets remaining in my possession was an open-ended ticket on Burma Airways, departing Calcutta and arriving in Bangkok, with one scheduled stop in Rangoon, Burma. On numerous occasions during my subsistence pilgrimage across the subcontinent I had been tempted to cash the ticket in and provide for myself a greater means of support. However, I had purchased the document with "black market rupees," obtained by selling the few American dollars I had brought into the country in my sock. I had learned as far back as Egypt that the people in these countries cherished and even hoarded dollars, gathering them up as they would gold. They had a definite value anywhere in the world should the inhabitants be forced to leave their homeland, something that was not always true of their own currencies.

Although this had allowed me to purchase the voucher at a tremendously good price, there was a worrisome catch on the other end of the transaction. Before boarding the plane, it would be necessary to produce a statement showing I had obtained the Indian rupees, used to buy the ticket, from a financial institution such as a bank and not from the shady moneychangers in the back streets, as I had. Furthermore, had I cashed the ticket in, it meant I would have to repeat the purchasing process all over again, undoubtedly at a premium.

I made successive daily visits to the Burma Airways office by bus, through the busy streets, where emaciated men lay begging, some completely naked and destitute on the sidewalks. The more fortunate of them slept on pieces of cardboard, while others directly on the concrete. There were also the spiritual devotees, *saddhus* and *yogis*, weathered souls of skin and bone sitting cross-legged, their eyes locked straight ahead in an undeterred meditative gaze. Some gave the impression they had reached their sought after state of enlightenment, while others manifested a more vacant look, indicating a result much more questionable.

Certain neighborhoods of Calcutta revealed an uneasy climate among the people in the streets. Were these the stresses resulting from the excessive temperature and humidity or was it something more political in nature? I wondered if the well-defined colonial legacy of discipline and social order left behind by the British might be wearing a little thin here. I had the same feelings when we encountered the mob mentality in Pakistan. I felt things could easily erupt around me with the slightest change in social mood. While on my rides across town aboard the public buses, there were several disruptions made by Communist agitators who chose these occasions to give fiery speeches to their captive audience. I had learned the radical Marxist-Maoist movement was on its way to becoming a politically dominant force in Calcutta's state of West Bengal at this time.

As I walked the long blocks to the airline office from the bus stop, groups of beggars approached me chanting, "*Backshish, Sahib, backshish.*" This roughly translated in South Asia, from the Hindi and Bengali, as a request for charitable giving or tip, by the *Sahib*, lord or sir. Nearly every one of them suffered from some pathetic abnormality, lost or deformed limbs and blindness being the most common. More than once, I had heard rumors regarding children, deformed intentionally by ruthless guardians to make them more productive as beggars. I found this idea difficult to comprehend and felt compelled to doubt its validity. It taxed my heart not to contribute when I encountered these pitiful beings, but I had little money left and their cups were too many and without bottoms. On those occasions when I did accommodate them, they mobbed me in mere seconds.

Burma Airways continued to delay my flight to Bangkok day after day due to the violent storms brought on by the monsoons. On one occasion the officials at the airline counter offered a humorous but chilling thought to those of us inquiring, saying, "Our prop-jets fly *through* the storms, not *over* them!" Touted as the cheapest flight to Thailand, their questionable safety record was a favorite topic of discussion among the budget travelers. It remained a possibility that on very short notice, the thermal and the bureaucratic clouds might part and my much-anticipated deliverance from these difficult circumstances would begin. At the end of the day, officials once again shook their heads, prompting me to make another trek to the American Embassy to check for mail, and another night in the park.

Disheartened by the continual delays, I discussed with consulate personnel some other alternatives, such as cashing in my airline ticket and traveling overland to Thailand through Burma. They quickly made me aware that, "Land passage was not permissible, nor possible!" Those who did so were never heard from again. Such a decision would place my life in great danger.

Taking advantage of the overhead fans in the reading room at the American Embassy, I took some time to learn more about the mysterious country of Burma (now Myanmar). The British had incorporated Burma into the Indian Empire in the late eighteen hundreds. Administered as a province of India until 1937, it then became an autonomous self-governing colony in 1948, declaring its independence from the Commonwealth. A revolutionary council then laid out the Burmese path to Socialism. At the current time General Ne Win, a military strongman and political kingpin, ruled the small country with an iron fist. This shed light on the consensus among the other travelers I had met at Burma Airways, who said we should get Burma behind us as quickly as possible.

The following day officials at the Burma Airways counter told me to gather my gear and stand by, restoring my faith in the process. In the confusion that ensued, they completely forgot to request a document verifying the legitimacy of my rupees for the purchase of the ticket. This was a stroke of luck as I did not have such a document nor did I have the money to buy a new ticket. A few minutes later, we packed ourselves inside a small and dilapidated bus. Like cattle on their way to market, we were slowly shuttled through the chaotic and polluted streets to the airport.

The aged and tarnished plane lifted off from the Calcutta runway and began its slow, wide spiral of climb into the dark layer of clouds hanging above us. The unpredictable monsoon weather fronts that poured down over the subcontinent from the Himalayas in the north had arrived. Pilots dreaded this run to Bangkok, and the many delays I experienced due to the inclement weather were indicative of their concerns. Extreme turbulence, thunderstorms, and icing plagued their flights.

The American predecessors in WWII who "flew the hump" to re-supply the Chinese government in the war against the invading Japanese had also experienced some of the same conditions brought on by such weather. This aerial lifeline continued for several years following the closure of the Burma Road in 1942. The Santsung mountain range was "the hump," proving to be an elevated barrier difficult and dangerous to traverse. Allied air transports effectively established a bridge between India and China with these flights, which helped end the war with Japan. Conditions had changed little since that time.

The flight was understandably rough and the erratic air currents tossed the plane violently about like a toy. Outside it was gloomy, and all I could see were the small beads of moisture that streaked across the outside of the window. The flashing vaporous blanket that was once above the aircraft had now swallowed us up entirely. It seemed like the buffeting continued for hours before we finally experienced a well-deserved hiatus from the tempest. Rangoon, the city of our stopover, now came into sight.

A sixth sense warned me there were more surprises to come. As far as I could see, my fellow passengers were a diverse collection of pilgrims, international wayfarers and business people. Vague aromas of curry, incense, and stale human perspiration permeated the cabin. As we made our approach to the Rangoon airport, the memory of a whimsical comment I once made to a college chum came to mind: "Someday I will send you a postcard from Rangoon." I had been expounding on my dreams of future travel. Now, just three years later, the forces of destiny led me to this faraway outpost, but there would be no postcards commemorating Burma. We touched down with a deafening screech of rubber tires on the tarmac and, oddly enough, the plane came to rest out in the open, some distance from any facility. Fuel trucks motored towards us.

The announcement came through a loud speaker from the captain insisting that passengers remain in their seats. Some time passed before a half dozen formidable looking soldiers dressed in drab army uniforms boarded the plane. Two of them waited at the door with their automatic weapons and the rest made their way down the aisle of the plane, spraying all of us with a pungent smelling disinfectant. Next, they began to search the passengers and their luggage, one row at a time. Obviously, they were intent on discovering something of a specific nature. I watched the unexpected violation of our privacy from my seat at the front of the plane. The search progressed up through the rows, conducted by harsh and ill-mannered military men who fired verbal commands to the passengers in an indistinguishable language.

The quiet young American seated next to me had become extremely uncomfortable and, from the ashen look on his face, my suspicions were that he might be smuggling precisely what the soldiers were seeking. In this part of the world illicit substances such as hashish would warrant an immediate arrest or even an "on the spot" execution. I was becoming very uncomfortable sitting next to him. As the search teams moved closer, I could see small droplets of sweat forming on my neighbor's brow, betraying a level of anxiety. "It will not be long now," I thought to myself.

Suddenly, just as one of the soldiers had begun to examine the passengers and their luggage in the row behind us, an order came from his commanding officer at the back of the plane. The harassing search ended abruptly as our refueling was now complete. The invaders lumbered to the rear of the plane where they then spilled out onto the runway. Our flight attendant shut the plane's door behind them with a decisive slam and then locked it. To the expressed relief of everyone aboard we made ready for takeoff, and the completion of our flight to Thailand.

The man next to me later confirmed my suspicions. Had the goons searching us found his contraband, there was a high probability they would have deemed me guilty by association, as I was sitting next to him. My life could have changed drastically over that one little incident and I was much relieved at having been spared.

Hours later, our pilots entered the glide path for the Bangkok airport and took us in for a smooth landing. I was grateful to be in Thailand at last.

Thai Song Greet

Bangkok Reflections
Chapter Twenty-One

There's a race of men that don't fit in,
A race that can't stay still;
So they break the hearts of kith and kin,
And they roam the world at will.
They range the field and they rove the flood,
And they climb the mountain's crest;
Theirs is the curse of the gypsy blood,
And they don't know how to rest.

From: *The Men That Don't Fit In*

—Robert Service

There was a well-known backpacker's rest in Bangkok by the name of the Thai Song Greet Hotel, and murmurings of its reputation had come to me while still in India. The stories told by travelers about this popular Mecca for shoestring sojourners were legendary. With my nest egg down to a meager sixty dollars, I came by bus from the Bangkok airport in search of this economical hospice as a matter of necessity. Although I knew the hotel was located somewhere near the train station, it remained difficult to find, and I found myself wandering the streets aimlessly. A kindly English-speaking Buddhist monk in a saffron robe came to my assistance and, after offering me a job teaching English at the monastery for $100 a month, he led me to the hotel. I thanked him and gave assurance I would seriously consider his offer.

The feelings of isolation that I had previously experienced in Calcutta, evaporated completely after crossing the threshold into the crowded and variant environment of the Thai Song Greet. The casually appointed main lobby was on the first floor and merged seamlessly with the restaurant and kitchen. They had designed these to serve both the hotel guests and the passersby on the street. A diverse cast of international characters occupied the many mismatched sets of well-used tables and chairs. Other patrons had seated themselves on the large wicker couches and chairs placed around the outside edge of the room, casually talking with one another over bottled beer. Coffee and end tables of lightly constructed split-bamboo were placed conveniently around for the clientele, and large overhead fans revolved at the base of long pipes extending down from the ceiling. Their slow hypnotic movement yielded only slight relief from the dreadful onslaught of flies, heat, and humidity that tormented the guests this time of year.

The hotel offered rooms with two beds for $1.50 per night, regardless of whether there were one or two occupants. Fortunately, on my second day, I happened on a fellow I had met at the Burma Airways office, and we chose to share a room, thereby reducing my cost by half. It seemed he was out on the town a good deal of the time after our initial dealings over the room, and his nightly marauding effectively left the place, for the most part, in my charge.

After checking in, I climbed the rickety narrow staircase from the lobby, up through the multiple floors, stopping at the appropriate hallway leading out from the stairwell. The rooms were spare and plain with whitewashed walls. There were wire screen transoms located in the upper sections of the wood partitions between rooms, leaving the walls virtually open at the top, creating a breezeway. Although this facilitated air circulation inside the building, such a configuration in wall construction drastically reduced the privacy factor. The guests occupying these living quarters could clearly hear all that went on in the neighboring rooms. In addition, there was the strong chemical odor of a sanitizer hanging in the air, the source being the large bucket out in the hallway holding a mop. There were two bathrooms for guest use on each floor, one at either end of the long hallway.

I stowed my backpack in the room, shut the door and walked down the squeaky wooden staircase to the first floor lobby. True to the stories, the Thai Song Greet was a one-of-a-kind hotel, acting as a home away from home for the many "odds and ends of humanity" who gathered here while passing through Asia. In the two weeks I would reside here, I would interact with a plethora of personalities having a variety of agendas. These included a desperate ruby smuggler, an international con artist, and a heavy equipment operator who roamed the world in search of adventure and high pay. I took a small table and ordered up some food.

The center of attention was an accomplished Chinese cook whom I came to know as Charlie. He worked feverishly, sweating over his several large woks, flinging sizzling specialties high into the air and then catching every tender morsel adroitly in his pan on their descent. The depth of Charlie's concentration was apparent although his demeanor remained relaxed, as if he had grown accustomed to this task over a great deal of time. I got the feeling that were he blindfolded the results of his food preparation would not be altered in the slightest. The menu he labored under was lengthy and assorted. The word around the hotel that amazed us all was that this heavyset man cooked single-handedly for everyone in the building. The waiters scrambled to keep up, dispersing his culinary delights with great dispatch, before they began to cool or acquire too many flies.

The plucked carcasses of ducks, geese, and chickens hung on the overhead iron hooks surrounding his work area. He could bone any of these masterfully in mere seconds with the quick and nimble strokes of his very sharp knife and cleaver. His noted specialty was a delightful dish listed on the menu as simply, "crispy chicken." After Charlie boned the bird, he diced the meat into small cubes and then breaded them lightly. Artfully fried in the wok until golden brown, he served the chicken bits on a heap of steamed vegetables over a bed of rice. He prepared the food quickly, his movements a blur, bedazzling the eye of the observer, not unlike a magician on stage when performing slight-of-hand.

The Thai name for Bangkok is *Krung Thep,* meaning "Heavenly City." It is the largest populated area in Thailand, marked by splendid physical beauty by day and replete with sinful pleasures by night. Givers and takers work in complementary complicity in this city of millions located on the banks of the Chao Phraya River. In the past it was called the "Venice of the East," reflecting the once vast network of canals used for transport that were now slowly being filled to support the growing need for streets and expressways.

Bangkok boasted many fascinating and interesting sights. One of these was the Grand Palace, once the home of Thai Kings. There were also hundreds of magnificent Buddhist temples, known as *wats.* The largest open-air markets in the world were here, and I enjoyed walking for hours investigating the many different stalls. Traditional shophouses bordered the colorful and congested streets as well. They had constructed these to satisfy the combination of needs required from a business and a home, with the commercial activities on the first floor and living quarters on the floors above.

My mind was overwhelmed with these sights and sounds as I walked through the confusing maze of streets and squares. The sidewalk vendors hawked their wares relentlessly. In the background, there were displays of traditional dancers singing the unique euphonies of Thai music in exchange for charitable donations. All signs appeared in a cuneiform-like script completely alien to me, making my extended walking tours of the city difficult passages that left me stranded and lost on numerous occasions.

On the afternoon of the second day I was having coffee in the lobby while watching Charlie the cook, when a man approached my table and politely asked if he might have a word. I nodded and pointed to the vacant chair across from me. He sat down and, after establishing my nationality, introduced himself as a fellow American by the name of Paul. He appeared uneasy and cautiously opened the conversation by saying that he needed to talk to someone he could trust, preferably an American. I proclaimed my trustworthiness and, very much intrigued, asked him to continue. Then he looked me straight in the eye and revealed he was in big trouble.

The man proceeded to divulge a suspenseful tale that I found completely captivating. He had been working for an obscure airline as a pilot, supposedly a subcontractor for a CIA operation out of Vientiane, Laos. Paul went on to explain that Vientiane was the "spook capital" of the world where countries who normally did not communicate with each other had spies and clandestine intermediaries who did. There, it was commonplace for the secret agents from the various embassies to be involved in meetings held between global antagonists, unbeknownst to the world at large. As a neophyte from Texas, he had taken an overseas job with this organization as a pilot because of the excellent pay. His main responsibility was to shuttle around passengers of unknown origin, flying them back and forth from as far south as Singapore and as far north as Vientiane. He kept further details of his employment vague, which I appreciated.

He was obviously a troubled man, perhaps made so by the circumstances he spoke of, those beyond his control. He was shabbily dressed, wore dark glasses, and sported several days' growth of beard. Then he mentioned under his breath, while anxiously scanning the seedy patrons over his shoulder, that he "feared for his life."

After pressing him further regarding his psychological health, I then asked what he wanted from me. He claimed to have worked for the "company" too long and knew too much. Now he wished to divorce himself from the operation and go back home, but there were those who had cautioned him that to do so would be a mistake. Paul seemed paranoid, constantly thinking he was being followed, and very pessimistic about successfully leaving the country at anytime in the near future. The overwhelming obsession that people were after him, real or imagined, had led him to his present apprehensive state. Paul claimed he needed the assistance of another party, if he were ever to escape.

He then disclosed to me that he had converted a good deal of his pay from his years in Laos into rubies, the prominent gemstone of that area. The rubies had appreciated and were now of great value, but he needed to somehow smuggle them out of the country to someone he knew in Texas. They in turn would keep the rubies in a safety deposit box for him until he could find a way to return home.

Since he was convinced he could not take them out of the country on his own, as he was "being watched," he proposed that I make a run for him, delivering the rubies to his Texas contact, which I assumed to be a family member. As consideration, he would pay me handsomely, in many thousands of dollars.

I seriously considered his offer, if only shortly, as I was nearly destitute. However, I decided the potentially negative consequences, even if Paul was telling the truth, in terms of risk, far outweighed the anticipated rewards. I figured either he had to be extremely desperate to trust me with his assets or he was trying to work some kind of illegitimate caper with me as the central player. I decided there were just too many questions and the scenario too convoluted for me to participate. I told him no, thanking him for the offer, and then disclosed I was staking my future on traveling to Australia. With a deep sigh, he abruptly stood, left some money on the table for his drink, and then hastened to the front door, where he disappeared into the crowded streets, as if swallowed up by human quicksand.

The following day a similar incident took place. This time the man who asked to sit at my table was neat and tidy, wearing a white sports coat and a panama hat. He was extremely well-mannered, and I detected a more-than-slight German accent to his English. After exchanging pleasantries, he introduced himself as Gerhardt. Then he asked if I were an American, which I confirmed. He opened his pitch by revealing he had a lucrative job opportunity that would be well worth my while to consider. I mentioned I had been pondering a job teaching English at the Buddhist Monastery to raise the necessary funds for the airline ticket from Singapore to Perth, on the west coast of Australia. I also mentioned in passing my alternate plan of working my way to Australia on a merchant ship. I then asked him to tell me more. He laid out his unique proposal in an accomplished manner, much like a professional salesperson might, overcoming objections before they came up.

The man informed me he employed a number of people who entered the villages of northern Thailand to dispense medical supplies to the native people. Before explaining what my part in all this would be, he offered me a generous salary of $400 per month, complete with a benefit package of room and board. In addition, he would provide me with local female companionship should I so desire. Then he paused, giving the "moment of silence" a chance to work, while looking me straight in the eye. He lit a cigarette, inhaled deeply and leaned back in his chair, then he continued.

At this point, the more unsavory details of his operation began to show themselves. His group prospected the Thailand countryside for suitable villages. Using a caravan of wagons and a flatbed truck, they would set up an attractive camp, complete with music and treats, much like the "snake oil" shows of our Old West. Without much encouragement, the curious local inhabitants flocked to see the show about to unfold on a stage that had been converted from the truck bed. An American or European, dressed in a traditional white doctor's smock, would stand above them on the platform, extolling the virtues of the latest "'wonder drug" from the Western world. They then sold the villagers low value items like aspirin in fancy bottles in exchange for money, artifacts, and sometimes even gold and small gems. The operation was clearly a swindle, as the medicines were relatively worthless.

Quickly, and without a second thought, I told the fellow that the very idea of such an enterprise went against my moral fiber. I declined his offer and asked him to leave my table. He seemed taken aback with my response, leading me to believe he had satisfactorily recruited others from the Thai Song Greet. It must have been an opportune place to mine for new employees. He scoffed at me as he briskly rose, exiting the hotel in quick strides.

The parade of fascinating personalities continued, when a few days later a broad-shouldered bull of a man with wrists the size of my forearms came up and asked if he could sit down. He brought with him two bottles of beer which he had taken from the self-service fridge provided by the establishment. He placed them on the table before us. The man wore a loosely buttoned sleeveless shirt with great amounts of curly red chest-hair boiling out from the front of it. His name was Mike and, like his predecessors, he had a riveting story to tell. He was a heavy-equipment operator from Illinois who had been away from home for several years, working in foreign countries. His specialty was operating the "big dozers," and recently he had been working D-9 Caterpillars in Vietnam. He was coming to Bangkok for some rest and recreation after putting in a long stint under very dangerous conditions.

Around one of his thick wrists he wore a 24 ct. gold bracelet composed of miniature ingots artfully linked together. The shade of this pure gold was a wonder to view, and its richness glistened beautifully. When I asked him about the unusual piece he told me it was priceless, and woe to the man who ever tried to separate him from this financial safety net. He knew if he were ever down and out, like he had been several times in his colorful career, the bracelet was better than cash. We enjoyed ourselves, trading stories throughout the afternoon. Mike checked out from the hotel a day or two later, after informing me he was heading back to Saigon.

The information pipeline that had first made me aware of the Thai Song Greet Hotel had neglected to inform me of one more of its unique flavors. Unaware occupants who happened to leave their door unlocked at night were more likely than not to find one of "the ladies of the night" snuggling up to them in their bed. These women occasionally lingered in the hallways after nightfall, and the guest's unlocked door was the accepted signal for desiring to do business or to engage in what they called *pom-pom*. One awkward and unexpected encounter was all I needed to remember to keep my door locked at night.

I spent the next several days sightseeing. There was the Grand Palace, the Temple of the Emerald Buddha, and the statue of the Golden Buddha. The most impressive of these was the last of the three. It was ten feet tall and cast of solid gold in the thirteenth century. It weighed a staggering five-and-one-half tons and reflected a polished satin patina, which left me in awe. The rich metallic casting was like nothing I had ever seen before, and it drew me closer, overwhelmed with the desire to touch it. At one time in history the Buddha was covered with plaster, and the memory of it being composed of gold became lost in time. Then, in the 1950s, after some of the plaster chipped off from the statue during a moving operation, people discovered its true nature.

It was just one more marvel to add to my collection of treasured memories.

My two-week Thai visa was running out, and they would not be renewing it due to my depleted funds. Therefore, the opportunity to teach English at the Buddhist Monastery was out. It was time to leave Thailand and head south by train down the Malaysian Peninsula to Singapore, the immense international port where I hoped to find work on a freighter. On the afternoon before my visa expired, I walked to the train station a few blocks way and purchased a ticket for the next morning.

The train was departing at 6:30 a.m. for the Malaysian border. My roommate had left the day before, resulting in my rent going up. I decided to spend the night prior to departure at the depot in order to save a little money and facilitate the early morning boarding. The ticket agent had warned me it could be hectic and seats might be hard to come by. Astonishingly, this seemingly small decision would soon lead to another extremely interesting experience.

I had Charlie's crispy chicken one last time, my final dinner at the Thai Song Greet, then paid my bill and walked to the train station. There I laid out my blanket on the hard wooden bench, making ready for the long night. Not much time had elapsed before a young Thai man, out walking his dog, stopped to talk. He asked if I spoke English. I answered yes, and shared with him I was waiting for the morning train.

He introduced himself as Ronarong. After some pleasant conversation, he asked me if I would like to come to his house to spend the night in a comfortable bed, rather than on the bench I had staked out for myself. He mentioned that he was a well-known Bangkok artist and would appreciate the chance to show me his work as well as practice his English. I was delighted to have this opportunity and quickly gathered my gear.

We walked into the darkness of the night and approached one of the larger canals where he had moored his small sampan. We navigated on the dark waters about thirty minutes before coming upon an enchanting thatched dwelling elevated over the water on pilings. After tying up the sampan at the small dock beneath the structure, we ascended the bamboo ladder into what I could only describe as "another world."

There were many interior walls in this house on stilts, each effectively covered with separate hanging canvasses. It was the most beautiful show of oil paintings I had ever seen, which I might inadequately depict as "impressionistic Buddhism." They were multidimensional and reflected a rainbow of soft pastel colors with transparent Buddha heads, positioned in the middle of the paintings like apparitions, overlaying complementary backgrounds. His work was harmonious in every way and I found myself overwhelmed, first by his style and then by the professional quality of the pieces. He was pleased I could appreciate his art and as his petite wife prepared dinner for us, we conversed about the role of the artist in the world of 1967. I described the following scene in a letter home to my parents.

(Mailed from) Panang, Malaysia   *June 9, 1967*

...I discovered upon entering that Ronarong was an accomplished artist. The paintings that hung on the walls were of a highly individualist style, represented a kind of modern impressionism with a theme of Buddhism. His wife graciously prepared dinner for us while he showed me the many local newspaper clippings and magazine articles extolling the quality of his artwork. It seemed he was a famous figure here in Bangkok. We had dinner on his veranda listening to the sounds of the jungle and enjoying the fireflies. It was a very special evening...

Ronarong had given me my own bedroom, and it was luxurious to have a comfortable night's sleep in a quality bed. We left his house in the early morning, just before sunrise. True to his word, the twenty-six-year-old Thai man delivered me to the station in plenty of time to catch my train south. When we parted, Ronarong mentioned that Lyndon B. Johnson had bought one of his paintings when he was Vice President. Then he told me that Vincent Price, the famous American actor and art collector, had purchased much of his artwork in the last few years. He suggested that should I ever look up Mr. Price, to be sure and say "hello from Ronarong." I smiled and we shook hands, bidding each other goodbye.

Although this little adventure lasted for only an evening over forty years ago, I have recalled it with fond memories many times since. As the train pulled away from the station, I thought to myself of how varied the Bangkok experiences had been. I smiled as I filed them away, to relive at another time, in another place, far into the future.

Rice Paddy

Road to Singapore
Chapter Twenty-Two

I shall be telling this with a sigh
Somewhere ages and ages hence:
Two roads diverged in a wood, and I—
I took the one less traveled by,
And that has made all the difference.

—Robert Frost

The southbound train glided over the two parallel ribbons of steel that traced the landward edges of a pristine beach off the Gulf of Thailand. From this point the same track would continue over the narrow peninsular corridor and down through the dense jungles that enveloped the south. The gentle sway of the cars had a mesmerizing effect on the passengers as they watched the series of inviting vistas that passed by outside. I had purchased the least expensive ticket on the slow train that would arrive in Penang, Malaysia, after approximately thirty-two hours.

There were many interruptions as the train made its customary stops in the small villages along the way. The hardwood benches of the third-class coach gnawed uncomfortably into my evermore protruding tailbone. Tropical scents drifted in through the windows, filling the car with nature's sweet perfume. The carriages squeaked and rattled in orchestral harmony as my mind drifted ahead to thoughts of Australia. Pleasant dreams are always the best respite for the weary traveler.

More and more I yearned to hear the reassuring sound of my own language and to feel the comfort that comes from conversing easily with people. In traveling, I had picked up a certain variant in verbal communication that I called "English of the road." Over time, the language of my homeland had morphed into an international tongue, one more elementary and basic. Primarily spoken in first person, using the simplest of vocabulary roots, it had become my parlance of choice. This form of speech was the common denominator used among the freelance global wanderers, providing "the greatest understanding for the greatest number." My language abilities had devolved, if not degenerated, over the previous ten months into this unique brand of "pidgin English." I had found that it did promote a better understanding among those using English as a second or third language. As a result, there were occasions when even other Westerners would ask me, "What country are you from?"

The train trundled over the tracks from dawn until sundown and then on through the dark of night. The heat was debilitating and I was grateful for the restful evening spent at Ronarong's house before my Bangkok departure. I held thoughts of the previous evening as I leaned my head against the wall and dozed. Periodically I awoke to the commotions of passengers disembarking at the different villages along the coastal route.

There had been a number of rowdy, professional, Thai boxers aboard, en route to a competition. Seeing I was the only Westerner on the train and without backup, a concerned Thai passenger had warned me not to engage this surly and cocky bunch. He implied they were confrontational and could be dangerous. It had been difficult to sleep while they were creating pandemonium, mocking and insulting passengers while they scuffled with each other in the aisles. Finally, they recovered all their gear from the designated luggage racks above the seats and exited at one of the stops in the night, leaving the annoyed passengers much relieved.

In the late morning of the next day the conductor's staccato message interrupted my daydreams and, though unable to comprehend a word of it, I searched the signs along the track for telltale clues as to where we were. As the train reduced speed, passengers began to move about, and I felt a gentle tug on my shirtsleeve. A young, clear-eyed Buddhist monk advised me, in very good English, that we were coming to Padang Besar, a city near the Malaysian border. I was beginning to see the Buddhist monks as angels, appearing just when I needed them the most. I gathered up my backpack and prepared to face Malaysian customs and immigration, a daunting endeavor I soon discovered.

My encounter with the border authorities brought me a great deal of stress. They were unwavering in their insistence that I produce proof of a means to exit the country once I entered. This meant a ticket to Indonesia or Australia. After the purchase of the Thai train ticket to Penang, my nest egg was down to a meager $15 and, according to them, this was not nearly enough to let me continue my journey into their country. Nor was it enough to take me back to Bangkok from where I had come. My mind raced at lightning speed, mentally scrambling to find a solution to this difficult predicament.

Before I had left home, I made a visit to my local banker and informed him of my desire to travel, making my way around the world as long as my limited funds held out. After that, I planned to work in different countries. I wanted him to know that I was leaving $500 in his bank to give me a start when I returned home. He suggested I take a "courtesy card" from the bank with me. This card was an official-looking document that provided an introduction and validated the claim that I had a certain amount of money in the bank. Initially, I rejected the idea, prideful in the denial I would ever have use for such an item. In the end, my banker convinced me to accept it, and I had reluctantly placed the card in a folding wallet at the bottom of my backpack the night before leaving Oregon. I wondered if the menacing Malaysian border officials I now faced would honor it. Since I was out of options, I presented the card to them and proceeded to state my case.

The level of intense chatter, simian in nature, escalated to a high pitch as four or five animated officials gathered in a close circle around my scrap of a document. I watched as an extended debate ensued with great fanfare, each minor bureaucrat having his say. I could only pray for a fruitful outcome as the civil servants made several phone calls, obviously to their superiors. I could not afford to take "no" for an answer. Then after extracting repeated assurances that I would wire for the money upon arriving in Georgetown, the British name for Penang, the officials reluctantly released me to return to the train. I was instantly relieved of the growing anxiety and was exceedingly grateful to have survived yet another unexpected trial.

Malaysia was different from Thailand. From the train I could see great portions of the jungles were now tamed, giving way to tailored plantations of date palms, bananas, and tropical fruits. There were rubber trees with buckets strapped to their trunks, catching the gooey natural latex that lazily dripped into them. The rice paddies, surrounded by a periphery of palms, reached out from the tracks to the jungles beyond.

I heard more English spoken among the passengers, and the people seemed friendlier. Once again, I was experiencing the positive legacies left behind from the rule of the British. Smiling schoolchildren, outfitted in matching uniforms, were taking the train to their school at the next stop. Pleasant hours passed as we journeyed deeper into this once crown colony of the British Empire.

At last, we pulled into Penang station, after which I followed the recommendations of one of the passengers on the train and found lodging at the Chinese YMCA on the outskirts of the city. When I arrived, I struck a deal with the overseers to do some chores around the place. This reduced my rent to mere pennies a day, an arrangement that pleased us both.

There were torrential downpours in the afternoons and the evenings brought massive invasions of mosquitoes, but I was comforted in the fact that I had some kind of shelter. However, it was a communal room, one which I shared with others, and having only a concrete floor on which to sleep. Each guest had access to a small locker, allowing me to use my trusty padlock.

One of the guests was an outrageous young Frenchman by the name of Jean Paul. We introduced ourselves upon waking one morning. He was shocked to find an American traveling under the same minimal conditions as he. "An American should be home having bacon and eggs, with cornflakes, after sleeping the night in a nice comfortable bed with sheets," he said mockingly. I mentioned to him not only was it out of necessity that I traveled as I did, but in fact, it was a matter of pride to see how efficient I could be in circling the globe. He roared with delight at my statement, and kept his sarcastic humor to a low murmur after that. We became instant friends.

For the next couple of days we explored the "Pearl of the Orient" together, visiting beaches and pagodas, and walking for miles through the busy rickshaw-filled streets. Jean and I challenged each other to nightly ping-pong contests at the YMCA, this being a national sport in Malaysia. We enjoyed the rich cultural potpourri that Penang offered as best we could without spending money, each day investigating new areas of the city on foot. In the evenings we traded the stories of our remarkable travel adventures with each other, becoming true "comrades of the road." The Catholic Mission in Penang had answered his call for help and was working on his behalf to reverse his failed repatriation efforts back to France.

The story I most vividly recall was the tale of his sojourn into Albania, that totalitarian Communist state on the southern border of Yugoslavia. This was the country I had navigated around after taking passage out of Dubrovnik. Jean Paul had secretly crossed the border into this mysterious country and traveled freely on the trains and trams for two weeks, ending up in the capital of Tirane. In the process of trying to cross back into Yugoslavia, the Albanian border guards shot him several times in the legs, with one bullet completely penetrating the knee joint. They dragged him back into the country from which he was trying to escape. When he regained consciousness, he was in an Albanian hospital recovering from a surgery performed by Chinese doctors.

It was a known fact that China had befriended Albania and was becoming a strong political ally. He was surprised to find the medical facility was both clean and modern, and Jean Paul had nothing but praise for the Chinese doctors who treated him. Released to live on his own after weeks of interrogation and months of recovery, he later was successful in his second attempt to escape, this time crossing overland, well clear of the border checkpoints. I asked to see his scars. He proudly showed them to me, providing some verification of his story.

The French government had repatriated him once after an extended excursion into Lapland where he disappeared to live under primitive conditions with a tribe of Laplanders. This previous record of assistance resulted in the denial of his current requests for repatriation by the French Consulate. They would take him home once, but not twice!

He was now formulating plans for an overland return to Europe with virtually no funds at all. I was down to my last ten dollars. I chose to make the altruistic decision of giving Jean Paul half of it, an act of extreme faith on my part. He became emotional over my gesture of goodwill and proclaimed that I could have unlimited lodging at his family's villa in Paris for as long as I wished at any time in the future. (It would be thirty-seven years before I was again in Paris, and by then my new friend's address had long since vanished.)

We parted good friends, wishing each other well. I was preparing to head south to Kuala Lumpur, while he proceeded north that day with plans to make the potentially deadly overland crossing of Burma. I had passed on to him what I had learned about that option, that it was a dangerously impossible route and, strictly forbidden by the Burma government. This did not deter him in his scheme, causing me to wonder many times through the years about the fate of this young adventurer.

Shortly thereafter, I checked out of the YMCA, walked out to the road and stuck out my thumb. As always, it invigorated my spirit to be hitchhiking again, and it was not long before a truck pulled over to pick me up. Throwing my pack in the back, I climbed up into the cab and was on the road to Kuala Lumpur. The driver had learned some English in school and I was soon plying him with detailed questions about my next destination. Being a Sikh, he told me of the Sikh Temple where travelers and pilgrims could stay without charge. I mentioned my experiences at the Golden Temple of Amristar, which excited him to no end. Staying at another temple was a reassuring thought, since I was now down to my last five dollars.

It did seem to me that my patron was wheeling much too fast down through the small clusters of jungle villages. I assumed my perception was clouded however, as it had been a while since I had hitchhiked. When I mentioned it, he said this was how everybody drove here. He called the villages "*kampongs*" and told me they populated the transportation corridors of the entire Malaysian Peninsula. If truckers were to maintain their right-of-way and make any time, they had to pass through them quickly.

This was not a well-maintained road, and it added to my concerns that there were people everywhere I looked. The roadsides were teeming with schoolchildren carrying books, old women with baskets of goods on their heads walking to and from the markets, and villagers on bicycles peddling through the mud. All of these aspects of humanity were jostling for their claim on the narrow thoroughfare. Suddenly we came around a corner to see the body of a child lying in a pool of blood at the edge of the road. The accident had just happened, and I could hear the villagers wailing in agony as we passed. My driver slowed down but did not stop. He told me it was very sad but that such things were commonplace.

The Malaysian Peninsula is bordered on the west by the Strait of Malacca and on the east by the Gulf of Thailand. From the gulf, the ocean spreads farther east, out to the South China Sea and beyond. I was now experiencing the intense tropical climate associated with my close proximity to the equator. A thick rainforest covered large parts of the Peninsula. It was very hot and humid, and the hammering downpour that came up drenched everything in sight, forcing us to pull the truck over to a thatch-roofed café alongside the road. Here we had tea and waited for the pelting torrents to dissipate. It was difficult to see through the sheets of precipitation to the other side of the road.

My driver, seemingly an educated man, continued to enlighten me as to the fascinating history of Kuala Lumpur. In 1857, some eighty-seven Chinese miners poled their way up the Klang River in search of tin. Huge reserves of the metal were found, which allowed the area to develop into the largest city in Malaysia. From these humble beginnings, the driver said with pride, Kuala Lumpur had become a vibrant commercial center for the world. Later, when we entered the outskirts of the city of his birth, we could see it was obviously a caldron of business activity. Everywhere I looked, people were tending their many enterprises, large and small.

The driver smiled and dropped me off at the local Sikh Temple. I was grateful to have come this far on so little. I did not stay long, as I was anxious to reach Singapore as soon as possible, in order to wire the bank back home for my remaining funds.

Kuala Lumpur nights were replete with the terrors that swarms of mosquitoes can bring. They enveloped me in a cloud and cast their misery over me throughout the long night. When I tried to retreat under my blanket for protection, the heat and humidity drove me back out, much to their delight. They were horrendous! They went into a feeding frenzy from dusk until dawn, and my poor body was appetizer, entrée, and dessert. I counted well over 150 bites on my face, arms, and legs from my first night alone. There was a high degree of malaria present in this part of the world, and I was concerned I might come down with the disease.

I hitchhiked to Singapore in the next few days, where I found lodging at another Sikh Temple. It was an overcrowded and unsavory scene of destitute world travelers. Thieves stole some of my things while I was taking a shower. After two difficult nights, I gratefully transferred to the Chinese YMCA, a slight upgrade for one dollar a night. Fortunately, I was able to start an account here, for food and my rent, while I anxiously waited for the bank to wire the $500 I had requested. In the meantime, I stalked the seaport daily in a relentless pursuit of shipping companies that would allow me to work my passage to either Australia or North America.

I managed to speak with several ships' captains, finding they each required *AB's* only—men with able-bodied seaman qualifications and corresponding papers. There were complicated matters of insurance as well. There was one exception. I found a job on a ship working my way back to England, room, board, and free passage being the only compensation. I respectfully declined, as this would be backtracking, and essentially without pay.

Singapore had declared its independence only two years before, in 1965, after its federation with Malaysia had disintegrated. The city-state was still reeling from the different political factions that were jockeying for control. The Communist Party held rallies and marched through the crowded streets daily, their members carrying large red flags. At the American Consulate, where I stopped for mail, guards frisked me roughly, before allowing me to enter the front of the building, where the large plate-glass windows had recently been broken out.

One afternoon, I walked down by the boat quay, viewing the miles of ramshackle two- and three-story shophouses near the water's edge. Acres of sampans and junks blanketed the serene waters, causing them to appear as mere extensions of the docks. I walked the waterfront slums that exposed the gaunt opium users, reclined and lifeless shells of men gazing out from the dens that faced the harbor. As I strolled along, I thought of the many great writers I had read, like Joseph Conrad, Somerset Maugham, and Graham Greene who had walked these same streets before me. Here, where world traders, men of the sea, and restless transients of all sorts sometimes mixed with the professional women of the night—here at the tail-end of Asia.

Waves of excitement broke over me as I made my way to the Australian Consulate one morning to obtain my visa. The visit proved disappointing, as well as unsuccessful. I suspect my haggard appearance and loose clothes worked against me. According to scales on the streets of Singapore, my weight was down to 167 pounds, some 88 pounds less than when I had left home. Furthermore, they required, as did India, that those entering Australia have sufficient means to leave the country. This meant that along with my ticket to Perth, I would also need an exit ticket to New Zealand. The strapping and efficient young Aussie officials quickly denied my entry.

To make matters worse, I came back to the Chinese YMCA to find that my appointed roommate, a young German man who had seemed quite pleasant at the time of our introduction, had left for Darwin in the Northern Territory of Australia with some of my things. This was the second time they had robbed me in the same week.

On closer inspection, I found he had absconded with my collection of foreign coins and some special curios I had gathered along the way from different countries. The coins were close to my heart, as I had once collected pennies as a boy. On this trip I had taken some pleasure in saving a few coins, left over from each country, in an old leather bank bag I had brought along on the journey. There were about 170 coins in all and, though they probably had little intrinsic value, there was a great deal of sentimental value. Those most memorable were the coins given to me in Nepal by the Tibetans. Coins were the only real souvenirs from the trip I had acquired, and now they were gone.

These thefts were cautionary lessons on placing too much store in material things, as they can often come and go. The irony was that the coin collection had been the last item for which I had any real attachment. My first inclination was to cancel my plans for Perth, change course for Darwin, and find this fellow to give him a good thrashing. Later, I realized that carrying this resentment would not be worth the trouble and I decided to let the events become part of his "Karma." I have often pondered if the thief's conscience ever got the better of him over his misguided deeds.

When my grubstake finally arrived by wire, the first thing I did was pay my bill at the YMCA, where I had been charging my food and lodging. Then I treated myself to a haircut and a shave at one of the salons in downtown Singapore. Following this, I arranged for a Chinese tailor in one of many street shops to fashion a pair of gray slacks and a white shirt for me. It was fun selecting the materials from the number of choices he presented to me. What took place next must have been a humorous sight to the casual observer, as several Chinese tailors with cloth tapes hanging around their necks mounted step-stools from all sides of me, to measure my lanky frame. I felt like Gulliver himself!

My clothes at the tailor's were ready early the next day so I proceeded to the shop, paid for them, and happily wore my new duds out into the street. I had a relaxing day, picking up a few items that I badly needed. That evening I went out to dinner, enjoying my first steak since Germany. I also had a Singapore Sling in a nice air-conditioned hotel before finishing the evening at the movies. This was a different kind of day than I was used to, and it felt wonderful.

Back at the YMCA one of the fellows mentioned my change in appearance, commenting, "You could well be the ambassador's son!" That night, before falling to sleep in my bunk, I wondered if that illusive Australian visa might just now be within my grasp.

I returned to the Australian Consulate clean cut and wearing my new clothes, with the remainder of my $500 in my pocket. I showed them my funds and, speaking with a more compassionate person than I had a few days earlier, I secured the needed approval for the visa. This was contingent on presenting to them the New Zealand airline ticket out of the country. By now, I was convinced of the futility in finding a way to work my way to Australia on a ship. Not only was there the AB seaman problem to contend with, but there was also the closing of the Suez Canal due to the recent Six-Day War with Israel. This had catapulted international shipping schedules into complete disarray.

I then purchased a Malaysian Airways ticket to Perth, on the western seaboard of Australia, and an exit ticket to Auckland, New Zealand. The ticket to Perth was $224, with the second undated ticket leaving Sydney for "Kiwi Land," costing another $75. I picked up my visa the next day and made ready for my flight "down under."

I was relieved when the Boeing 707 finally lifted off from the Singapore runway that evening, feeling liberated from my long and taxing Asian journey. Would this flight to Australia be my deliverance into a paradisiacal land of plenty? My nest egg again significantly reduced, I was aware I needed to find work soon. I settled back into the well-cushioned reclining seat of the aircraft and jettisoned all my concerns, not realizing that the next little challenge was only a few minutes away.

Standard Gauge

Down Under
Chapter Twenty-Three

Australia is too big to comprehend. It's too barren, too rich, too foreign, too far away—which of course is also why it's so appealing. The island-country-continent baffles the imagination through its mere presence—its age, aridity, the searing red of its deserts, the luminescent green of its rain-forests, the deep blues of its tropical seas, the crisp clarity of its ethereal light. Australia entices, seduces, and seeps into the bloodstream until there's no choice but to go see for yourself. —Larry Habegger

The flight to Perth was far from a normal operation. Passing over the Straits of Singapore, the crew discovered we were unable to reach adequate cabin pressure. As we gained altitude the temperature in the plane plummeted, spawning multiple requests from the shivering passengers for additional blankets. Passenger responses ranged from a slightly agitated state to the beginnings of a maelstrom of panic. An apprehensive flight attendant announced they were looking into the temperature problem. Apparently assuming I could handle the information, she leaned down close to me and, speaking in a soft voice, shared the lead pilot's latest explanation with me.

They suspected the lower cabin temperature was the result of one of our exterior doors being slightly ajar. Since the freezing atmosphere outside the craft was currently seeping into the cabin, the pilots decided to reduce the altitude drastically. In this way, they hoped to negate the effects of the ruptured seal and eliminate the major risks to the passengers and plane. Conditions stabilized to something that was tolerable and we continued in the direction of

Perth rather than returning to Singapore. Our craft jetted through the airspace just above the earth's surface, flying at a moderate level over the mountains of Sumatra and then dropping lower out over the Indian Ocean.

Snuggling up in Sofia's blanket, I gazed out the window at the carpet of moonlight glistening off the choppy seas. We streaked through a cloudless night sky, low enough for me to make out the wave definition. It was somewhat disconcerting to be flying this low is such a large craft. My thoughts turned to home, reflecting on the times when Dad and I had faced dangerous situations in his Cessna 210.

Once, while flying in Northern California, yellow-jackets suddenly filled the cabin of our small plane. Whether the wasps had hatched out of the airspeed indicator tube or from one of the fresh air vents, we never really knew. However, they were agitated and soon began to sting. Dad, a sure and steady man, kept his hands on the controls and his eyes straight ahead while I killed the flying menaces, first with my bare hands, then with the folded flight-plan map. We eventually landed without the aid of the airspeed indicator, causing us to suspect this was their port of entry. My hands were sore and swollen mitts for the next few days, but it was a small price to pay to be safely down on the ground.

Another time we flew into a storm near the summit of Mt. Ashland, close to Wagner Gap, one of the topographic folds in the Siskiyou Mountain range. An unexpected summer storm had erupted just as we flew north over the Oregon-California border. Lightening crackled through the air all around us and hail pelted the curved windshield making an ominous sound, much like popcorn popping. Enveloped by a dark, wet cloud, we had zero visibility and flew on instruments and prayers. Years later Dad told me how relieved he was when we finally put down at the small Ashland airport. He was always cool in a pinch, strong and in control.

Suddenly, the voice of the flight attendant cut short my musings into flights of the past. They were now beginning to serve dinner. A young lady with a charming Australian accent passed me my dinner tray. She asked if this was my first time "Down Under." I replied an enthusiastic "yes." Then I told her how relieved I was to finally be so close to the country I had thought about so much.

"Down Under" refers to those two major land-masses in this part of the world that fall below the equator, namely Australia and New Zealand. The path of our flight had delivered us across zero degrees latitude as it passed over Indonesia, just north of Jakarta. We were now in the Southern Hemisphere. The hours passed.

When I thought of Australia, I had always conjured romantic images of kangaroos, friendly people, and a young land that held the last pure chance of opportunity on earth for its residents. It was a land equal in size to the United States, yet only lightly populated. Australia represented a place where people were free to discover their destiny, impeded only by the degree of their own personal ambition. For me this country characterized freedom from the poverty, sickness, and hopelessness that was beginning to take root as I passed through Asia. The equator was the fulcrum off which my new world would be tipping. It signified emancipation from the circumstantial bondage I passed through in the Northern Hemisphere and presented me with the opportunity for rebirth I craved.

I took some time to ponder on what all this traveling had done for me. Despite all my trials and tribulations along the way, I still clung fast to the proposition that travel was a crucial element in a person's overall development. It could even represent a certain rite of passage that brought with it a new mental toughness, increased levels of maturity, and a greater emphasis on self-reliance. From this process alone, there is a creeping and incremental enlightenment that gradually invades one's being, an accompaniment that develops almost without the traveler's awareness.

Now, I had learned to compare and contrast the conditions of foreign environments to those in which I grew up. My critical senses were more acute and I was increasingly aware of the consequences of my actions. Europeans had long since seen the importance of sending their offspring abroad to acquire a wider worldview, to learn other languages, and to expand their awareness of other cultures. Adults simply saw this as furthering the educational benefits in their youth.

Americans, on the other hand, seemed to have given only moderate weight to this option, not really seeing worldwide travel as a viable opportunity. Of course there were the exceptions, as myself, who managed to have had the "summer holiday in Europe." Generally speaking, we as a country seemed more preoccupied with our own lives, tending to disregard the rest of the world and its treasures until later in life, when retirement came upon us.

I was jolted from this line of thinking back to the present moment by the sound of the landing gear locking into position with a loud "thump" that vibrated under my seat. This signaled that the long flight was at last coming to an end.

Our plane touched down in Perth, the City of Lights, the lovely capital of Western Australia. Many on the plane expressed relief in completing our harrowing little flight, as passengers shed their woolly layers and prepared to disembark. Clearing customs went smoothly and it was a pleasure to see the chipper "Aussie" faces and to speak with such warm, obliging people. This was the day that marked the beginning of my life-long love affair with Australia.

I felt almost like a returning prisoner of war, coming in from the cold of a Gulag archipelago that had nearly pushed me beyond resuscitation. But how could I be returning to a place I had never been? Along with those thoughts came the realization the end was now in sight and my goal of circling the earth one step closer to completion. Now, there was only one more ocean to cross.

I recalled that once when running the high hurdles on the high school track team, I mistakenly stopped at the wrong finish line after having surged ahead of my competitors. I wondered if Australia was that first line for me. Would I again stop before the final finish line? Regardless, I was beginning to take comfort in knowing I had completed the most difficult portions of my global journey.

During the entire previous eleven months on the road, I had been nagged by curious nostalgic yearnings for food from home.

Suddenly, my mind filled with the simple images of a glass of milk, a hamburger, and a clean room with a large bathtub. These dreams were soon to materialize. I marveled at the new and clean facilities at the airport and took my time in the restroom to clean up with hot water, before boarding the shuttle bus into town.

There I found a small, reasonably priced hotel that had rooms with a tub for three dollars a night, located on the outskirts of Perth. There was an inviting restaurant attached, and, after stowing my gear, I made the ceremonial walk to the café. Here a lovely blue-eyed blonde brought me a menu, and after smiling exhibited the most delightful manner of speaking.

I ordered my favorites. First came the glass of milk, fresh and cold, like the milk from the dairy farm I once worked on as a boy in Oregon. It trickled slowly down my gullet to settle in my empty, growling stomach. Next, the hamburger arrived, the one I had fantasized about since leaving home. Yet this one was quite different! The burger sat about four inches above the plate, unexpectedly stuffed with a surfeit of garnishes I had never seen on a burger before. They called it a burger "with the lot," packed with beets, mushrooms, bacon, a fried egg, and a variety of vegetables. Hanging out over the whole-grain bun was a large rough-hewn beef patty. There were coarse cut chips on the side which they served with mayonnaise of all things.

The hamburger was pure ambrosia. I consumed it in a state of ecstasy, as a man might savor his first kiss. The egg yolk squirted out and ran down my fingers as I devoured the creation slowly, in measured bites, prolonging the delight. I feared that taking in so much nutrition at one sitting was sure to bring on a severe case of protein shock.

Completely satiated, I returned to my room where I drew up a steaming hot bath and stripped down. I stepped into the vaporous water, lowering myself down into the high-sided white porcelain tub. My eyes brimmed with tears of joy as I totally immersed myself in the soothing waters. I saw it as a blissful baptism, establishing a holy covenant between this new country and me, one that already was beginning to transform and heal me. Lying in the clear steaming liquid, I surveyed the gunnysack of bones that was my thin, emaciated body. Overwhelmed by the good fortune of this luxury, I continued to let feelings of ecstasy wash over me as I draped a hot dripping washcloth over my face and slowly exhaled.

In a letter home, I described a walk I took the following morning.

Perth, Australia   *June 28, 1967*

...I got up the next morning and had a big steak, two eggs, beans, salad, a side of cornflakes, toast with butter and jam, coffee and a newspaper, all for sixty cents! I then walked to North Perth wearing my pack and seeking a certain boarding house, recommended to me by a hitchhiker I had met at the YMCA in Malaysia. On my way, I was amazed at how clean everything was, and how friendly strangers on the street were to me. "G-day Mate," came at me from all directions! When I stopped in the various shops to browse, I found nearly everyone to be an immigrant from some country where I had already been! I spoke with Germans, Greeks, and Italians. It reminded me of the innocent, wholesome and healthy lifestyles in the USA during the 1950s...

I promised myself I would never forget the simple but monumental pleasures of those first few glorious days in Australia. In the days that followed this marvelous country proved a saving sanctuary for me where my health improved and I quickly regained my strength. Securing a room in the boarding house in North Perth, I began my search for employment the next afternoon. I picked up a newspaper and scanned the classified ads.

In the next two weeks I interviewed with fifteen different companies, many of them specializing in oil extraction or mining operations in the pursuit of the ores for iron, gold or magnesium. They repeatedly informed me that immigrants had been streaming into the country from all corners of the world to take these jobs, most of which were situated in the isolated work camps of the northwest outback. However, I soon learned that the country was currently entering a recession, and the big companies had stopped hiring just a few weeks before I arrived. I filled out application after application to no avail. I also heard many more times than I wish to recall, "Ah, you're just a Yank, you'll work a bit and then be off for home!" This was probably true, although the thought of staying in Australia was growing stronger.

The "blokes" at the neighborhood barbershop told me about a job as a warehouseman's helper for $10 a day, which I quickly took, but it seemed they only needed someone for one week. This paid the room and board at my new home, the Butler Place. I continued my job search in my spare time.

Australia, for a variety of reasons hard to explain, had ended up with three different rail track gauges throughout the country. The direct result of this incompatible gauge problem was that a good deal of the freight shipped out in containers and truck trailers fixed atop flatbed rail cars. Men laboriously switched these goods from the arriving train to the departing one, usually at the state borders where the dissimilar track widths met. The problem was widespread, and great efforts were at hand to make all the track widths the same. One old fellow told me, "There is always a standard gauge job going on somewhere in Australia."

A recently completed mixed standard and narrow gauge, called the Eastern Railway, opened in 1966 through the Avon Valley, just east of Perth. Now they were constructing another major line that involved laying a new standard gauge line from Kalgoorlie to Perth. For this job, I would need to apply in Kalgoorlie, 372 miles to the east.

Perth, the capital and business center of the state of Western Australia, lies along the beautiful Swan River. A picturesque city of tree-lined avenues and spacious parks, it has as one of its borders the shores of the Indian Ocean. It was a relatively young city, designed and laid out with much forethought and high purpose. Perth's warm Mediterranean climate and noteworthy sandy beaches made it an ideal place to settle for new immigrants. Many nationalities had come here from the crowded and aged quarters of Europe to stake their claim on the fresh opportunity that was Australia. These adventurers brought with them a new gene pool, ready to mix with an already vigorous population. I felt it was not unlike the development of our American West. This was new blood for a new world and, as far as I could see, these arrivals accepted the country's offerings graciously and harmoniously. I was beginning to feel a part of this family of immigrants, and this was reassuring.

The abundance of ethnic restaurants available to me was comforting, and I found myself stopping to eat four or five times a day when I was not working. These charming eateries existed side by side down the streets as far as I could see, each with their daily specials in the window or on sidewalk signs. Every kind of cuisine one could wish for presented itself, and all were reasonably priced. Many of the restaurateurs and shopkeepers took an interest in where I had come from. This made it easy to talk to them.

I frequented the restaurants often, in addition to taking meals at my boarding house at night. My weight was slowly climbing. The color came back to my skin, and I continued to regain my vitality. Australia was an elixir of life for me, nourishing my body, soothing my mind, and letting the sunshine into my spirit. Juxtaposed to this was the seeming impossibility of finding a permanent job. Nevertheless, the benefits of being in this new country far outweighed the temporary challenge of employment, although my meager funds were starting to dwindle again.

After giving more than sufficient time to the job search in Perth, I made the decision to travel east on the Great Eastern Highway to seek my fortune in the isolated and historic gold mining town of Kalgoorlie. It was here that I would check out the standard gauge opportunities for possible employment. I looked forward to getting back on the road again, and I felt much stronger from the many nutritional meals I had eaten in Perth. My attitude was positive, and I was optimistic regarding what I might find ahead. There were still a few dollars in my pocket when I packed my things and said goodbye to my mates at the boarding house. Walking across town, I found the highway leading out of the city and put out my thumb. I was free to hitchhike once again.

Aboriginal Stamp

Kalgoorlie and the Frozen Chickens
Chapter Twenty-Four

At the beginning of time, the earth looked like a featureless, desolate plain. Time began when the supernatural beings awoke and broke through the surface of the earth. Totemic ancestors moved about the earth bringing into being the physical features of the landscape. Before their disappearance from the face of the earth, the sun, the moon, and the rest of the earth-born celestial beings rose into the sky, and man was left to wander the earth.

—From an Aboriginal story of Creation

The initial ride carried me away from the suburbs of Perth towards Midland, clipping the border of the gorgeous Swan River Valley. My Aussie benefactors were extremely personable and acted as able tour guides, escorting me through section after section of impressive scenery. The ride lasted several hours before they dropped me off at a wide spot in the road and made their turnoff. Barely had I swung my backpack down to the ground before another driver came along and picked me up. This time the ride was longer, carrying me farther into the Darling Range with its thick eucalyptus forests, sporadically broken up by open fields. The quality of beauty was astounding, and I continued to soak up the majesty of the Australian countryside from every direction.

Recurring feelings of gratitude flooded over me, stimulated by the vast openness of this new land. At times, I imagined I had been reborn. The immigrants from the pages of Australian history could have felt no greater delight upon their arrival than I was experiencing. I suspected the feelings of the sentenced prisoners who originally settled this country were much to the contrary, condemned to sail from England against their will to a harsh and unknown land.

Now, I could not help but speculate, "Could Australia become my future home?"

While gliding along the country highways, I reflected lightly on my experiences in Perth. Few could have tried harder to pursue a successful course than I, vigorously throwing myself each day to the task of seeking employment. Ultimately, I had found three small jobs there. One of these was with the owners of the boarding house where I did small carpentry repairs on the place for my rent, nothing permanent. I finally resolved that there are certain times when external events just do not fall a man's way, and Perth had been one of these. The story would undoubtedly have been different had I arrived a month earlier, before the influx of foreign labor and the advent of a mild recession. I dismissed my concern, concluding that it was all "meant to be" in the larger scheme of things.

After a couple of additional rides and another day of easy motoring, I reached Kalgoorlie. This dusty frontier settlement seemingly transplanted from out of one of our western movies was complete with boardwalks, dirt streets, and saloons. I would later learn there was even a house of ill repute on one of the back streets. Climbing out of the car at the front edge of town, I began the long traverse down the main street, surveying the physical layout while scouting for a place to stay.

I stopped at the historic Exchange Hotel and entered the pub where, without exception, only men stood at the long bar, downing their ale. Still others were playing darts, a game dear to my heart. I had a cold beer and asked the bartender about cheap lodging. He mentioned, in a thick Australian drawl, that he had seen a sign down the street earlier in the week. Later, I walked in that direction.

This was a region hewn from the traditional lands of an aboriginal people known as the Maduwangka. The name Kalgoorlie actually translated from their fascinating language to mean "silky pear bush." The native people freely walked the streets, and I was surprised when I engaged several of them in conversation, inquiring about a boardinghouse, how distinctly Australian were their accents. Their eyes reflected a deep sensitivity, as if they connected with forces in nature far deeper than I could even imagine. There was a gentle demeanor among these indigenous Australians, and I instantly felt a deep respect for them and their place in the history of this vast country. In the ensuing days, I would learn more about their beliefs, with respect to *songlines*, those meandering footprints of ancestors, and *dreamtime*, the complex song-cycles that identified their crucial landmarks.

Back on the street, just off the boardwalk, I spied a small sign in the front yard of a two-story house, a common structure slightly Victorian in design. The sign read, "Room for Let." The exterior of the boardinghouse had a wrinkled skin of clapboard siding and the roof wore a cap of rusty corrugated metal. This was typical of the other residential dwellings I had seen around town. A sitting veranda wrapped completely around the front of the structure. "Spoke quarter-rounds" of gingerbread aesthetically connected the porch posts with the horizontal beam supporting the slanted roof of the porch.

The dry hinges of the weathered screen door assaulted my ears with a loud screech as I opened it. I stepped in and followed a well-worn carpet runner down a dimly lit hallway leading to a counter, behind which sat an older man sound asleep. As I walked up, his leathery face came to life and he looked up with a start, lifting his hat slightly with one hand while scratching his suntanned neck with the other. He cordially welcomed me and, after commenting on my "Yank" accent, was quite interested to hear that I had just hitchhiked in from Perth.

The establishment rented rooms by the week or the month, and the rate included two meals a day. The morning meal was a continental breakfast of tea, fruit, toast and jam. They served the evening dinner family style at the large table in the dining room. These were communal affairs attended by all of the other boardinghouse guests.

I took the room for a week, impressing upon him I needed to find work to stay any longer. He told me, "Lots of blokes are looking for work right now." That night at supper, my fellow boarders made me feel right at home. They were all single men, and we traded stories while passing large bowls of hearty food around the table to each other. I would soon learn that lamb, potatoes and beets were common table fare. Each diner had his own suggestions of where I should seek employment, though many had revealed to me that they themselves were unemployed.

One man told me to try the gold mines, but on second thought, he said I would most likely be much too tall for the tunnels that burrowed 1,500 feet below the surface. The same fellow informed me that due to the dangerous nature of the job they usually needed powder monkey helpers, and that I might try exploring that angle. One of the other residents told me to try down by the railway station, where he unloaded boxcars occasionally for fill-in work, but nothing steady. I assured them I would check it all out in the morning.

That night I took a walk downtown and explored some of the pubs, stopping in for a game of darts with a few of the locals. It reminded me of some of the rough bars I had frequented in the logging and lumber towns where I had worked in my younger days. These fellows were a tough lot, with scarred faces, misaligned noses, and missing teeth, but once it was evident I was proficient at darts they all wanted me for a partner on their team. Darts had become a passion of mine from the old San Jose days where I had worked part-time at nights in a dart pub, a business started by a colorful expatriate from England. I would manage the place evenings while the owner made unusually long phone calls to his girlfriend back in Britain. Winning free "grog" in the Kalgoorlie pubs was a cinch given the skills I had previously honed with this indoor sport. Suddenly, I realized I was socializing and having fun. It had been a very long time, and I welcomed it!

Early the next morning I hustled over towards the railway freight-yards, where I came upon a couple of stout looking older men deeply engaged in conversation. Their accents were strong, and I understood little of what they were saying to each other. With those isolated in the bush for a long time, the language evolves into a bizarre collection of narrow colloquialisms that become nearly indecipherable by someone from the outside. Their lack of interest when I introduced myself was uncharacteristic of the people I had met so far. They continued to visit while ignoring my presence.

Finally, one of the gents looked over at me, presenting just the window of opportunity I needed to state my case. Using far too many words for the occasion, I anxiously explained my situation and the need for employment. In garrulous tones, he said there might be something for me in the morning and then resumed talking to his mate. I committed to returning the next day and walked on into town to do some more exploring of this colorful gold rush settlement.

The next morning I found my new employer in the same general area where I had left him. This hard man seemed oblivious to my cheerful salutations and only responded with a mouthful of gibberish that left me dumbfounded.

"Hitintheutemate," he said. A deep furrow ran across my brow as his words painfully and effectively short-circuited my brain. I then asked him to reiterate what he said, which proved to be a great mistake. He hollered back instantly, "I speak the Queen's English, and if you can't understand me then that's your problem!" The fellow was a bit red in the eye and definitely had a disheveled look about him. From the smell of his breath, it was easy to surmise that ale had been his beverage of choice for breakfast.

Confused and offended, I stood there waiting for further clarification. The intolerant fellow glared as he repeated his words, this time slightly easier for me to grasp, "Get in the *ute*, mate." I was soon to learn a *ute* was an Australian breed of utility wagon, a cross between a pickup and a car, something like our El Camino, the utility coupe built by Chevrolet.

We drove on down to the railroad siding while he explained that much of the food came to Kalgoorlie in boxcars by train and was then later distributed by trucks to the surrounding areas. He mentioned he had some temperature-sensitive items that needed unloading right away from a refrigerated rail car. These I could then place into the delivery trucks that would soon arrive. When he had finished with his orientation, I expressed my gratitude for the job. I went on to reveal my boarding house rent was due soon, and I would greatly appreciate it if he could pay me at the end of the day. He grunted. Making conversation, I prattled on about how I had paid for a good deal of my college education loading boxcars with lumber in Northern California. His mood remained truculent; he obviously was not the least bit interested in the details of how I acquired my higher education.

We came to a raised loading dock alongside the tracks. My Aussie boss got out and, opening the door of a refrigerated boxcar, nodded to me saying, "There ye go, mate!" He told me I would be working with frozen chickens all day, and that the delivery drivers would provide the invoices that had the quantities needed for the trucks. Then he vanished, leaving me to sort out what he had said.

Using my socks for gloves I stacked the heavy cases of frozen chickens onto the dock while waiting for the first truck. The driver showed up a short time later and gave me instructions on how to load the chickens properly for shipping by crisscrossing the cases so they interlocked at the end of each row, much like the stacking of cordwood. He also lent me his pair of gloves, a welcomed act of kindness. I kept my head down and worked hard, taking great comfort in the knowledge that I would be paid at the end of the day and all would be well.

I had not packed a lunch so I worked straight through, only knocking off for a short rest at midday. It felt good to have sore muscles again. I fantasized about advancing to a trucker job from this humble beginning. Maybe down the line I could become a supervisor, working my way up in his small operation. A few days later, I realized these speculative dreams were widely premature and overly optimistic.

The effects of exhaustion and hunger had overtaken me by the end of the day. The boss returned, did some tallying up and informed me that we were finished with the chickens. He told me to knock off but not before mentioning we would be unloading some galvanized pipe in the morning. I agreed to be there early the next day and then watched him make a move towards his *ute*. Then I reminded him about my request for compensation. He mumbled something indistinguishable under his breath then grabbed an empty cloth bag from the back of his rig and stepped into the boxcar. The man emerged with the large bag half-full of frozen chickens and handed it to me!

I was flabbergasted! He told me this was how he was paying me as his last payroll had left him short of cash. I let him know this was not what I had had in mind. I then made a cynical remark about trying to pay my bills with frozen chickens. He grinned, saying, "You just might be surprised." After futile protests, I agreed to take the chickens, chalking the incident up to just another page in the Australian adventure. My thoughts then switched to my landlord.

It seemed the straightforward approach might be the best bet and I rehearsed my lines while proceeding on foot to the boarding house. It was a longer than usual walk down the hallway to the main desk, the heavy bag of frozen chickens over my shoulder. I just could not imagine coming out on the winning side of this discussion.

Much to my amazement, after hearing the "tale of the frozen chickens" the innkeeper entered into serious negotiations with me, but only after he uncorked a good laugh or two. Soon I found myself in the ridiculous position of bargaining with a hotel manager in the middle of the Australian desert over how many frozen chickens should equal one night's lodging. Since I did not have a refrigerator, there was a decided advantage on the side of the opposition. The "law of diminishing returns" would certainly come into play as the chickens began to "age" in my possession. Nevertheless, I considered myself a master bargainer now, trained in the backstreet bazaars of Old Delhi. Equipped with this experience, surely the advantage swung back to me.

In the end, I cannot recall just what finally constituted parity between room rent and "due and payable" chickens. I did relinquish a good number of the frozen fowl to him though, taking only a few to the pub with me to see what kind of commotion I could stir up down there. Much to my surprise, I found that after hearing my story the pub owner gladly traded one frozen chicken for a pitcher of beer. I also gave the proprietor of a small restaurant nearby one chicken as compensation for cooking one of my birds for me, which by this time was starting to thaw.

After that, there was no doubt in my mind that frozen chickens were acceptable "legal tender" in Kalgoorlie. The price I paid for this enlightening epiphany and associated experiences was enduring the profusion of chicken jokes unleashed around the supper table in the week that followed. My fellow boarders took so much pleasure in rehashing the story however, that I thought it might very well become a part of modern Western Australian folklore.

The job of unloading boxcars continued for the next week, with my employer at last paying me in Australian currency. This was not before nearly crushing me in the boxcar with a load of pipe swinging from the boom of a forklift he was maneuvering carelessly. The money earned allowed me to stay current on my bill at the rooming house with some left over for incidentals.

My next job came after interviewing with the owner of a metal fabrication shop, a contact recommended to me by one of men at the rooming house. Directed to the main office, I found myself seated in front of a Goliath of a man with a thick bushy mustache, leaning back in a swivel chair. With his large gnarly hands clasped across his chest, he listened patiently as I made my request for work. I explained to him that I would be willing to tackle almost anything for a fair day's pay. At that, a faint smile broke over his weather-checked face.

Speaking in an outback accent that I was becoming increasingly familiar with he said, "Almost anything, eh? Well then, I might have something for you." Once again, I had foolishly led with my chin, and even though this did elicit a positive response, I would soon regret it. Promptly raising his girth from the squeaky chair, he led me out the back of his building. There, at the rear of his property, was a concrete slab equal in size to a tennis court. He mentioned it was six inches thick and reinforced with rebar. The task he contemplated for me was breaking it up, using a twelve-pound sledgehammer.

I took the job, working harder than usual for the next several days, for ninety cents an hour. It was not long before I discovered there was a definite technique to swinging a sledgehammer. With a steady and measured rhythm, I proceeded to break up the oppressive monolith foot by foot, with sure and repetitive strokes. I found that it took six heavy hits before the slightest crack in the concrete began to show. I worked, soaked with sweat, while the palms of my hands continued to produce a number of ugly water blisters. Each day my hands got worse until at last, after making significant progress on the slab, I gave myself permission to "resign."

The wanderlust had been nipping at me again, and I yearned to investigate the great expanse I had heard about to the southeast, known as the Nullarbor Plain. Kalgoorlie had been an instructive experience, but it seemed like a dead-end with only a bleak array of opportunities for work. After a last breakfast with some of my mates at the boarding house, I settled my account and then made the long walk to the edge of town.

Soon I caught my first ride, and was headed down the road with new friends, swapping stories while moving south in the direction of Norseman, a town on the Coolgardie Esperance Highway. Those liberating feelings returned, and I was excited at the prospect of discovering what new adventures awaited me.

Road Train

Hitching the Nullarbor
Chapter Twenty-Five

We are all travellers in the wilderness of this world, and the best we can find in our travels is an honest friend.

—Robert Louis Stevenson

A young couple had picked me up on the outskirts of Kalgoorlie, and we were now rolling south in the direction of Norseman, another old Western Australian mining town. Looking out the window of the car at the extensive open area of land, I pondered on how different this was from the crowded cities and thick jungles of Southeast Asia. To me, the people here seemed like settlers living on the edge of modern human history, forging new lives in a young country. Even the air that streamed in through the car windows smelled sweet and fresh, carrying with it the aromatic fragrances of the natural and untamed countryside around us.

The idea of hitchhiking across the Nullarbor Plain began building in my mind from the moment people told me not to attempt such an enterprise. This topographic region, characterized by loose desert soils laying over the largest piece of limestone known to the world, represented a 70,000 square mile section of picturesque outback. The entire stone slab, a former seabed, had been thrust upward by incremental shifts in the earth's crust. Then, the erosive forces of wind and rain smoothed it out over eons of time. Now that flat and wind-sculpted surface, directly south of the Great Victoria Desert, was what I wished to cross. In addition, and equally significant, was the fact that I did not have the forty dollars for a train ticket across this barren expanse of the continent.

In talking to different locals in Kalgoorlie about the prospect of hitchhiking, I encountered absolutely no one who had done it, nor did they know of anyone who had. In fact, people were quick to discourage me for a number of reasons.

Of primary concern was that in early July, the middle of the Australian winter, the empty plains of the Nullarbor were exceedingly cold, bathed in the Antarctic winds blowing landward off the Great Australian Bight. The Bight being the extensive bay south of these minimally populated portions of the western and central mainland. Secondly, hitchhiking across this portion of the country was unquestionably illegal, and likely to result in my arrest. The police in Norseman, our next destination, were specifically on the lookout for hitchhikers.

In addition to this, a 600-mile stretch of the formidable 1,840-mile distance to Melbourne was dirt track, unofficially closed during the winter due to the deep mud that stalled even the "road trains." The more determined drivers of these massive trucks, pulling three and sometimes four trailers at a time, did not let such restrictions hinder them. They merely went out on the road, remaining undeterred by the harsh and forbidding conditions that existed on the plain.

Furthermore, the route was rife with dangerous sorts who managed to keep themselves one step ahead of the law. Communications between the authorities in different regions were poor and moving from state to state provided criminals an optimal solution for leaving their lawless past behind them. These fellows were a tough class of criminal swagmen who would gladly separate you from your purse. They were very different from the original kindly transients who had walked the country in search of work during the years of the Great Depression.

Lastly, and most importantly, the "road train" drivers had specific instructions from their employers not to pick up hitchhikers. This was a matter of policy regarding the driver's personal safety and a requirement of the company's liability insurance. These arguments only served to enhance both my curiosity and determination to pursue the venture. There were no longer any lingering doubts in my mind about the crossing, for now I had committed to hitchhiking the distance to Melbourne.

After a long day's drive, we pulled into Norseman. I could see on my map that this was the last major opportunity to stock up on provisions before embarking over the long Eyre Highway, the road I would come to know well in the week ahead. My patrons let me off near a grocery store in the center of town. Here, with the few dollars left in my pocket, I purchased some canned goods, spaghetti and beans, a loaf of bread, some oranges and apples, and a block of cheese. I treated myself to one last supper in a local cafe, having a burger with "the lot," my new favorite. The waiter kindly filled my canteen with water before I stepped out the door. Knowing my plans, he warned me about the police, adding that once on the road out of town I should be all right. Then I hiked to the edge of town and waited patiently for that first ride, the initial spark that always provided my momentum.

Some research in Kalgoorlie had helped me better understand the area I was about to enter. Everything I had read told me the Eyre Highway leading across the Nullarbor was one of the memorable Australian road journeys. This route passed through some of the most desolate and inhospitable land on earth. In 1841, Edward John Eyre, the road's namesake and first European to make a successful crossing, had referred to it as "a hideous anomaly, a blot on the face of Nature, and the sort of place one gets into in bad dreams."

The Nullarbor Plain is an enormous wilderness, stretching out flat and nearly treeless farther than a man can see. Nullarbor comes from the Latin meaning "no trees," and reflects the kind of spaciousness that reaches into the horizons and beyond. Only the hardiest of scrub vegetation existed in this arid country, the kind that could survive on little water and thrive under harsh conditions. Bluebush and saltbush were two such plants, growing up in irregular patches alongside the road and vibrating in the wind beside me while I waited for a ride.

My first lift out of Norseman came from out of nowhere, seemingly a serendipitous gift from fate. A sun-weathered soul with a long grey beard pulled over in a rusty, dilapidated old Holden *ute* and motioned me in. The ride lasted for about an hour before he dropped me off and then vanished in a cloud of dust down a side road leading to the sheep station where he worked. I naively thought this to be a fortuitous sign of the good things to come. Little did I know I would be marooned at this spot in the desert for more than a day.

It got very cold on the plain that evening, too cold for the one thin blanket Sofia had given me in Nepal. I sat up most of the night huddled over the fire I had built, the blanket doubled across my back. By rotating positions every so often, like a pig on a vertical spit, I held at bay the brutal shivers that would periodically sink into my body. These dry and debilitating conditions chilled me to the core. I recalled goose hunting in eastern Oregon as a boy with Dad, when it got so cold I could barely make my hands function well enough to cock the shotgun. Now, each time I had to leave the fire for a fuel run, my internal body temperature would plummet drastically.

The constellations of the Southern Hemisphere provided a pleasant distraction from the hardships of the desert night. They were new to me and I could not remember ever having seen the stars in such vivid clarity. The crisp, cold night air held pleasing herbal aromas of the native flora. These fragrances were intoxicating as they came and went with the intermittent breezes of the night. Occasionally, sets of glowing eyes reflected back at me from the darkness, pausing for several minutes before they disappeared. These were the eyes of the curious kangaroos that, drawn by the fire, had come to share my lonely night. I occupied myself by making entries in my travel journal by the flicker of firelight. Never had I felt more alone. Never had I been so cold. Never had I experienced such total silence.

The following morning, a couple of "road trains" passed me in a flurry of dust and sound, shooting through as if I did not exist. These awesome titans exploded down the road more like locomotives than oversized trucks. They were the unique transportation phenomena of the outback arteries of Australia, and supreme rulers of the roads. It was their responsibility to service and supply a nation, as vital blood flowing to the extremities of the land. Like prehistoric colossi returning from extinction, they imposed their territorial imperative on the isolated tracks of Australia's wilderness. Their mammoth size was impressive. They rolled the back roads at high speeds, carrying sheep, ore, farm equipment, machinery, and even houses on their long backs.

On the afternoon of the second day, I heard the distinct sound of one of these great trucks in the distance. As it came closer, I realized my water supply was nearly gone. I was not eager to spend another freezing night in the isolation of the outback wilderness. This time, I initiated a different approach to hitching a ride. Instead of passively standing at the side of the track with my thumb out, trying hard not to look like some wanted criminal on the run, I took up a position in the middle of the road. There I laid down my backpack and stood with my arms spread wide, staring intently at the oncoming mass of steel. I was calm and focused, feeling like a young matador facing his first bull. "I will hold my ground at all costs," I said to myself. The closer the giant came, the more pronounced the sound of its air horn. Soon a steady and constant piercing blare took precedence over all other sound. Each time the operator started to maneuver to the right or left of me, I would sidestep in that direction. We engaged in this deadly dance until, in the end, the mammoth rig came to a dramatic halt in a cloud of dust and fumes, its air brakes squealing and hissing.

A red-faced man climbed down from the cab, shouting to me in a language much too emotionally charged and accented to understand. We confronted each other boldly in the middle of the road. I honestly believe it was in times like these I cultivated the sales skills that I would use later in life. I stood still as the livid oversized Aussie fired nonstop questions at me. It was not long before I detected a measure of respect from him for the degree of creativity I had displayed in causing him to stop.

He continued with his diatribe about company policy regarding riders, explaining the liability insurance rendered it impossible for him to accommodate me in any way. I told him I was hitching as much of the distance around the world as I reasonably could and that he had the chance to play a unique role in history by helping me with this Herculean task. I went on to say that I might even write about him in a book some day. He grinned, showing great stained tusks for teeth, and then, after a bit of a laugh, he said, "Good on ye, mate."

His name was Ray. As we spoke, I fixed my eyes on the automobile sitting on top of his full load, facing backwards. After his third attempt to tell me no, I challenged him to let me ride in the car perched above us. He scratched his head some and proceeded to walk around the rig, kicking the tires and checking the tie downs. Then he looked up, "Mate, you're a determined bloke, aren't ye?"

The ice had broken and the face of the glacier was melting; capitulation was at hand. He nodded and I was up the sideboards dragging my gear behind me, employing another one of life's lessons that Grandfather Hardy once thoughtfully shared with me. "Don't wait around for someone to change their mind or they will!" Then he added, "Grandson, most deals are lost after they are made." A great amount of experience in life transpired before I was able to comprehend the wisdom of this statement, but he was right.

I took up temporary residence in the old car riding on top of Ray's load, facing the western track to our rear. The inside was warm from the heat of the sun radiating through the windshield. There was a pleasant scent of old upholstery and the front seat provided plenty of room for me to sleep comfortably. I had my own little watchtower on high from where I was able to survey the wide scenic vistas of the Nullarbor Plain. I took a deep breath as the sound of Ray progressing through the gears in the "prime mover" faded away. A great friendship was about to bloom from the seeds planted there in the middle of that desolate road.

After a full day of driving, Ray pulled off the dirt track early that evening. We set about building a large fire from dried bushes that looked something like American tumbleweed. Ray's "billy" was a pot that hung from the apex of a tripod, composed of steel rods he placed over the crackling fire. With this simple affair, he heated up his stew for dinner. Remembering the line in the song of Harry Nathan's turn of the century version of the Aussie national anthem, "Waltzing Matilda," it all suddenly came back to me.

"Once a jolly swagman camp'd by a billabong
Under the shade of a Coolibah tree

And he sang as he sat and waited till his billy boiled
You'll come a waltzing Matilda with me."

I opened my can of beans and warmed it near the fire. When it started to simmer over the edge of the can, I pulled it back with a crooked stick. The smells of our camp cookery filled the night air. Never had beans, bread, and cheese tasted so good. We traded food and stories as the brisk night rolled in over us. The conversation always seemed to come back to the Nullarbor. Ray related that the entire crossing would take six nights and seven days. He laid out the journey ahead by drawing a map in the sand with his large forefinger. Our destination was Adelaide. I enjoyed the informative conversations about where we were going and how long he estimated it would take to get there. Already, I felt we were becoming a team with a common objective, and I was quick to help with the chores around the truck.

It got very cold after dinner, prompting Ray to walk over to the truck and climb in. He told me his idea of a night's sleep was an hour or two lying down in the cab. I stayed close to the fire, implementing my rotation ritual to stay warm. After his nap was finished we broke camp, but Ray did not completely extinguish the fire. I asked him why. He said water was too precious and the area was so immense it did not matter; the fire would just burn itself out. Being from Oregon and always conscious of forest fire danger, I never really accepted this idea but followed his instructions on the water. However, I did manage to kick some sand on the fire before we loaded up and roared off into the darkness of the winter night.

That night I nearly froze to death sitting on the load in the old car, catching the brunt of the cold night air whistling by. I was wearing every single piece of clothing in my possession, but having come from the equatorial heat of the Malaysian Peninsula, I did not possess many warm items. I wrapped myself up with my only blanket like an Egyptian mummy and tried not to think about the wintry conditions. Rubbing my hands together and stamping my feet on the floorboards all night offered little relief from the bitter cold that had rolled in after sundown. It was a long night.

In the morning, I was elated to see in the rearview mirror of my car facing backwards, the molten orange orb peeking out from the eastern edge of the desert. It shed a golden-copper light across the land, and I knew I would be feeling the warmth of the sun's rays soon. I had survived the night.

Later, we came to the fueling station of Caiguna, one of the few stops along our route. While Ray grabbed some snacks, I topped off his jerry cans with life-giving water. After a chat with the proprietor, gleaning the latest news and weather conditions, he filled the mammoth tanks with fuel. I was very careful in the early days of our journey not to linger in the washroom after we stopped, over concerns he might leave me behind. I kept a sharp eye out for Ray and the rig at all times.

My thoughts wandered back to J. D. Lowe, the casehardened old farmer I had worked for in my early teens who, in his own way, had made me painfully aware of the importance of paying attention in life. "Many troubles are of our own making, Bob," he would say, "Most of them can be eliminated just by being observant."

Mid-afternoon of the second day I felt a twinge of excitement when I spotted a plume far in the distance behind us. In time, the column of dust drew closer. I wondered if Ray had seen it. Was it a dust devil? Could it be another road train bearing down on us? The better part of an hour had passed since the appearance of this mysterious apparition, and I remained consumed with speculation. Folks in the restaurant at Norseman had told me about the camel caravans that were used in the early days to cross these forbidding lands. I wondered what ceremonies might have taken place when different travelers met under such isolated conditions. I felt like my ancestral pioneers who, in their 1843 trek to Oregon, might have discovered another covered wagon following them in the wilderness.

Soon it was plain to see the object of my interest. It was another road train. Over time, the behemoth closed the gap between us, even though I detected an increase in sound and surge of power in our own rig. I figured Ray had seen the challenger by this time and had decided not to "give way." During my high school years we called what was about to unfold a drag race, usually held out on the old airport road late on a Saturday night, after bolstering one's courage with a few cans of beer. The Australian version was similar but decidedly more exciting, shaping up to be a monumental competition between two enormous masses of machinery. I was delighted to have a front row seat! The car seemed safely perched high above the contestants, though at times it had shifted precariously. I wondered if it was possible to bounce off from where I now sat, and what might happen if the truck diverted off the road?

The pursuer gradually pulled alongside, and now the two charged headlong over the narrow dusty track at top speed, each with outside wheels off the hardpan surface. The tightly wound diesel engines screamed at full pitch and a great spinning cloud trailed behind us like a horizontal cyclone. As they say in Australia, the race was "full on!" Overall, the match remained dead even for quite a while. When one of the trains would nose ahead by a few yards, the other would quickly respond by pulling along side. Later, heavy rains began to pelt us and the road became slick and extremely muddy. This made things messy and slowed us down. Suddenly, some distance up ahead I could make out a large obstacle in the road. I wondered if the drivers could see it, too. As we approached, it became clear it was another road train, buried to its hubs in three feet of mud, lying still in the road like a wounded animal.

Understandably, the "great race" was over, ending in a draw. Forced to stop, there were friendly exchanges between Ray and the other operator. Then we chained our great trucks together and pulled the stranded rig out of the bog so we could all move forward again. Ray later told me contests of this nature were common and often eagerly engaged in to breakup the monotony and stress of the long and protracted road trip.

That evening we "boiled our billies" while basking in the radiance of the campfire. After dinner, Ray informed me I could ride in the cab with him for the rest of the journey. The benefit of having a heater was the first thought that came to mind. I also looked forward to more communication with this tough trucker. He then went to the cab and took his regular two-hour after-supper nap while I tended the fire and wrote in my journal.

After Ray awoke from his rest, I noticed him popping some white pills. When I asked about them, he told me that he used them to stay awake on the weeklong job. This explained how he could drive all day on only a couple hours of sleep. We roared off into the night telling stories by the dim light from the instrument gauges on the rig's huge dashboard. First, he wanted to know everything I knew about American trucks. I told him about the logging trucks that Dad had bought to haul logs to his sawmill in Happy Camp, California. I continued to feed his curious mind with the stories of the lumber trucks that Yreka Western sent down the narrow and dangerous Klamath River Road to pick up the mill's lumber. I told him about the great freight-liners that rolled over our nation's freeways and turnpikes, serving the nation through all seasons and conditions. He was fascinated and made me promise to send information on trucks back to him when I finally reached home, something I was happy to do.

After the truck stories Ray and I shared the accounts of our lives with each other. The great loves of our life, the challenging trials, and other fond memories filled the cab hour after hour. We had the time to explore the many facets of our separate backgrounds, growing up in different hemispheres, under dissimilar circumstances. He was older and had survived many difficult situations. His stories fascinated me.

Ray began to act strangely after the fourth day. He brought the rig to a complete halt once to remove a wire fence that someone had dragged across the road. The only problem being, there was no fence! There was another time at night when he stopped to view a nine-foot tall "roo" he claimed to be sitting in the middle of the road. It did not exist either, although we saw scores of large kangaroos as we crossed the plains. Folklore or fact, I had heard stories in the Kalgoorlie boarding house of truckers who, after too long behind the wheel on the Nullarbor, would "lose it and go mad." I was beginning to worry about my new friend.

Ray continued downing the white pills in the days that followed and his driving correspondingly became more erratic. Finally, on the morning of the sixth day, he completely collapsed over the steering wheel of the fast moving rig. This shocked me into action. We went off the road as I frantically tried to pull him away from his slumped position over the great wheel and regain control of the oversized truck. I hit the air brakes and slowly brought the big rig to a halt. Fortunately, I had averted the real danger of us overturning. Ray slept through the entire ordeal.

Upon waking, he could remember nothing of what had happened. I impressed upon him the seriousness of his condition and insisted on driving while he caught up on his sleep. He finally agreed and, after some instruction, I took over the wheel for the rest of the day while Ray slept. There was a tight schedule for him to keep and to delay our movement east was unthinkable, as bonuses would be lost, employers upset, back-hauls rescheduled.

On the seventh day, although it seemed it had been much longer, we finished the crossing and pulled into Adelaide right on schedule. A tremendous feeling of accomplishment welled up inside of me. Ray and I had become great friends during the crossing. After trading addresses, I thanked him one last time, then gave him a firm handshake and swung down from the cab. Looking back I could see him grinning from ear to ear as I waved a farewell to my travel mate. Then, as he pulled away, I stuck out my thumb and started walking down the road, looking for the next ride.

It is with cherished memories that I think back on the experience of crossing the Nullarbor Plain. Ray and I corresponded for several years after my return to the States. I sent him great amounts of literature on American trucks for which he was very grateful. He shared with me, just before we parted, that he was happy he had violated the company rules just this once, when he decided to pick up the young American "Hitching the Nullarbor."

Kangaroo

Into Melbourne
Chapter Twenty-Six

The call of the horizon finds quick response in the heart of every wanderer. —Louis L'Amour, "The Walking Drum"

The air was cold and the rain came down in transparent sheets, as if spilled from a great bucket hinged from a cloud. I had been a week crossing the desert on very little sleep. Now, this sudden deluge out from the dark gray nimbus overhead left me frustrated and wishing I were back in the warm dry cab of the truck. Soaked to the skin, I stood at the muddy apron of the roadside near the outskirts of Adelaide, waiting for a rescue ride. A shiny blue Holden sedan pulled over, stopping on the road just ahead of me. "Relief at last," I said to myself, dashing toward my warm and dry reprieve. After catching up, I flung open the back door of the vehicle and tossed in my wet pack, then piled in the front seat, grateful to be out of the unforgiving weather. The driver introduced himself and then quickly turned back to the wheel, negotiating the car back into the long line of late afternoon traffic.

I reflected to myself, that returning to civilization represented a major change from the stark unpopulated milieu of the outback. I could see that stepping up to the quicker pace and crowded conditions of the population centers might take a few days of adjustment.

His name was Greg, and he opened the conversation by joking he had picked me up because I looked so miserable standing alongside the road. "Ah, a man with a heart," I thought. Greg was a university student, on his way to his parents' home for a few days break before resuming classes the following week. He made it very clear that picking up hitchhikers was not something he regularly did, but he had altered his personal guidelines only because of the wretched weather. I mentioned I was making my way to Melbourne after hitchhiking across the Nullarbor on a road train. That was all it took for him to come to full attention and initiate an onslaught of questions. He told me crossing Australia had been one of his great dreams in life.

The more I shared my recent experience with him, the greater was his enthusiasm. I began to wonder seriously if I had infected him with a wanderlust that might become a detriment to his educational aspirations. He especially liked the stories of the great drag race and Ray's hallucination of the nine-foot kangaroo in the middle of the road. The young man remained thoroughly consumed by even the smallest of details regarding my road-safari of the previous week. For the next hour, this topic consumed our conversation. He asked, "Was it dangerous? How did you get the different rides? Was it cold? Where and what did you eat?"

It sometimes puzzled me how little most people traveled outside the circle of their immediate environments. On numerous occasions during the trip I had asked directions from someone regarding the next town or village, often a mere hundred miles away. They would respond, "I can't tell you. I have never been there." This seemed true whether it was Kansas, Cairo, or Kathmandu. Regardless of where I had roamed, I found that the majority of people seemed confined by the complications and responsibilities required in their basic survival and rarely had the time or inclination to venture out.

I further speculated that most of them settled down within a confined range almost by accident, decisions born primarily as a result of love affairs, job searches, and the location of other family members. Without question, most people seemed content to sprout their roots and commence the journey of life almost blindly. The option of travel was usually far down on their list of priorities.

For whatever reason, the calling to travel had haunted me like an unfinished book, for as long I could remember. Old friends have informed me that traveling the world was all I ever talked about in my youth. The current odyssey, antithetical to my peers in so many ways, came about from nurturing the dream and then making room for it to come true. In addition, as I have observed before, it may have just been in my pioneer genes to scout and to seek. In any event, I knew my strengths would continue to come from fulfilling my desires to explore the globe. I could not conceive at this time that I too would settle down one day for the very same reasons as those homebodies I had met along the way.

I had long since conceded that traveling was not for everyone. Yet, in the short time I had known Greg, I had the feeling I represented the embodiment of his travel dreams, a sort of Johnny Appleseed of the road. His imagination had now been titillated, if not challenged, with what was possible. I sensed I had inadvertently planted the idea, and wondered if he too might someday become a traveling man. For me I had discovered the value of life deepened incalculably with the new realities grained from my travel experiences.

Greg had determined I was a curiosity worth sharing and insisted I come with him to meet his parents. Intuitively the suggestion of such a detour did not set well with me, but it was getting dark, I was hungry, and I found it easy to acquiesce. Soon we were cruising through the tree-lined and upper class residential neighborhoods a short distance out of Adelaide. We pulled onto a cobblestone driveway and passed through open wrought-iron gates flanked by large carriage lanterns atop the brick gateposts. A multistoried palatial estate with walls of stone and windows trimmed in white millwork came into view just ahead.

The full magnificence of the structure appeared as the car came to rest in the spacious courtyard adjacent to an entrance designed for valet parking. Without question, I was decidedly under-dressed, which added to my apprehension. I had patched my loose fitting Levis numerous times, and my well-worn sandals were looking a bit shabby. We passed under the arched foyer leading to the two massive hardwood doors at the front of the house. I thought it odd that Greg rang his own doorbell. Through the beveled crystal-glass window set in the door, I could see a shadowy figure reaching for the door handle from the inside. The large door opened, and a middle-aged butler greeted us with a restrained smile. Shouldering my backpack, I received a quizzical nod from him as we entered.

He obligingly took Greg's bags in hand and toted them to the cloakroom nearby.

The butler then led us to the study off the main hallway where the patriarch of the family, Greg's father, greeted us. The furnishings were lavish but tasteful, with a marble-topped sideboard against one wall and the father's large desk in the middle of the room. There were two large leather chairs on either side of the fireplace. The surrounding walls were nearly all composed of bookcases, veneered with glass doors that encased a great number of volumes. Floor-length draperies of burgundy velour, fastened back with a strap furbelowed in golden filigree, hung evenly on each side of the colonial sash windows. The room was without a doubt well-maintained and all was in perfect order.

Physically, Greg's father was an older clone of the younger man, but for having less hair and a protruding stomach. The man of the house sported a closely trimmed mustache, one that definitely had a distinguishing quality about it. He wore a heavily starched white shirt and loose tie, complemented with suspenders that held up his well-pressed wool trousers. He had a lit cigar in one hand and a half-full snifter of brandy in the other.

Greg did the honors, introducing me to his father and making him aware that I was a weary traveler in need. Greg further asserted that he wished me to stay for dinner, as well as the night. The older man reserved his approval on the lodging and quickly gained control of the conversation by plying me with questions about my background. After awhile, feeling a bit uncomfortable with his interrogation, I averted any additional queries by requesting the whereabouts of the washroom.

Upon my return, the drama escalated slightly as I again found myself on the unpleasant end of a unilateral conversation with Greg's father. Greg, my defender, had apparently gone to his room to clean up before dinner. The older man expounded on a multitude of topics while drinking heavily between loquacious outbursts. Initially, he spoke of his position in the community as one of Adelaide's leading industrialists. Soon after that, he imparted his personal philosophy, a brand of social Darwinism, in a somewhat tedious "survival of the fittest" soliloquy. I was already familiar with a good deal of what he was espousing and was frustrated to think he might be directing his emotionally clad lecture toward me. By now it was obvious the man had been imbibing too much and, as a result, he was losing me as a listener.

The older man nattering on in his cups reminded me of *Babbitt*, the satirical 1922 Sinclair Lewis novel portraying the vacuity of middle-class conformity and striving. I had also read *Buddenbrooks*, the profound first novel by Thomas Mann, during my winter in Greece. Here Mann interestingly portrays the pressures and twists of fate confronted by a wealthy German mercantile family in decline. My thoughts wandered to what the future might hold for Greg. Would he tread in his father's footsteps? I wondered if the charitable gesture of bringing home a "vagabond of the Nullarbor" comported with how his father thought the evening should unfold.

I recalled an unexpected conversation with my own father when he offered me a position in the family lumber business, a business I had come to know quite well. I had only recently graduated from the University of Oregon when I respectfully declined his gracious proposal without sufficient consideration. My response was born out of an instinct "to be on my own," rather than one calculated from reason. I was motivated to make a separate start in the world, and I was far too young to realize the gravity of such a decision at the time. I just knew deep down that I sought a different path.

Just then, the butler sounded the dinner bell and we all shuffled into the dining room where I was to meet Greg's mother. We spread out around a beautiful long table, with place settings for four. The walls of the dining room were dressed in vertical wood panels of Padauk, a rich dark-red Indian hardwood used in the interiors of the early Pullman railcars. A magnificent crystal chandelier hung over the center of the long table. The carpets were soft and thick, of a vintage Axminster design. The room was impressive and the table could have comfortably seated a dozen or more people.

Mrs. Babbitt (as I referred to her in my mind) entered the dining room wearing a lovely evening dress that fell to the floor. I could only assume the couple dressed for dinner each night. There was something very wholesome and athletic about her, as if she played a great deal of tennis or golf at some exclusive club. I guessed her to be in her late forties and was impressed by her charm and radiant beauty.

Appearing slightly younger than her husband, Greg's mother was warm and congenial in a subdued sort of way. After an exchange of pleasantries, she shared some tales of growing up on a sheep station in the "outback," up in the north, just outside of Port Augusta. Her cheeks glowed when I mentioned I had come through that area only the day before. She told me she had met Greg's father while attending the University of Adelaide. Her then husband-to-be was working at the time in his father's business part-time while attending school. On the surface, their stories resembled a series of pleasant experiences strung together like the pearls on the necklace she wore. Yet, on closer inspection, I thought I could see a price paid in both their faces; they obviously lived an existence peppered with stress and pretension.

We all took our seats. The waiter brought the delectable courses, one after the other, serving us individually. First was a large tureen of soup, then salad served on chilled plates, after which came the entrée of assorted vegetables and roast spring lamb. The meat was seasoned with rosemary and garnished with small buttered potatoes. The gravy boat was brim full of thickened dark brown drippings from the baked lamb. Appetizing smells permeated the dining room, and I could hardly contain myself.

I was famished and wanted to grab the food off the serving platters, devouring it on the spot. I restrained myself. This was a very different menu from the subsistence Nullarbor *tucker* Ray and I had eaten the previous week on the road. Although the evening was divine in many ways, I was still trying to dispel the uncomfortable feelings and budding resentments that continued to surface while listening to Greg's father pontificating at the head of the table.

Eventually, I found myself inextricably tangled up in a political discussion with Mr. Babbitt. I politely persisted in changing the subject and yet, he pursued the topic vigorously, in the manner of a predator focused clearly on his prey. Essentially a political neophyte at the time, all I can remember saying was something about "the poor conditions of the people of India." This set the man off on a tirade regarding the virtues of personal determination and individual responsibility, all of which I agreed with, but was unable find an opening in the conversation wide enough to note. The evening went downhill from there.

I began to eat a little faster with my head down, not quite knowing how much longer the opportunity for such a tasty feast might last. It was then that Mrs. Babbitt ever so slightly leaned in over to her husband and whispered just loud enough for us all to hear, "Dear, I think you have had too much to drink." The man seemed stunned, as if suddenly discovering he had been relieved of his clothes. He did not take it well. The last thing I wished for was to be engaged in a *kafuffle* (Australian for commotion) with the head of the household. I was beginning to see that the best solution was for me to take my leave.

Shortly after that, I excused myself from the table, expressed my gratitude to all, and conveyed a pressing urgency to get back out on the road. I slowly and gradually made my way to the mammoth front door, fending off requests from Greg and his mother to stay longer. The butler, for reasons unknown, had taken a great liking to me, and imparted a few kind words of encouragement under his breath as he handed me my things.

Greg followed me out, and we shook hands in the driveway. He mentioned once again his wish to cross the Nullarbor and to see wilds of Western Australia. I told him that having the desire was the first step and that I sincerely hoped he would someday act on his long-held dream. He apologized for his dad and, with neither of us quite knowing what to say next, Greg disappeared back into the confines of his parents' residence.

I was relieved to see it had stopped raining. Stepping off the manicured grounds, I found myself eagerly seeking the main highway south. The hearty meal had renewed my strength. I walked for a couple of hours in the cold night, reviewing my actions and thinking about what might have gone wrong with the evening. At last, I caught a ride with a long-distance delivery truck driver on an errand to Mount Gambier. Apparently he drove for a company with a more lenient policy toward hitchhikers. Heading southeast, he was as happy to have some company, as was I.

We pulled into Mount Gambier in late afternoon the next day. It was July 16, 1967, my twenty-fifth birthday. I decided to celebrate by taking the rest of the day off from traveling. I secured a room in a backpacker's youth hostel, stowed my gear, and lay down to sleep for many hours. There were dreams of my homeland. The great loneliness that had tormented me periodically returned. My thoughts focused on family and home, and I thought about my brother Bill who had shipped out in the Navy for Vietnam. I wondered about my parents whom I had not heard from since their letters had caught up with me back in Singapore.

In the next two days, different rides shuttled me from town to town along the southern coastline of Victoria. There were stops in Dartmoor, Portland Bay, Warrnambool, Colac and Geelong. The last ride brought me to the western edge of Melbourne where a vacancy sign in red neon captured my attention. It was well after dark when I walked into the old hotel, having spent my last dollar on the road.

A sharp young man came to the counter, and greeted me with a heavy European accent. I told him I had been traveling for much too long, I had no money, and I was in need of a room. He smiled, and then told me that I reminded him of his first night in Melbourne, four years previous, when he had first arrived from Switzerland. He had quickly spent his nest egg and he knew about being broke. His name was Fritz, and he had a plan for me.

Fritz offered to cover the cost of my room for the first night and lend me bus and train fare for the next day. The room was not one of the regular hotel rooms but one often used by the hired help and given to me at a reduced rate. Then Fritz carefully laid out a list of instructions for me to follow, promising that if I complied with them, all would be well.

He told me he was imparting the same suggestions that someone had extended to him. I was to take a tram and then a train early the next morning to arrive at a place of business in Melbourne where I could expect to find work. The establishment was a car wash. If the sun came out and business picked up, they would put fellows on to wash cars. The boss was a friend of his and would pay me at the end of the day if I mentioned Fritz's name. He further instructed me to bring my day's pay packet back to him, from which I would reimburse him for the room and the transportation. How lucky I was to meet this young immigrant.

I settled into my small room at the back of the hotel and after a hot shower, slid into bed. What a luxury after sleeping in the sitting up position all those nights on the Nullarbor. The sheets smelled clean and felt good on my tired body. From what little I had seen, Melbourne was a beautiful city. In the morning, I would be out there negotiating its busy streets to find a new job. I slept better that night than I had in weeks.

Gangplank Photo
Peter, Helen, Eddy

Photographed on board
s.s. AUSTRALIS

At the Car Wash
Chapter Twenty-Seven

Each blade of grass has its spot on earth whence it draws its life, its strength; and so is man rooted to the land from which he draws his faith together with his life. —Joseph Conrad

Rising at dawn after my long comfortable sleep, I quickly showered and dressed. Then I made my way down the poorly lit hallway leading from my room to the hotel lobby. Fritz, the nightshift manager, was still on duty and after we exchanged pleasantries he wished me well. His dayshift counterpart would soon relieve him. Map in hand, I sallied forth into the great living, breathing city of Melbourne. Like me, the city was waking up to the breath of fresh sea air rolling in off Port Phillip Bay and from Bass Strait beyond. As I walked to the tram stop, there was a sense of order and tidiness everywhere I looked. I had never really been keen on large cities but already I felt this one would be different.

The city tram Fritz had recommended pulled up on time, and I took a window seat among the other early risers. The tram whisked us through the canyons of tall buildings that rose up on either side of the track. The sun's rays broke over the city, casting more light on the attractive parkways and well-maintained public lawns interspersed along the boulevards. I had read some brochures at the hotel before falling asleep, learning more about the Royal Botanic Gardens, Queen Victoria Gardens, and the Olympic Park. These were all places on my list to see. In addition, there were the many charming vistas and numerous restaurants along the Yarra River that Fritz had mentioned. I was becoming aware that Melbourne was a city well-known for its magnificent sights, cleanliness and international cuisine. I promised myself I would take the time to explore this new world just as soon as I found employment and settled accounts with my recent benefactor.

I followed my new friend's instructions to the letter, first taking a tram and then a train to my destination. I arrived at the car wash on the corner of North Road and Nepean Highway, in the small suburb of Gardenvale, shortly before 8:00 a.m. I introduced myself to Mark, the young manager, and quickly laid out the short version of my story. A man of few words, he simply grinned and promised that if they got busy he would try me out. He was a wiry and energetic fellow in his middle twenties and, like most of the Australians I had met, spoke in a rapid-fire manner. As he turned to leave, I mentioned Fritz. He paused to muse, and said, "Oh yes, Fritz got his start here, too!" I then asked that he pay me at the end of the day, a request I was getting used to making in Australia. Without hesitation Mark agreed and then disappeared into the car wash to tend to a ruptured waterline.

I would quickly learn that sunny days translated to lines of anxious customers waiting in front of the vacuums. So it was on this first day when the sun came out and the cashier at the drive-in started to get busy. As he had promised, Mark put me to work, suggesting that I quickly learn the ropes from the other workers. He wanted the cars to come out sparkling clean, with as few reruns back through the wash as possible. I would discover in the following days that Mark was a tough manager who took pleasure in keeping us all jumping. He started me out on wheels, which included the tires and hubcaps—not an ideal position for someone of my height, but I was grateful to be working just the same.

The seven hours of that first day seemed to fly by and I mastered the responsibilities of my menial job without a problem. Mark paid me my ninety-seven cents an hour in cash at the end of the day. I took my pay envelope back to Fritz, where I reimbursed him for my transportation fares and the room as we had agreed.

Fritz smiled broadly, as I thanked him for his help in referring me to the new job. He told me, "It was nothing," as he was just passing on what someone had done for him when he first arrived. After a few more days at the hotel Fritz let me know there were certain rooming houses around St. Kilda, a suburb of Melbourne much closer to the car wash, where I could rent a small flat by the week at a more reasonable rate.

A few days later, I bid farewell to Fritz and moved into one of the flats he spoke of, located at 52 Grey Street, just off the main avenue of Fitzroy in St. Kilda. It was a long, two-story building that stretched perpendicular to the street. The hallways were dim, even in the daytime, with just enough light coming from the stairwell and the one bare light bulb to reveal the dilapidated condition of the place.

The room was not much larger than the swayback bed it held. The furnishings included an old wooden dresser, a cracked mirror on the wall, and a small nightstand. The single window presented a view of the small parking lot at the side of the building. There was only one bathroom, with perpetually dripping faucets, located at the end of the long hallway. The derelict men who lived on the second floor all shared this one facility. For now, this was my new home.

I was soon to learn there were a number of overqualified fellows working at the car wash. Several had university degrees (including me), accomplishments they had achieved well before coming to Australia. The car wash was a catchall for many individuals working in the country illegally, victims of bureaucratic red tape that delayed or prevented them from obtaining legal status. It provided an acceptable venue for well-intended people to survive, while at the same time existing as an incremental step in an immigrant's backdoor-rise to full status. Those employed at the car wash were essentially "building a work history," even if it was technically illegal.

In addition to the car wash providing an economic safety net, it was also a site where talented people bonded easily around a unique work culture. We were as survivors of a shipwreck practicing the unique Australian concept of *mateship*, where loyalty and closeness came from a shared misfortune. In just a few days I came to know them all and, with relish, we entertained one another with stories and histories taken from our individual backgrounds.

On further inquiry, I discovered we had a displaced architecture student (himself a certified draftsman), a boilermaker, and even an engineer among our working group. Each of these men had fallen through the cracks of the Australian immigration bureaucracy, a system that had failed them in refusing to recognize their qualifications. Some at the car wash said it was due to the exclusive nature of the powerful unions already strongly established in the country. Others claimed they were on the wrong end of the social engineering policies of a government that was trying to plan the country's growth in certain directions. Whatever the cause, we were as one and felt tied together due to our shared circumstances.

Big Peter was from England, and he was in charge of "cut and polish" or the waxing department. Shicki was the youngest of the group, still in his teens, and because of his small size and agility was responsible for "hook ups." This involved diving under the car as someone drove it off the turntable and fastening one end of a hook and chain to the tie-rods under the front end. The other end of the tether he quickly secured to the main chain that pulled the vehicles through the various washing and drying applications.

Ahmed, who was French-Algerian from North Africa, spoke very little English and just smiled a lot. He was an expert window washer. Eddy, also from England, was the master tail-off and detail person, seeing that the cars were perfect as they rolled off the line. He was also the proud owner of an older Holden, a car that looked suspiciously like a Chevrolet with rearranged chrome strips. I later learned Holden had become a subsidiary of General Motors back in 1931. Owning a vehicle gave Eddy the noble distinction of being our transportation man, though we rarely needed a car.

St. Kilda was a rough, unconventional, Bohemian area, and many nights I could hear the voices of drunken men yelling in the streets. Fist-fights between toughs and the proprietors or bouncers erupted in the late hours when the pubs began to close. Extricating the piss-pots (Australian for heavy beer drinkers) against their will was a difficult and unenviable task. Some nights I awoke to the sounds of men returning to the apartment house after a night of drinking. They fell on the stairs in their arduous climb to the second floor, loudly cursing the darkness, the coarseness of their language sounding like the pirates and convicts of bygone days. It was not an easy place to get a good night's sleep, but then the rent was affordable at $6.50 a week.

After a couple of weeks on the new job, I graduated to full-time employment. Our work schedule was six days a week with payday falling on Mondays. Peter, Eddy, and I elected to take every Tuesday off and frequently took the tram into the city on that day to look at the pretty girls of Melbourne, drink beer, and play away the day with darts and pool. Coin after coin went into the jukebox, playing *"Up, Up, and Away"* by the Fifth Dimension until I thought we would wear it out. We borrowed our motto, "all for one and one for all," from the *The Three Musketeers*. We worked hard and played hard, always looking forward to those carefree days we had off. Sometimes we would go to the George Hotel or the Prince of Wales, down on Fitzroy Street, for a night of team darts, but those places were a bit too expensive for our budgets.

Aside from the camaraderie of the workers that surrounded the car wash, there was the fascinating operation itself. After the cashier, the vacuums and driving on, the cars entered a long narrow tunnel of temperamental machinery that we seemed to service and repair constantly. The crew was continually in competition with itself to set new production records, one of the few ways to make our boss smile. If a machine broke down, we quickly performed that function by hand, often never missing a lick on the production line. Occasionally a very nice imported car of superior quality and value came into the wash, causing us all to take notice, be on our toes, and make sure things went just right.

It was on a day such as this that a man dressed in a suit brought his pristine Rolls Royce, a Silver Cloud III, into the car wash. The sleek lines, rich nickel chrome, and impeccable detail presented a remarkable and impressive sight. We all wondered why he did not have someone wash it by hand. I suspect the same thought crossed his mind a few hours later. The front-end fellows carefully vacuumed, paying attention to every detail. One of the men drove the Cloud onto the turntable for positioning. There the beauty pivoted to face the dark cave that housed the mechanized internal workings of the wash. Shicki hooked onto the tie rods and fastened the other end of his hook into the main chain. Now, the driverless masterpiece began to move slowly into the open jaws of the whirling brushes. First, there was the pre-spray; next, the soapsuds came down from above in a flurry of foam globules; then the exquisite piece of rolling artwork disappeared into the machinery. However, all was not well.

I was working out in the tail-off area that day. It was there I first heard the worrisome and ear shattering screech of steel against steel. I ran back to the washing tunnel to investigate. There amidst the showers of sparks and water was the vague profile of the Rolls Royce as it moved slowly and methodically into the housing of the large bumper brushes, then crawled on to take out the metal side panels of the drying machine. The main chain pulled the vehicle relentlessly forward, according to its purpose and design. Everyone scrambled for the "off" switch at once, but it was too late.

The right front wheel of the Cloud had climbed over the guide track and had taken out one machine after another, cutting a swath down the side of the car wash like a bulldozer. Later we learned that the Cloud's engine needed to be running for the power steering mechanism to allow the front wheel to track properly. This was a requirement of which the drive-on man was unaware. There was an ominous silence after what transpired, with every man holding his breath. Although it was a relief to no longer hear the sound of clashing metals and broken glass, neither the Rolls Royce nor the car wash would ever be quite the same after that day.

The veins on Mark's forehead were visibly throbbing, and his face reddened with anger as he yelled and flailed his arms in a fit of rage. None of us had ever seen the calm and collected young manager so out of control. The owner of the Rolls Royce was understandably hysterical. The two men exchanged a sharp barrage of words. Mark was unaccustomed to being on the defensive, and it was an interesting sequence of events to observe. He shut down the wash immediately, ordering a few of us to stay behind and finish the cars in progress by hand. Mark then sent everyone else home. The Cloud was left stuck in the drying machine, waiting for the insurance investigators. After that, our young manager made the long walk to the office where he called the owner of the establishment to inform him of the calamity. The wash remained down for repairs and out of operation for the next week. Mark fired the drive-on man.

The unexpected time off work gave me the opportunity to revisit Port Melbourne to make inquiries with ship captains about working my passage back to the U.S. This had been my routine on the mornings of my days off, but increasingly it seemed a fruitless activity. I had also enlisted the help of the American Embassy in finding such an opportunity on an American freighter, something they occasionally did for those wishing to work their way home. My searches thus far had always ended in vain.

Much to my surprise, after six weeks on the job, Mark promoted me to assistant manager. Always grateful to be working, I had mastered the various positions in the wash with zeal. In addition, I think he liked the fact I was an American with a varied resume of work experience. Mark had an ardent admirer, a devoted girlfriend who lived in Sydney. Several times a week he would ask me to keep an eye on the wash while he wooed her over the phone. During these periods I continued to familiarize myself with the intricate workings of the operation.

I was pleasantly surprised to find that, rather than being resentful of my new status, my fellow workers seemed to prefer working under me rather than Mark. They taught me all I needed to know about maintaining the machinery. Increasingly, Mark relied on me to handle minor breakdowns, personnel problems, and production flow while he was on the phone or out of town to visit his "Sheila" (an Aussie term for girls). Soon, I began to handle timecards and the payroll worksheet. A small pay raise came with the additional responsibilities, which allowed me to increase my savings account.

On one of my weekly sojourns into Melbourne with Peter and Eddy, I spied a turtleneck sweater in the window of a men's store. It was an off-white, cable knit, thick and heavy, and made of pure Shetland wool. The price was fifty-five dollars! This was a small fortune to me at this time but I thought it might raise my spirits to buy something new. Impulsively, I put the sweater on layaway,

CONSULATE GENERAL
OF THE
UNITED STATES OF AMERICA

14 Commercial Road
Melbourne 3004, Australia

August 30, 1967

Mr. Robert V. Hardy
Siskiyou Mills
Box 527 Happy Camp
California, U.S.A.

Dear Mr. Hardy:

I received your telegram on August 29, 1967, and immediately contacted
your son, Robert, who calls to this office regularly to receive his
mail.

Robert is presently working at an automobile car wash and service station
while waiting for a vacancy in the crew of an American vessel returning to
the United States. Your son is well and happy and the reason for not
writing to you was his work, which appears to extend beyond the regular
working hours.

A letter was mailed to you two days ago, from Robert, and he has promised
to write you again today.

Please be assured that this office will assist your son in returning to the
United States by signing him as a crew member of an American vessel which
will be en route to the United States, but a vacancy must occur in the crew
of such a vessel before we can assist Robert. It is not unusual to wait
several months for such vacancies.

In the meantime, it would seem that your fears for Robert's safety are
groundless and in the meantime your son has promised to keep in close
contact with this office.

If this office can be of further assistance to you please do not hesitate
to write us.

Sincerely yours,

Edward C. Murphy
American Consul

agreeing with the proprietor to make payments of five dollars a
week. I continued with this payment plan until one day I walked
into the store and paid for it in full. The garment was finally mine. I
proudly took it home to my dingy apartment house. Although I did
not frequent those establishments fancy enough to wear the sweater,

it became a small but important symbol of hope and achievement in my life. The sweater remained a bit of an anomaly among my possessions, but I would occasionally take it out of the closet and lay it on the bed. I liked the scent of the lanolin in the wool and I looked forward to a special time when I might wear it.

After about half a dozen trips down to the port, I came up with a job on a freighter to Los Angeles. This met with my criteria to work my way back home, and I would arrive with a little money besides. The ship was to leave in a week, so I gave notice to Mark and anxiously prepared for the next adventure, this one at sea. When I again visited the port for my boarding instructions, a few days before sailing, the captain was nowhere in sight. Another man claiming to be the captain confronted me harshly, saying there were no positions open. I told him my story. "Sorry, mate," he said. "That must have been the retiring captain you talked to. I am the new out-going captain and I am telling you here and now, there are no positions available."

With those few discouraging words my hopes of working my way across the Pacific were dashed. I went back to the car wash and promptly got my old job back. In the ensuing week I purchased the cheapest ticket available on a Greek registered passenger liner leaving for Acapulco in several weeks. At least this would give me the chance to seek out my grandfather's trunk, I thought to myself. I had now committed to leaving Australia, even as I vowed to return someday.

On different occasions, I had noticed a medium-sized, white Chrysler Valiant coming into the car wash, seemingly more often than needed. That is to say, the car appeared when still reasonably clean. The driver was an attractive, well-dressed young woman with long, dark, shoulder-length hair. I guessed her to be in her late teens or early twenties. She nearly always wore dark sunglasses with thick frames, making it impossible to ascertain in what direction she might be looking. Always cordial to me, this female presented herself as a tad bit mysterious. Handing her keys off to me, she would offer a slightly mischievous smile before walking over to take her seat in the customer's waiting room.

My friends, who never missed a thing, often teased and challenged me to strike up a conversation with the mystery woman. I managed a few words on her next visit, learning her name was Helen and that she was a student. On Helen's following visit there was an even greater connection between us, this time causing me to share more of my situation with her.

As we talked I could see Helen's quiet exterior masked a daring and vivacious spirit on the inside. She seemed to be completely absorbed in the information imparted to her. I was emboldened by her intriguing smile and the attention she was giving me. I asked her if we might get together sometime and her answer came quickly with a reassuring "Yes."

This would be my first formal date since leaving home, a year before. I found myself somewhat nervous when the big day arrived. My old patched jeans managed to hold together as I washed them one more time. I put on a clean pair of socks to wear with my sandals that I had just shined with Vaseline. In addition, I wore my new sweater, without regard to how warm it was.

Helen picked me up in the Valiant on my day off, and we toured the sights of Melbourne, taking a long ride. She was twenty-one and living at home while attending school. Her father was the owner of a large clothing establishment, manufacturers of men's trousers, shorts, college wear and shirts. It was fascinating to talk to this young Australian girl after spending so much time with the "blokes" from the wash. Excitement ran through my veins as I realized from the many questions she asked, that I had sparked her curiosity. We talked about the exotic places I had visited: Greece, India, and the Middle East in particular. (These would all be places she would visit in the years to come). Finally, I revealed to her I was planning to sail very soon on a ship bound for Mexico. I did express my mixed feelings about leaving Australia, a country to which I had become strongly attached.

Helen took me to one of her favorite restaurants where we had a wonderful meal and explored a variety of subjects in our dinner conversation. Afterwards she delivered me back to my Grey Street apartment, a place I preferred she didn't see just yet. I leaned over and gave her a light kiss, then got out of the car. She drove away slowly, looking back to give me a little wave.

After I had given my second notice at the car wash, my friends planned a going away party for me. I asked Helen if she would honor me by attending as my date. She happily agreed. We saw each other once more before the day of the party, becoming even more comfortable in each other's presence. What cruel twist of fate, I thought to myself, that after living in Australia for nearly four months and not meeting anyone, this should happen only a few days before I was set to leave the country! Still, I very much looked forward to seeing Helen again.

On the day of the party, she picked me up wearing a spring dress, with October in the Southern Hemisphere marking the season. Her effervescent personality and overall attractiveness energized me. The boys at the party were impressed. They thought it wonderful I was seeing the "lady in the white car." It was a glorious sunny afternoon and we all had fun, with Helen becoming the center of attention. I could see she was enjoying herself. Again, I wore my new sweater. My "mates" delivered eloquent speeches and sang old songs from their homelands, lightly primed by the modest three liters of beer we all shared. At the end of the festivities, Helen and I said goodbye to my comrades and drove away in the white car. She then posed the question if I might read to her from my travel journals. I was delighted to accommodate her, and we proceeded to my apartment from there.

We sat on the edge of the bed, my austere room having no chairs. She was poised, with her hands in her lap, appearing totally engrossed in the tales I read to her from my tattered notebooks. The overall journal was now nearly 400 pages in length. I was flattered that she was so taken by my stories, drinking them in as if quenching a great thirst from somewhere deep inside. The readings continued to spark her interest and I felt the matched innocence that existed between us was increasingly stirring our emotions. The shy and awkward feelings we mutually held initially were dissolving, overcome by the growing desire to know more of each other.

I found her long hair beguiling, especially when she inadvertently let a lock of it hang over one eye, like Lauren Bacall in an old Bogart movie. She exuded a freshness, and the alluring sparkle in her brown eyes that I had seen earlier at the party, remained. I sensed she was a searcher, a risk-taker, with an inquisitive spirit like me. Yet, through all of this, I detected a hint of sadness. Could it be from the knowledge of my leaving, or was it from something deeper, farther back in the past?

She had moved to the top end of the bed now, leaning back against the headboard. I stopped reading and seamlessly the conversation moved to romance. Briefly, we shared some history with each other. I spoke of my first true love from high school, a country girl who brought about feelings in me I had never before known. Bashfully, she revealed there had been only one other boyfriend, who no longer was a part of her life. Silence filled the little room as my lonesome eyes betrayed me. She must have sensed the emotional vacuum left inside my heart, a vacuum created from the endless solitary months on the road. In a soft feminine voice, barely perceptible, she expressed the murmurings of understanding I had so longed to hear.

Our eyes locked in a warm visual embrace. The moment we had both dreamed of had come at last. We kissed lightly, then again and again. Moments later our fingers walked together in slow motion down the front of her dress, delicately unfastening one button after the other. Now it was her heart that was being unveiled. The flawless porcelain skin of Helen's lovely slim body gave way to the shapely ripe fruits of her youth. Tenderly I caressed her slender nakedness, the scent of pheromones calling me closer. Then we became lost as one, spinning and entwined in a lover's ecstasy, before inhibitions might call us into retreat. Afterwards, we fell into a deep sleep, unaware of the emotional heartache that would trail us into the future from these few blissful hours.

I had only dated Helen for a total of three weeks before my time in Australia came to an end. In the days prior to my leaving, I paid my rent and closed my bank account. When the sad day of my departure finally arrived, Helen picked me up at my apartment in her white car. She was lovely, wearing a pale blue dress with white buttons. We spoke quietly, again sitting on the edge of the bed.

She took me to the ship where we met my workmates, Peter and Eddy. Port security was virtually nonexistent in 1967, and guests of choice could share in departing celebrations with the passengers aboard the ship. Helen, Peter, and Eddy had accepted my invitation to come aboard the *SS Australis* to see me off. We all congregated in the passengers' lounge where we proceeded to build a pyramid on our table, composed of the empty Alsops Ale cans. We reveled in merriment for an hour or two before the sorrowful reality of my departure came upon us.

Suddenly, there was an announcement from the loud speaker in the lounge asking the visitors to leave the ship. We walked to the port side. Helen and I lingered in a long embrace. Then she joined my friends as they walked away, down the gangplank to the crowded dock below. For just a moment, Helen, Peter, and Eddy stood there looking back. Peter had his arms folded, and Helen was standing in the middle of them both, next to Eddy. Just then, the ship's photographer came along and snapped a photo, freezing that emotionally charged moment forever in time.

The great engines somewhere deep inside the bowels of the liner shuddered and we gently pulled away from shore. The air filled with the sounds of horns, sirens and bells. Confetti rained down from the upper decks, fluttering through the air and obscuring the view of my friends standing on the dock. Rolls of colored streamers stretched between the hands of those on land and the passengers aboard ship, unraveling to astoundingly long lengths as we continued to pull away. Another wonderful segment of my around-the-world passage was ending, and once again it was distressing to leave my cherished friends behind. I waved one last time to Helen as her image diminished, only to be embedded in my mind forever.

My father had frequently spoken to me of "turning points" and "mileposts" in one's life. These two terms were among his favorites. He often discussed the importance of acknowledging these, but added, "Many times, we can only identify them in retrospect." Leaving Australia that day was without any doubt a turning point.

The date was October 12, 1967 and I would be a full eighteen days at sea. Torn by two great callings, I felt a fracture running down through the center of my being. On one hand, I yearned to stay in Australia, to see more of Helen, and explore a frontier bursting with opportunity and promise. On the other was the more dominant call to complete my journey, seek out documents concerning my grandfather's life in Mexico, and return to the country of my birth.

No longer able to see my companions standing on the dock, I turned and began to walk the decks, wondering if I would ever see Helen again and, if so, when?

SS Australis

Pacific Crossing
Chapter Twenty-Eight

The most difficult thing is the decision to act, the rest is merely tenacity. The fears are paper tigers. You can do anything you decide to do. You can act to change and control your life; and the procedure, the process is its own reward.

—Amelia Earhart

The *SS Australis* was now moving steadily through channels away from Port Melbourne towards the great watery expanse of Port Phillip Bay. From there, our course would lead us out into Bass Strait and then eastward toward the Tasman Sea. I leaned out over the rail to see the distant crowds dispersing from the docks. The skyscrapers of Melbourne rose from the city like elongated crystals, their height diminishing and fading into the shoreline as we sailed further south, away from the mouth of the Yarra River.

Standing on the main deck, I watched as the flagship of Chandris Lines gathered momentum, leaving a trail of dark smoke behind us from her two mammoth stacks. The Newport News Shipbuilding & Drydock Company, of Newport News, Virginia, had built her in 1940, just two years before my birth. The ship weighed in at 34,339 gross tons and sported dimensions of 723 feet by 93 feet. The steam turbines and colossal twin-screws were built to propel the great white lady through the waters at 20 knots. It felt good to finally be underway and there was a definite comfort in knowing my fate, at least for the short term, had been decided.

The "Melbourne days" flashed through my mind like an old movie as the great liner steamed farther away from the port, transporting me into a new world. The rich experiences of living in the Victorian capital had filled my time with pleasurable events.

Of primary importance was the satisfying camaraderie stemming from the many friendships associated with my employment at the car wash. The wash was like a second home for me, and my friends like an adopted family. It had been delightful meeting Helen during my last weeks in this garden state of Old European elegance and New World style. We had shared some very special moments together, even though they were much too short-lived. It had been captivating to learn about her life and already I was beginning to miss her. Once again, I was departing a country, taking with me a treasure-trove of fine memories. I pondered on how these experiences might weave themselves into my future.

As the crowds on deck thinned out, I made my way to the purser's counter to inquire about my sleeping quarters. They directed me down to the lowest deck of the ship, or "steerage," where I would find my cabin. This was where the least-expensive accommodations were located. I had saved just enough money from the car wash to finance the voyage, with a little left over for Mexico. My ship passage across the Pacific cost less than $300.

I descended the endless metal staircase down into the belly of the ship in search of my cabin. Behind the door with my number on it, my three new roommates had already marked their chosen bunks. The place was deserted. The beds were hammock-type affairs composed of a heavy seaman's canvass stretched with light rope woven through a periphery of brass grommets. The rope, lashed over a superstructure of two-and-one-half-inch painted pipe, kept the canvass taut. I took the one vacant "upper" that remained. The bulkhead walls of the cabin were of plate steel, which I assumed was some part of the vessel's skin. A head with a shower was just down the hall. I covered my bunk with the worn green blanket that Sofia had given me when she left Nepal. The realization then struck me that this small cubical would be my home for the next eighteen days. I went topside to scout out the decks.

By now, we were well out into the Bass Straight, and I wondered how long it would be before we changed course and sailed north to Sydney, located one-fourth the way up Australia's eastern seaboard. Our itinerary showed a scheduled docking there for at least a day to take on more passengers, and I was looking forward to exploring the famous capital of New South Wales.

The smell of the sea air invigorated me. A few seagulls trailed us, like so many white kites gliding effortlessly on the wind-wake of the ship. The sun was now setting behind us. The crimson and orange light glowed with brilliant intensity, casting flat trajectories of illumination across the irregular horizon line of the mainland. Whitecaps reached high in the air in futile efforts to break loose from the grip of the sea. A strong wind blew in my face, and I could feel the air currents flowing through my hair.

I recalled a favorite line of mine taken from *The Prophet* by Kahlil Gibran: "And forget not that the earth delights to feel your bare feet and the winds long to play with your hair." Walking on deck gave me time to reflect on the exhilarating feeling that now filled my veins, one I had known before. It was an extremely emotional sensation that I associated with feeling free. Now it ran to the core of my soul transfusing me with a new vitality that I savored, hoping it would last longer on this occasion than in times past. It was the same addictive sensation I would chase over the globe again someday, but only after decades of the self-imposed commitment to building a career. I stopped walking laps around the ship and lingered with my hand on the rail, reconnoitering the endless dark ocean undulating before me. It was boundless and foreign, frigid and unfriendly.

This would be the longest voyage I had ever undertaken. In 1962 my sailing to Le Havre, France, from Montreal on the *Saxonia* of the Canard Line had taken seven days. On that journey my college friend Tom and I gave assistance to a stowaway, until they caught up with him on our fourth day out to sea. He had accosted us from out of the shadows one dark night while we were walking the deck. He asked for our help. For several days, we took him food and calculated safe places for him to sleep. The purser's men apprehended the poor fellow one morning when he overslept in the movie projection room, where we had guided him.

It was a relief to ease back my grip on the constant chore of survival for a few days and trust in the captain for the remainder of our time at sea. With my meals served at precise times and my lodging covered, I was looking forward to a relaxing voyage ahead. For now, my immediate destiny was in his hands. He was the accomplished master whose task it was to shepherd our vessel safely through what troubled waters might exist between Melbourne and our destination, Acapulco, Mexico.

I reflected on the personal goals I had fulfilled in Australia. Having gained some twenty pounds, my health was now vastly improved. I had secured employment with a number of small operations, but the car wash job had enabled me to earn the necessary funds to complete the next segment of the journey.

I walked to the front of the ship and looked over the bow of the SS *Australis* as the prow sliced through the waves like a giant knife. One of the officers had informed me we were now "all ahead full," due to our late departure out of Melbourne. Ocean spray burst up over the bow occasionally, providing a sobering douse in the face. It had turned cold, and I shielded my icy cheeks from the numbing Antarctic winds that blew north from the white continent at the bottom of the earth. The winds cut through my jacket, making my bones ache. Shivering, I turned back to the stairwell and disappeared into the sheltered levels of the ship. It was dinnertime. I followed the other passengers, who were marching through the hallways toward the dining room, called by the melodic tones of dinner chimes.

I chose a table. They were large, round, and formally set, dressed with white tablecloths, the facilities being the same for passengers of all classes. There were six seated at my table including myself. After cordial introductions, the conversation moved through an interesting array of international passengers. Several mentioned they were sailing on to England, via the Panama Canal, following our stop in Acapulco. It was not long before I began to field the questions that came from all directions regarding my stay in Australia. Initially, I kept it simple, making the effort to learn more about my new acquaintances than they might learn about me.

I felt completely out of place. It was obvious my table-mates were not budget travelers, but people of greater means, taking a longer voyage for leisure or to visit friends and relatives. Our waiter provided me with the required "dinner jacket" for the evening sitting, and I wore socks with my sandals. In the days to come, I would emerge from my unsuccessful anonymity as their "fascinating world traveler" whose "interesting stories entertained us at dinner." However, in a short time I bonded with the group, and we all looked forward to seeing each other several times a day to exchange the latest gossip extracted from the daily events of ship-life.

After dinner, I explored the ship's library, catching up on the current events back home and finding some books on Mexico. The ship was large, and I became lost a couple of times that first day before finally orienting myself as to its configuration. Late in the evening, I followed the narrow corridors down to the bilge and entered my "stateroom." Everyone was fast asleep. I climbed the foot ladder to my bunk and collapsed, exhausted from the day of two worlds, Australia and my new life at sea. I rested with open eyes most of the night, serenaded by the chorus of snoring shipmates whom I had not yet met.

Early the next morning I awoke to the announcement on the public address system, "Would Robert Hardy please report to the purser's office." The constricted electronic voice from the speaker box in the hallway repeated the message. Perplexed, I nodded to my new roommates, introducing myself while quickly dressing. I soon made my way down the hall and up a number of decks to the purser's office. A radio-telegram was waiting for me in a sealed envelope with a Chandris Lines logo on it. I opened it, and then felt my heart jump a beat! It was a message from Helen.

"Bob, disembark the ship in Sydney-STOP, Come back to Melbourne-STOP, You can work in my dad's factory-STOP." The serene feelings of yesterday were now beginning to evaporate. Taking the message with me to a secluded section of the passenger lounge, I settled uneasily into a large overstuffed chair by the window. After several deep breaths, I tried to assimilate the full context of the message. Suddenly my mind filled with questions, and it seemed my clear direction was no longer clear. I realized this needed some careful thought before I answered Helen's call. I sat quietly, reading the radio-telegram repeatedly.

I weighed her heartfelt request, realizing a change in course now could possibly mean a change for life. My Australian visa had nearly expired. Would I even be able to get back into the country? Turning around at this time would surely involve some aspect of the immigration process. My ambition had been to travel entirely around the globe. Returning to Melbourne conflicted in a major way with my original plans. Increasingly double-minded on the subject, I continued to consider her option.

Completing the voyage to Mexico was important to me in fulfilling dreams of researching the life of Grandfather Moray. I remembered hearing about the trunk of papers and letters that he had left behind. Then there was my family and the anticipated return to Oregon after being absent for so long. Helen was presenting me with a wonderfully romantic opportunity, but it had simply come at the wrong time. I concluded that it was better not to change the progression of events at this point. I had faced another "turning point" in life and I wondered if fate was smiling over placing such a test before me.

When I next appeared in the dining room, my table-mates peppered me with questions. No longer could I maintain a low profile. My new acquaintances had come to know my name, and each one of them had heard the announcement that morning. Reluctantly and hesitantly, I revealed the situation to them, whereupon I immediately had five qualified relationship advisors, none of whom agreed with the other. I was relieved to find escape from the well-meaning voyagers as I retired to the library. I wrote in my journal at a table near the window. Later, looking up, I spied land. Excited, I moved out on deck to see more.

Now sailing north, we moved past the mouth of Botany Bay, first visited by Captain Cook voyaging to Australia in 1770 on the HMS Endeavor. The bay was so-named from the plethora of unusual plants found in the general area by his botanist. It was near here the early penal colonies, established by the British, spawned the first European habitation at Sydney Cove. We continued north, later docking in picturesque Sydney Harbor.

I left the ship and hiked the good distance to Kings Cross. At this time, October 1967, "The Cross," as it was affectionately known, was a center of rest and recreation for American service members during the Vietnam conflict, which had been escalating. Just a short walk down Darlinghurst Road and Victoria Street exposed me to the red-light district and its associated trappings. Crime and open prostitution shuffled themselves together with the stylish restaurants and hotels. This area had been part of the Bohemian heartland in the early decades of the twentieth century. Over the years, it had attracted the curious of all kinds from many different countries. Some came and left, while others decided to stay. Now, it was a most fertile venue for "people watching," an avocation I had long since cultivated and thoroughly enjoyed. I walked the streets, taking it all in, stopping to take a table at a sidewalk café. Here I reviewed my overall situation once more.

I spent some of the afternoon in deliberation before I began the letter to Helen. I let her know that I treasured our experiences together. It meant a great deal getting to know her and I went on to thank her again for taking such an interest in my life. A little further into it, I shared that regrettably my quest must continue eastward, as I felt it my destiny to stay on my course. I mailed this just before boarding the ship, hardly content in my decision.

Back aboard ship, I discovered an older man pouring over a chessboard in the passenger's lounge. He had a book and was replaying some of the famous matches in chess history. Chess was another unique gift passed to me from my father. He had learned the "Royal Game" aboard a destroyer in the South Pacific during WWII. He shared his knowledge of the game with me when I was old enough. I can remember winning only on rare occasions while growing up, but the game remained a pastime we both enjoyed. Now I was crossing the South Pacific myself, some twenty-four-years after his encounters in the same part of the world.

Some had said the ancient pastime of chess dated back as far as 760, with the more modern forms of the game having evolved since the late fourteen hundreds. It incorporates the keen use of survival instincts with the best use of basic game philosophy. Formal matches usually take place under time pressure. There are three fundamental principles to remember when playing this game. Control the center of the board, develop your pieces quickly (knights and bishops first), and king safety, as exemplified by a move made fairly early in the game called "castling." Castling places the king behind a field of three pawns with a rook at his side for protection. The budding chess aspirant must continue to learn tactics and formulate strategies. There are many openings to become familiar with and middle game skills to develop. Then there are the endgame exercises to master. Above all else, a player must avoid blunders! Chess, it seems, is a mirror of life itself. He who forgets any of these important lessons, invites disaster.

The man looked up and smiled, then introduced himself. "I am Yuri; I am from Yugoslavia," he said. I immediately sat down with him at his request and soon we were intensely engaged in a match. His game was incredibly strong, showing his ability to see moves and combinations well in advance. I was a victim repeatedly to his skewers, forks and traps. He offered to help me with my game in the days to come. I humbly accepted.

Suddenly my concentration was broken. "Robert Hardy, please report to the purser's office." Helen had sent another missive with a new request. This time she requested that I disembark in Auckland, New Zealand, our next port of call. She generously offered to pay for my airfare back to Australia from New Zealand. She asked for more time for us to get to know each other, mentioning the constrictions put on us by these outside events.

I thought I had resolved the issue in Sydney but then realized she possibly had not yet received my letter. The heartstrings were now stretching across the sea and turmoil returned, causing a dull pain to develop in my abdomen. Although now resolute in my decision, I could not help but consult several of the other passengers at dinner. They were sympathetic to both sides of this complex emotional equation, but I knew in the end the decision was only mine to make. Moreover, painful as it was, I had already made it.

By this time, my fellow voyagers were coming to know my name quite well. The word spread fast on the ocean liner! The status of this drama was becoming a serial entry in the daily saga aboard ship. Helen, and the sentimental circumstances surrounding our situation, became the topic of conversation regardless of my diversionary tactics at the dining room table. The story captivated people, and I was invisible no longer. With each announcement I was gravitating more towards being the center of attention, a position I did not want, but from which I could not escape.

At last, we arrived in New Zealand, entering Waitemata Harbour, then docking in Auckland. I was happy to go ashore for a long walk after several days' confinement to my circular strolls on deck. Any break in the journey was one I would celebrate. I disembarked to explore the picturesque seaport. Later, after obtaining some maps at an information stand, I made a comprehensive exploration of the city on an isthmus. It seemed a fresh and wholesome place populated with fast-talking, quick-thinking, and friendly people. I visited as many points of interest as possible in my allotted time ashore. The day had passed quickly, and reluctantly I returned to the ship. New Zealand was enticing and I vowed to return someday and investigate further its many prizes.

Helen sent one final radio-telegram to the ship. I received it after leaving the "land of the kiwis," well out to sea and steaming almost due north towards the Fiji Islands. Suva would be our last port of call before reaching Acapulco. Helen encouraged me to "get off in the Islands." However, Australia was now falling back into the fond memories of the past and becoming obscured by time, distance, and the new experiences each day aboard ship. My nervous stomach was getting better, and though I often thought of Helen and our times together, I had come to terms with my difficult decision. There had been a stronger call, and it was time to move on to Mexico and beyond. This homing instinct would eventually pull me back to Oregon, back to the beginning.

The Fijian island of Viti Levu came into sight just off the bow. The shoreline was a Gordian tangle of mangroves and inlets.

I disembarked the ship for the day in Suva. The heat and humidity were devastating. Looking for relief, I found myself on the second floor of an open-air restaurant, sitting at a wicker table positioned under a large fan. The building was a rustic affair with foundation and walls composed almost entirely of bamboo. It reminded me of the house where I had stayed in Bangkok. In an effort to organize my thoughts, I pulled out my journal and began to write.

The views from my perch, looking out over the hustle and bustle of the crowded streets, gave me a great perspective on the port. I could even see our white ship moored at the dock in the far distance. There was a perpetual sea of movement in the foreground. I saw pushcarts stacked high with the long cut stalks of sugar cane. There were multitudes of rickshaws and people carrying bamboo cages occupied by colorful island birds. Heat marshaled the tempo as people slowed their pace through the hottest hours of the day. The restaurant fans were a blessing, swirling over me just enough to keep the incessant flies that hovered above slightly off their course.

I struck up a conversation with a fellow at the next table. He was a cane cutter enjoying a day off. He explained the challenges of his job while we had cold drinks. Entering the fields, he chopped at the thick walls of vegetation all day with the long machete he now packed at his side. The hardwood grip of the great knife was worn smooth. I could not help but notice the numerous scars and recent cuts on his powerful arms. He spoke of the many hardships endured with the cutting of the cane. Other workers stripped and gathered it into carts, hauling the bundles to the railcars where they shipped out to the mill. He worked on little sleep in order to use all the daylight hours to cut. There were terrible bug bites to cope with and the sharp leaves of the cane sliced into his flesh like razor blades. However, the money was relatively good. This captured my attention, and we talked at length. I told him I was off the *SS Australis* for the day and would be boarding later to continue the voyage on to Mexico. A smile broke out over his face upon hearing this.

Seemingly, out of nowhere, we began to hatch a silly plan to exchange places! More a dream than a reality, we both enthusiastically pursued the scheme for fun, yet with some measure of sincerity. This fellow would take my boarding pass back to the ship, whereas I, in turn, would show up for his job in the cane fields the following morning. We continued to dare each other deeper into the depths of this cockamamie idea throughout the afternoon. I postulated that after working a couple of months in the cane fields, I could catch another ship coming through Fiji for Mexico and eventually arrive home with plenty of money. Besides, I had always enjoyed the stimulation of hard physical labor.

The afternoon passed into early evening when I heard the deep blast of the ship's great steam whistle, bugling the call for passengers to board the vessel. Looking around, my new Fijian friend was nowhere in sight. I promptly made my way through the busy village and back to the ship. Grinning as I walked up the gangplank, I continued to wonder just what it would have been like to make such a swap and cut cane in Fiji. "Now that would have made a good story," I thought to myself.

In the following days, sweet smelling south sea breezes wafted gently across our decks. Great thunderheads projected vertically into the stratosphere to the south of us. The ship was closing in on zero degrees latitude, that imaginary ring around the midsection of the earth called the equator. This invisible belt, equidistant from the North and South poles, held unique surprises for those who had never crossed this line of demarcation while at sea. That was, the small matter of King Neptune's Court! Passing over the equator for the first time, I was required to take part in certain ceremonies, long established by maritime tradition.

A mock courtroom was set up. Following this, the court enumerated, in a decidedly humorous manner, my alleged crimes, and then meted out the appropriate nasty punishment.

In our case, for there were a good number of us crossing for the first time, we were pelted with the revolting leftover food slops from the galley. This continued while costumed members of the crew, holding tridents, hurled good-natured insults and accusations. Afterward, the officers of the court liberally washed off all the debris from our clothes with buckets of seawater dipped from the swimming pool. It was all a good bit of fun, and the celebration helped break up the monotony of the many days at sea.

Yuri and I persisted with our chess games up until our last day. He revealed that he was once, at some level, a Yugoslav champion. Of our twenty games, I succeeded in winning only one, yet I had learned much from him. It was a wonderful way to spend some of the time crossing the ocean, when I was not reading in the library or writing. I said goodbye to my chess partner, who was sailing through the Panama Canal and then to Southampton, England. From there, he would be traveling back to Yugoslavia, his final destination.

After the extended time aboard ship it was evident that most of the passengers were anxious to disembark. I felt the same. Those I spoke with who were going ashore in the morning expressed their relief at the prospect of walking on firm ground again. There is an unstable feeling that comes with being at sea so long and I was soon to learn that it would persist well after leaving the ship. It would take a couple days for the effects to disappear after reaching Acapulco.

The next morning, under a golden dawn, our ship anchored in Acapulco Bay, exposing us to a flawless semi-circle of sandy beach. From there I could see the expanding concentric layers of hotels and small businesses rising into the hills beyond. It appeared that all levels of society mingled within these close lines of luxury and poverty. The passengers exchanged departing words with each other and one by one, they began to leave the ship. Ashore, I found myself shuffling from one customs and immigration line to another. The long Pacific crossing was over and I felt proud to have made the voyage. I embraced the fact that I was back in North America, and much closer to my home.

The Flying Men of La Quebrada

Mexican Holiday
Chapter Twenty-Nine

*Only that traveling is good which reveals to me the value of home,
and enables me to enjoy it better.* —Thoreau

The colorful history of Mexico had been of special interest since my youth, due to the adventurous life pursued there by my grandfather. During the long voyage, I had used this opportunity to absorb as much as I could about this fascinating country from the volumes in the library aboard ship. Now I found myself at the very same inviting natural harbor as did the Spanish galleons arriving in Acapulco during the sixteenth century, laden with their precious spices, porcelain, and silk from the Orient. This port had represented the primary gateway for the valuable trade from China and the Philippines. In Acapulco, the cargo was off-loaded and then shipped overland to Mexico City, en route to the eastern Gulf port of Veracruz, where it was again placed on ships to continue its long journey to Spain.

The aftermath of the Mexican War of Independence with Spain (1810–1821) saw the end of the galleon trade and Acapulco slowly receded into obscurity until the first half of the twentieth century, when it began to grow in importance as a resort town. It had been isolated from the world until the late 1920s, when they reconstructed the initial road linking this coastal village with the rest of Mexico. Now the alluring harbor, lovely beaches, and attractive climate were becoming accessible to people from the outside. Airlines soon began to service Acapulco, and the once sleepy port community continued its transformation. Soon the rich and famous began to arrive and enjoy the many enticing natural wonders of the region.

Now, I had come to these idyllic Mexican shores like the throngs before me, to seek out a treasure chest laden with wonders of my own, a trunk of letters belonging to my grandfather. What a thrill it was to step onto Mexican soil after being at sea for almost three weeks. Cleared through customs, I walked into town with my pack, hoping to quickly secure a room. Within minutes, a friendly vendor approached, hawking his wares. I asked him what was happening in this special place that might be of interest to me. He immediately mentioned the cliff divers. Then he added that many of the younger people enjoyed the beaches about nine miles north of the city where the scenery was spectacular and the lodging cheap. The place he spoke of was *Pie de la Cuesta*, which translated in English to, "at the foot of the mountain."

Making a mental note, I continued walking through the narrow and picturesque streets that surrounded the bay until I found a modest looking hotel several streets in from the beach. For a few pesos, I took a room and stowed my gear. Later I had lunch in a small restaurant by the sea and reflected on the voyage. I walked the streets for the rest of the day, happy to be back on land, and then came back to my room for the night.

I awoke refreshed. The morning brought with it the unmistakable scent of salty sea air mixed with the pleasant fragrances of the tropics. In the background were the random sounds from a noisy street. Then, there was a knock at my door. I opened it to see a young boy standing there in front of me.

"Hey, mister; you want to see the cliff divers? Come with me—I show you now." This dark-eyed lad with straight black hair looked like he could well have been a direct descendant from the ancient Aztecs. He was eager and persistent, his white teeth glistening when he smiled. Did the hotel alert him a guest had checked in? Was I a new prospect?

Soon I was following him down the cobblestone streets toward the historic district of town. We came upon an old fort, Fuerte de San Diego, built in 1616 to protect Acapulco's busy port from the dreaded pirates. From there we veered over to the craft market where I inspected a variety of goods on display while fending off the merchants who aggressively tried to peddle an attractive array of products. They were polite but shrewd, badgering the steady stream of potential customers who filtered through the maze of commercial activity. The boy obviously knew the best route to the La Quebrada cliffs, towing me at times behind him by the hand as he weaved expertly through the crowds of people.

Upon arrival, he pointed to the divers. They were perched like tranquil seabirds in the warm sun on the sharp rocky outcroppings. The men were poised high above the narrow blue-green ocean inlet. Pleased with the results, I tipped my young guide after which he disappeared into the gathering of onlookers that had been forming.

I studied those positioned on the cliff. They were relaxed, standing tall and looking down into the distant churning waters. Some of them were praying at a small shrine. Then suddenly, as if imitating a diving cormorant with wings outstretched, one of the daredevils plunged in perfect form, 100 feet into the constricted tidal channel below. His headfirst descent was precisely calculated to catch the heaviest inbound flow from the surf, preventing his destruction on the rocks beneath the surface. More divers followed his lead, exhibiting a level of courage and skill that was astonishing. The vivid images of the magnificent flying men of La Quebrada would long remain in my memory, inspiring me to return some four decades later to see a different generation of divers perform these same death-defying feats.

The Acapulco buses displayed evidence of many hard miles, and the one I took north out of the city was no exception. I peered through the glassless window at the jungle-like settings as we followed a dusty road north. We shared this dirt track with stray chickens and feral dogs as our driver negotiated the narrow strip through a string of sparsely populated villages before completely escaping the margins of the city. Farther down the road, we passed small taco stands and *palapas*, or thatched huts, with a backdrop of white ocean beaches to my left.

The right side of the road featured a beautiful freshwater lagoon where it was rumored the original Tarzan movies had been filmed. Coyuca Lagoon lay under a thick tangle of vines creating a woven green canopy that nearly blotted out the sun. I spotted natives in the shadows, wearing only loincloths, spearing fish from their dugout canoes. A colorful variety of tropical birds peppered the air with their strange calls and shrieks. Later I viewed a large snake coiling down from a tree limb, suspending its rounded kinks just above the surface of the dark lagoon.

Pie de la Cuesta was a small fishing village located at the base of the Sierra Madre, situated primarily on the ocean side of the road. Although it consisted of only a few shacks, I was impressed with the vistas of open sea, the strong pounding surf that shook the ground, and the dunes of white sand that tapered gently down to the water.

I rented a small *palapa* with walls of bamboo stalks tied closely together. The corner posts supported a rope hammock that hung diagonally across the middle of the room, and the sandy beach made for an adequate floor. This minimalist beach house was mine for the tidy sum of thirty-six cents a day, and I was quick to reserve it for the next week. I used the restroom facilities at the cantina nearby and bathed in the sea. I was mindful of the dangerous undertows that pulled at me from below the surface. The collapsing waves of oscillation ran up the steep beach and then, seemed to sweep everything back into the sea with a mighty force.

Long morning walks on the beach with fellow travelers from all over the world brought a sense of fellowship similar to what I had experienced in the youth hostels of the Middle East. Most members of this transient community occupied their afternoons reading and blissfully bathing in the sun to the repetitive reverberations of the breakers. Sundown brought with it spectacular vermillion, orange, and yellow sunsets, a captivating and mesmerizing conclusion to the day.

Each evening the cantina offered the "catch of the day," the fresh *pescado* brought in continuously by the fishermen. They served the fish with slices of fresh lime, tortillas, and beans at the small open-air restaurant near the road. Sometimes the local *mariachi* band would entertain our assemblage of international travelers, playing for tips.

The moonlit evenings were opportunities for impromptu sessions of storytelling that informally progressed from person to person around a small fire pit made in the sand. This compelling comradeship lifted the spirits and increased the sense of joy and unity among all participants. It was an ideal forum in which to share some of my unique travel experiences. Discovering *Pie de la Cuesta* and the merry band of wanderers who lived there was a perfect climax to the long trying odyssey that had consumed me for the last fifteen months. It was all shaping up as the ideal holiday. That is, before the *Federales* arrived!

Their harsh commands pierced the calm night air as they invaded from different directions in their military jeeps. They came to search the individual *palapas* and our personal belongings for marijuana. There had been reports of usage among some of the young people on the beach. An older officer walked with me to my hut and then proceeded to empty my backpack while carefully examining each item with a high degree of focus, as a scientist might inspect important specimens in a lab. From there he thoroughly searched the place, finding nothing. By this time, while continuing to field his questions, I was unfolding my tattered world map, my trusted and time-tested "document of substantiation." Upon inspection, he seemed impressed as his eyes followed the jagged line that traced my route through the different countries around the globe. With a glimmer of humanity, he commented enthusiastically that I was almost home.

He then turned to me with a menacing smile that proclaimed the naked power of his professional rank. He warned, "You must be very careful in Mexico; it is easy for a foreigner to get into trouble here!" This statement was a bit unnerving and while I was still digesting what he had said, my interrogator turned and strode outside to join the rest of his night raiders.

His men did at last find a quantity of "Acapulco Gold," the highly prized local cannabis, in the *palapa* of one of the Canadian fellows. His name was Danny. They shouted at him in Spanish before dragging the young man off into the darkness. There he was roughly loaded into the back of a jeep, wedged in by armed guards on either side. Feeling violated, some of us followed the soldiers out to their vehicles. I will never forget the distressed look on the young Canadian's face. They drove him off into the night, handcuffed.

The stories we had heard about these kinds of circumstances were not encouraging. In the best-case scenario Danny's family back home would pay large bribes extorted in return for his release. In the worst case, he could spend years as an incarcerated *gringo*, enduring terrible living conditions. None of it was good.

Distrust and depression followed this traumatic assault, and the congregation of international travelers soon began to disperse, exiting the once peaceful shores of *Pie de la Cuesta* for other parts of Mexico. The "utopian atmosphere" we had all enjoyed quickly evaporated. One evening, not long after Danny's arrest, I stepped aboard the midnight bus for Mexico City; it was time to move on.

During that long ride I had the occasion to converse at length with a highly educated teacher from the interior. He described Mexico City as a colossal sprawling megalopolis that was stimulating, unpredictable, and plagued with many social, political, and environmental challenges. He went on to say the population was burgeoning, the pollution often burned your eyes, and political unrest at the Mexican National University was growing. There were also rumors of corruption at different levels of government. Furthermore, he warned me to be on guard for pickpockets and petty thieves at all times. I kept what he had told me in mind, but decided I would set out to see if I could discover some of the more positive aspects of the city.

A repository for the country's wealth and power, the city boasted a strong patronage for music and the arts. There were theaters and galleries, magnificent and spacious parks, markets and museums. The beauty and opulence of this flourishing capital fostered respect and admiration from all the visitors I met. There also seemed to be an undying love and devotion from its own inhabitants. Each day I ventured out from my small hotel room with a map of the city to wander on foot for hours and behold the interesting sites.

The downtown area, Centro Historico, exposed me to both the squalid and the grand. There were people living in abject poverty in the shadows of architectural marvels amid a thriving business district. The public filled the many squares surrounded by a perimeter of colonial mansions, small business establishments, and the occasional historic Catholic Church. These all presented enticing vistas, and I wished I were an accomplished sketch artist able to capture these scenes with pencil and pad. As I sat in an open-air cafe bringing my travel journal up to date, I soaked up the views of lovely stone facades and the decorative ironwork that graced their verandas on the upper stories. This was a capital city comprised of many exquisite facets and fascinating contrasts.

On Sundays, there were promenades on Plaza de le Constitucion and late afternoon bullfights in the Plaza Mexico. Families came out to stroll together hand in hand and join in the *fiestas* all over the city, but especially in the beautiful and well-regarded Chapultepec Park. It was here I discovered the imposing National Museum of Anthropology and History, its construction completed in 1964, only three years before my arrival.

In the days that followed I was absorbed in examining what some considered then "the greatest museum in the world." The sheer size of the complex overwhelmed all who entered. I found the architectural effects soothing to the eye, with the efficient use of central and open-air patios, unlike any museum I had ever seen. Each room was clearly dedicated to a particular culture or period, which motivated the viewer to discover even more secrets in the rooms to follow. The ancient origins of early civilizations in Mexico's vibrant history found representation here. The Mayan and Aztec rooms seemed to be unquestionably the favorites of the visitors, with a mammoth twenty-four-ton Aztec stone calendar being the obvious treasured centerpiece of all the displays.

Walking eight to ten hours a day in the world's largest city, I investigated the Chapultepec Castle, the Museum of Modern Art, and Independence Monument. On another day I visited the Palace of Fine Arts, and the Cathedral. These were just a few of the highlights that kept me immersed in this new culture for over a week. I tended to my daily food needs by eating from the busy street markets, which presented themselves as a visual feast as well.

The scorching sun created an air inversion over the city, and each day I could feel the increasingly negative effects of pollution. I was becoming light-headed, my chest was tight, and I was developing a bad sore throat. I had a nasty cough and after a week, I checked out of my small hotel room at the top of the third floor staircase and climbed aboard one of the now familiar decaying buses. I was anxious to visit my uncles, who had lived on the west coast of Mexico for many years. I prepared for the long journey to Puerto Vallarta by picking up some tortillas, fruit, and cheese from the market place.

Leaving the Ciudad de Mexico behind, the old bus weaved through the snarls of city traffic, eventually finding its way into the countryside. We were moving northwest in the direction of Guadalajara, a distance of approximately 350 hard miles. I can remember passing through the narrow streets of many small towns, the bus sometimes just clearing the walls of the main buildings. There were occasions when we retreated some distance so as to permit the on-coming vehicles to pass, as much of the time the roadway was composed of merely a single lane.

The bus transported an interesting variety of passengers including, but not limited to, small goats, noisy fowl in vine-woven cages, and the aged inhabitants with their weather-scarred features. There were large parcels scattered about on the floor, the result of the shopping pilgrimages by those who had descended on the city for those hard-to-find provisions. There were laborers who commuted for only short distances and then jumped off quickly when reaching their workplace. In every small village new people climbed aboard while others departed, causing the complexion of passengers to be constantly changing.

We traveled all day and into the evening before reaching Guadalajara. From there the journey continued in the direction of Tepic, a place I had heard my grandfather speak of many times. The driver encountered several difficult sections of road after making the turnoff towards Puerto Vallarta. The rutted and narrow dirt track was well past the given abilities of our bus or any vehicle for that matter. I assisted the driver in changing flats on two occasions. Other times we jacked the bus up and out of ditches, sometimes building a bed of stones under one of the wheels. We followed the well-worn artery that had been previously carved through the jungle. The original intent for the road had been to funnel the forces of civilization into this secluded coastal village, located in the state of Jalisco.

The bus bounced us roughly through the night as we bridged the uneven gullies that cut across our route. At dawn I observed many native inhabitants of the jungle communities walking by the side of the road, carrying with them their machetes and water jugs. Some were busy setting up stalls in the local farmers' market, while still others were tending their small garden plots nearby. It was interesting to observe this slice of life in the small villages as we passed through.

The next morning the road followed a small stream or arroyo that gradually broke through the last of the Sierra Cuale range leading to the misty coastal plains below. My spirits elevated as I viewed the narrow strip of land that tapered out to the flat and pristine waters of the Pacific. A prevailing sea breeze from the southwest poured in through the windows of the bus, signaling my entry into this tropical realm.

We crossed the threshold into the city, which had a population of less than 20,000. The bus progressed into a relatively unspoiled section of the old part of Puerto Vallarta, accented by its traditional whitewashed adobes capped with the ubiquitous red tile roofs. My heart filled with the anticipation of looking up my two long lost uncles.

After some tortillas and *huevos rancheros* in a small restaurant by the water, I began to inquire around town about my uncles. People directed me to Casa Moray, a quaint little dwelling near the ocean at the southern end of the main Vallarta beach. As I walked up to the steps of the patio area I spied my uncle Bernard engaged in a business meeting. It had been a number of years since we had seen each other and initially he did not recognize me. He was overjoyed when he realized who I was and soon, after his acquaintances left, we fell deep into conversation.

We continued to reminisce, telling stories and updating each other for the remainder of the afternoon. My chronicle was far too long to try to recount in just one session so we left most of it for the days that followed. Relocating to his main house up the hill from one of the central avenues in town, we found Aunt Teresa busy preparing dinner. My aunt and uncle extended every courtesy to me, which included allowing me to stay in Casa Moray on the beach for the next month. The naming of houses is a strong tradition in Mexico, and they had named this dwelling after my grandfather.

The next day I sought out my other uncle, Richard Applegate, who had for years lived up in the "Gringo Gulch" area. This was a traditional residential area where Elizabeth Taylor and Richard Burton had built a house around the time of their movie, *Night of the Iguana*, in 1964. Uncle Richard's home was located up the narrow street, and away from the busy center of town, on a low ridge just above the Cuale River.

He was also delighted to see me, extending a warm welcome and taking me into his home. Later we went for a tour of Vallarta and the surrounding area in his open-aired jeep. We stopped at a small shop where he purchased some shorts and a white sport shirt for me. I wore my new acquisitions out of the store, relieved to be in something besides the well-worn and patched Levis that had been my uniform of the road for well over a year. Already I was sensing the forces of transition that would eventually guide me back into the world from which I had come. I was beginning the integration process, on the outside at least, soon blending in with all the tourists around me.

In addition, Uncle Richard was kind enough to lend me his jeep for the duration of my stay. Over the next few days, a wave of sentiment swept over me as I experienced that warm feeling projected from my mother's branch of my family after such a long time on the road alone.

Richard and Bernard Applegate had come to Puerto Vallarta from northern California in 1956 to conclude my grandfather's affairs after his death. Each of these enterprising men found themselves seduced by the balmy breezes, swaying palms, and the gentle spirit of the Mexican people. So too, had it been with Moray, their father. The cobblestone streets that spread out between the lovely old buildings exuded a charming atmosphere impossible to resist. After selling their respective businesses in northern California, they both later decided to make their permanent homes in this revered paradise.

Over a period of time they became building contractors, creating splendid homes that hugged the jungle-strewn cliffs and shorelines that overlooked Banderas Bay. They built these homes for the many retirees and snowbirds that flocked to populate this enticing coastal village. These stunning houses often received special acclaim in well-known architectural digests of the time. From humble stem-walls of concrete grew up the elegant casas in white, accented to perfection with hardwood shutters and tile roofs, with many of the attractive handmade fixtures and furniture inside originating from the small cottage industries in Guadalajara.

One evening Richard and I were enjoying a delectable seafood dinner and a leisurely game of chess at the Oceano Bar near the shoreline of the large circular-shaped bay. While comfortably seated in our wicker chairs, I shared with him that one of my objectives in visiting Puerto Vallarta was to discover more about my grandfather's life. I further explained I was on a "mission" of sorts to investigate the contents of a "trunk of letters" I had heard existed among Moray's things. I wanted to learn more about our family history and hoped it might provide interesting insights into my own. His eyebrows shifted slightly at hearing my request.

Uncle Richard revealed that there was in fact a trunk full of grandfather's documents, the family heirloom for which he considered himself the principal custodian. He mentioned he would be happy to let me examine it as long and as often as I wished. The one stipulation was that I not remove any of the papers without placing them back in the trunk before I left. He informed me that Moray had always kept copies or originals of his most important business transactions. The trunk also contained many personal letters written to close friends and family members over the years. Adrenalin pumped unrestrained through my veins upon hearing Uncle Richard's words.

I told him that, as a boy, I could remember Moray's long visits with us in Ashland, Oregon. I mentioned the trunk of letters and documents that was always close by his bed. Richard told me the old trunk could very well be the same one I saw as a child. I eagerly anticipated the discovery of the priceless secrets that I hoped might be unlocked. The first half of November had already passed, and I realized if I was to be home for Christmas I needed to get started immediately on the review of these documents.

In the next four weeks of reading and compiling, I reconstructed some of the extraordinary accounts that made up my grandfather's exciting years. Moray Lindsay Applegate was born in 1876 of pioneer stock and raised on the ranch home in the Klamath Basin of Oregon. He was destined to live his daring life in the spirit of his grandfather Lindsay who had come with his two brothers to Oregon by wagon train in 1843. Already I was feeling a generational closeness to this line of men, sensing my journey around the globe was much like the wagon train exploits of my ancestors.

One passage I had read from his many writings particularly stood out for me, as it went a long ways in capturing the essence of his personal philosophy of life.

If you regard death as a calamity, then life itself is a calamity and there is no consolation. Wouldn't it be better, and more logical, to regard the whole thing as an adventure, meaning both life and death? The whole is at least as interesting and romantic and wonderfully mysterious. All we can do is to play the game and that should keep us cheerful, if our scheme of life is right.

In another note written just two years before his passing (at the age of eighty), he was feeling the burden of his years when he communicated this reflection to his wonderful lifelong friend of nearly fifty years, H.C. Thompson.

Am in excellent health, but realize my days are numbered. Yet it is hard to believe I am at last an old man. I have always felt young and romantic until my sickness last year, when the Angel of Death was breathing down my shoulder. But I am becoming reconciled, and I am overhauling my philosophy of life.

Sheer joy and fulfillment welled up inside of me from those satisfying discoveries gleaned daily from the old weathered trunk. It had served effectively as a time machine, transporting me back through the events of my grandfather's life. I felt as if I had been personally conversing with him once again. The unique kinship I had always felt to his legacy had now grown even stronger. From this time on, I knew I was never alone or without his presence close to me. We would forever be kindred spirits.

I have continued to consult with him about the marvelous adventure that is life, as I too, his grandson, have begun to feel the burden of my years.

Mt. Shasta

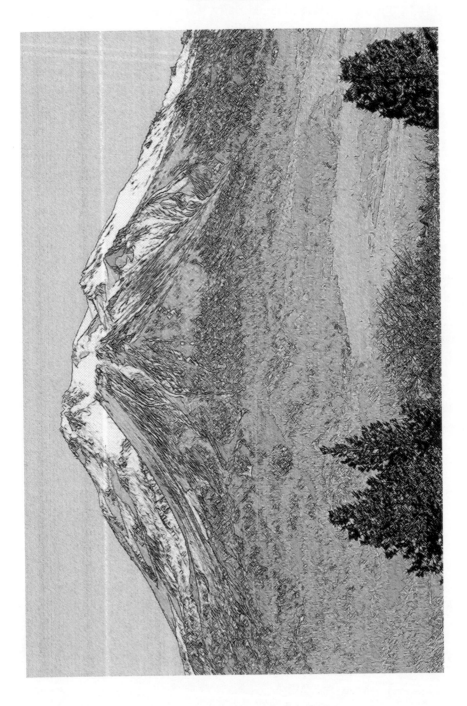

Back to the Beginning
Chapter Thirty

*The perfect journey is circular—the joy of departure
and the joy of return.* —Dino Basili

Gentle sea breezes swept off the bay, rattling palm fronds and unrolling an invisible carpet of cool air over the sandy beaches. The scenery enchanted me, from the international beauties sporting their minuscule bikinis in the daytime to the sedating seaward sunsets at dusk. Each afternoon, after wrapping up my research for the day, I digested my discoveries on *Playa Los Muertos*, "The Beach of the Dead." Contrary to its rather morbid namesake, this location was alive with vigorous activity.

The beach had derived its designation from a notorious historical battle between the local natives and the ruthless gold smugglers of the time. Legend recounts that innumerable bodies once littered the beach as the result of a major conflict between these two determined factions. Now this fashionable and prime shoreline property was littered with the bodies of the numerous sun-worshippers who lay on the sands like iguanas, absorbing the warm restful rays. Tourists and patrons of nearby upscale hotels strolled casually along the sea walk that divided the beaches from the private commercial patios and restaurants. Day after day, I found myself engaging in conversation with a fascinating variety of Vallarta visitors.

On one pleasant afternoon, I struck up a dialog with an American man whom I had seen on the beach in previous days. He was engrossed in a book, and an exotic rum drink with flowers hanging out of it sat on the small table next to him. He appeared to be in his late thirties, tan and relaxed. Upon inquiry, I discovered he was waiting to take delivery of a new 100-foot yacht on its way to Puerto Vallarta from its construction site in San Diego.

As we continued chatting, he divulged that delivering yachts was his sole occupation. He mentioned that he was now gathering a small crew to assist him in taking the craft on her maiden voyage through the Panama Canal and eventually to her new owners in Florida. He then asked if I would be interested in such a position. I answered with an enthusiastic "yes!" His principal point of persuasion was the "no experience necessary" caveat he had added at the end of his pitch. This would delay my return to Oregon by a couple of months, but would enable me to fly home from Florida at the end of the voyage, at his expense, and with money in my pocket. It was an appealing idea.

Each day he patiently made efforts to get through to the States on the public pay phone, of questionable working order, in the town square. After several unsuccessful attempts at calls to San Diego, he changed his approach, using cablegrams instead. Daily we met at the beach to discuss future procedures aboard ship and to see what new information he might have. The week of intense anticipation passed at a snail's pace.

I awoke as usual to the blended sounds of street roosters crowing in concert with tolling church bells in the background. Later I heard the repetitive calls of the town knife sharpener who summoned his clients in a perfected mournful cry. Then I walked to the beach looking for my soon-to-be employer. He arrived appearing glum and disheartened. Finally, some news had come, and it was all very discouraging. From sketchy accounts, he had learned that the yacht had caught fire while en route, suffering severe damage, with her skeleton crew forced to abandon the ship. My dreams of an extended sailing adventure had literally gone up in smoke somewhere off the coast of Baja.

With no job in sight, there was little reason to delay my departure north. I set out on one of my last days in Vallarta with my uncle Richard's jeep, heading south on the narrow coastal road leading to Playa Mismaloya. I felt the need to view the scenic rocky coves and offshore outcroppings of Los Arcos one last time before leaving this paradise. The contrast of the golden sands and aquamarine water spliced together at the shoreline reflected a memorable radiance. Parking the jeep, I walked to the water and plunged into the gentle surf, then swam out around one of the large offshore stacks. The water was warm and clear, and I could see many colorful schools of fish swimming beneath me.

Later, back on the beach, I let the warm rays of the sun dry me off before purchasing a *taco con pollo* from a vendor at one of the beach *palapas*. Several pleasant hours passed, after which I climbed behind the wheel of the jeep and began the drive back to town.

I carefully maneuvered the short wheel-based vehicle around the sharp curves that hugged the cliff above the ocean. As I rounded one of the bends, I could see a man and a younger woman climbing onto the road from the steep embankment that fell to the surf below. A warm feeling came over me when, to my great surprise, I recognized it was Philip! He was one of the world travelers I had met around the tables of the Blue Tibetan Restaurant in Kathmandu. I was jubilant to see him again, and we started updating each other right there in the middle of the road. He and his lady-friend were visiting Vallarta before making their way to the mountainous state of Oaxaca, a popular destination for young people, located in the southeast portion of the Mexican Republic.

They soon piled into the back of the jeep and we headed for town, with each of us talking non-stop over the other. Emotions ran high as we discussed all that had happened in our lives in the seven months since Nepal. I asked him about Sofia. He informed me that word had come to him of her safe return to Copenhagen. I felt a great sense of relief upon hearing this news. We had dinner together that night in a cantina near the beach. That evening we said goodbye, never to see each other again.

It was mid-December, and my extended global passage was now in its sixth season and sixteenth month. Voices inside of me whispered ever-stronger hints of a Christmas at the family home in Oregon. Mexico had provided me with a brief respite to the growing road weariness that had begun to totally grip my being. My initial and primary quest of seeing the world was now nearly complete.

In the month of reading Moray's papers I had come across an old discolored cablegram announcing my birth in 1942, sent to him from Ashland by his sister. This little document instantly took me back to my roots, and touched me deeply. It was liberating to discover that my romantic and adventurous tendencies might well have been a gift passed down from a hereditary tree. I had come to Puerto Vallarta in search of this kind of knowledge and information. Now that I had found it, the time had come to say goodbye to my relatives and look towards home.

My uncles and their families flattered me by throwing an exquisite going away *fiesta* the day before my departure. There were colorful tables set with great quantities of tasty treats, including seafood, black bean soup and some memorable enchiladas. The *mariachi* band filled the air with the music I had come to love. All social life in Mexico revolves around the family, and I experienced this as only one of the many pleasant aspects of the Mexican culture. I could not have been more grateful to all of them for their warm acceptance of me, which was in a sense the start of an assimilation process that would manifest itself in the months following my return. It was reassuring to know I was a part of a larger circle, rather than just the vague and rootless "citizen of the world" that I had come to be for so long.

The morning following the party, my relatives dropped me off at the Puerto Vallarta Airport where I boarded a Martin 404 Skyliner, the designated plane for the "mail run," to Tijuana. This inexpensive flight would shuttle me several times, back and forth across the Gulf of California, between the mainland and Baja, on its irregular path north to the U.S. border. It provided my best chance of arriving back in Oregon before Christmas.

The two 2400 hp Pratt and Whitney Double Wasp prop engines created a deafening roar, propelling the forty-four passenger plane skyward with a powerful surge. In my talks with the hostess I learned the aircraft was one of only 103 built, designed to replace the DC-3 as the stalwart of commercial airliners in the 1950s. These workhorses of the air were eventually sold into the smaller fleets maintained by foreign countries. This one had found a busy life in Mexico.

Far below, I could distinguish the hardedge line between sea and shore, occasionally obscured by a patch of floating mist. Nearly all of my fellow passengers were indigenous to Mexico, many holding large parcels on their laps with additional belongings overflowing into the aisles.

After several hours, we were over Baja where we initiated the first in a series of bumpy landings on the crude dirt runways that scarred the surface of the land. Our mission was multi-faceted, dropping off passengers and mail in exchange for new versions of each. There were the old and infirm, those wrinkled and bent from a hard life eked out in the shady crevices of this sun-burnt peninsula. The prevalent sound of babies crying provided a symphonic background to the "mercy flight" that served these outlying areas.

As the plane dropped down out of the sky, I looked out the window to view "small varmints" fearfully scattering across the scorched ground beneath us. The Martin 404 swooped over them like a great winged predator, casting an ominous shadow. With each landing we bounced roughly on the uneven terrain, coming to rest in a cloud of dust. There were often delays when the pilots waited for the booked passengers, many making their way to the plane in dilapidated vehicles from the outlying villages. This aircraft was their primary link to the rest of the world. The saga continued on into the day, back and forth between Baja and the mainland until we at last entered into the glide path for the Tijuana Airport.

Shortly after walking my backpack across the U.S.-Mexican border, I collapsed to my knees and literally kissed the terra firma below. I was in a ceremonial state of bliss, feeling a curious mixture of emotions. There had been times when my homeland had devolved to but a slight and indistinct memory, a distant benchmark of my former history. I had succumbed several times to the idea that I might never see it again. On different occasions, I had seriously pondered starting a new life, on my Greek island so dear, or in The Kingdom of Nepal, or in my beloved Australia, never to see American shores again. Each of these alternatives presented me with an alluring turning point in my life, a fork in the road, a detour that could well have led to a personally conceived "Promised Land" or "Shangri-La."

In the final assessment, these options fell to the scrap heap of idle dreams, and I felt overpowered by an intense homing instinct that now possessed me. I was compelled to place ever-greater emphasis on my return. No longer did I see myself as a man without a country, a vagabond of the world, but rather, a tired son of Oregon who had walked a unique and varied path for an interval of time. I was returning to the starting point, to the place where it had all begun. My hometown of Ashland was for now, the final destination, where the circle would close.

In the beginning, it had been the inexhaustible commitment to a personal liberation, a global exploration, and a passage into spiritual discovery. Now, the original luster of those ideas had dimmed, worn down by the abrasive stones of reality. Unpredictable forces of destiny had shaped me as I passed through a gauntlet of novel experiences. Though tired, I was emerging from this ordeal, more confident, more adaptable, and considerably more self-reliant. Although I felt I had been endowed with an expanded view of the world, my once great thirst for knowledge had temporarily been diminished. Now what I sought most was a place of tranquility that would allow me to prepare for the next stage in life, whatever it might be.

I seasoned the trip north to Oregon with visits to those close to me at the time of my departure. First, there was my younger brother Bill, stationed in San Diego with the Navy. We had a warm reunion in my modest hotel room in Coronado, later going out for dinner and bringing each other up to date on family affairs. It was great to see him, and I passed on greetings from the uncles to him. The emotion-filled evening ended much too soon. Once again, I found myself frustrated when trying to attempt the impossible task of recounting even small parts of my traveler's tale. It was much easier just to listen.

The Greyhound bus ride to San Jose was soothing, and I dozed off, inoculated with a sense of well-being as the weight of the travel concerns that usually occupied my mind slowly lifted. Upon arrival,

I contacted the girl I had left behind, our relationship one of the sad casualties of my choice to travel. We sat down over tea while she explained in a very kind way that her life had gone on, and there was now a new man. We had agreed she was not to wait. She graciously presented me with the cards and letters I had posted to her during the early stages of the journey. After a light kiss, we said goodbye.

Nervous with excitement I knocked on Kirby's door in Menlo Park, for I had not made contact in the ten months since leaving him on the Greek island. There were many sentimental moments as we sat down and talked through the hours that followed. Kirby, more than anyone else I had met, could comprehend the long-term stresses that traveling abroad could bring. He understood the ceaseless toil of constantly being on the move over foreign landscapes with marginal finances and few facilities. It was relaxing to rest at his cottage near the Stanford campus for a few days.

My last visit was with Tom, my college friend and travel partner on my initial trip to Europe during the summer of 1962. He and his charming wife put me up for several nights at their restored Victorian home in fashionable Los Gatos. For many reasons I found it fascinating to see how the lives of my close acquaintances had progressed while I had been away. Tom had moved up the ladder in his father's business, developing a large circle of friends and associates. Already he was a respected member of the community, poised to forge ahead in accepting prestigious positions within local civic groups. "No one stands still," I thought to myself. I wondered if the time spent on the road had caused me to fall behind. Was there a way to affix a value to what I had done? I had to conclude that only the future could answer these questions.

One evening Tom, with his whimsical sense of humor, mentioned I looked like a "male model," a comment reflecting my dramatic weight loss. Although I had gained back thirty pounds since stepping on the scales in Singapore, I was still fifty-five pounds less than when I had departed for Europe. Tom and his wife feted me with delectable dinners and stimulating conversation around their dining room table. Taking my leave, I expressed my gratitude for the "returning hero's reception," and bid farewell to my friends. Then I caught the Greyhound north for Ashland, Oregon, for the last leg of my journey.

Everything seemed somehow different. I sensed this was true whether moving through metropolitan areas or cruising down the freeways. I was absorbing a new world whose pace and direction had most definitely changed in the sixteen months I had been gone. Advertisements stood out as more colorful and clever. It even appeared that people were walking and talking faster. The country was embroiled in a great debate regarding a war and our place in the world. The once minimal evidence of a growing subculture had expanded and displays of the "flower children" and "alternative lifestyles" abounded on nearly every street corner. It was definitely a much different country than when I had left.

The long bus ride north up through California to the Oregon border afforded me time for flashbacks over the rich tapestry of my travel odyssey. I was still a rolling stone, and the idea of settling down in one place and stepping back into American life seemed unthinkable. I knew I would miss playing the part of the roving international observer, the roaming humble ambassador, the refugee in search of his next sanctuary.

For me, it had been the year of two winters. The first one I had experienced in the Southern Hemisphere while I was in Australia. Now, December's gale buffeted the bus as we glided over the icy hard-pack that gripped the surface of the road. Outside the window, new fallen snow blanketed the aprons of the highway as the sleek Greyhound racked up the miles, past Red Bluff, then Redding, and points farther north.

The great white prominence of Mt. Shasta loomed up before me, its steep brawny white shoulders reflecting in the moonlight. I focused on the 14,161-foot silhouette of the peak that punctured the night sky. It had always been a mountain of significance to me, towering above my world. I had dreamed many times of climbing its icy ramparts to the frigid summit above. Someday I would, several times over.

Blasting up new sections of highway built since I had left, the bus strained on the uphill curves as we neared the 4,310-foot pass that sliced through the backbone of the Siskiyou Mountain Range. My heart jumped as landmarks like Pilot Rock came into view. I recalled passing by the great rock on the skyline at the start of the journey, after Kirby and I caught our very first ride hitchhiking, back in August of the previous year.

We were over the summit now, and the bus driver shifted into the lower gears, cautiously descending the slippery lanes leading down into the Rogue River Valley, the place of my birth. I could see Emigrant Lake, and the snow-clad crest of Grizzly Mountain. We passed the site where the old Callahan's Lodge used to be before the new freeway took it out. It was a place filled with warm memories. Later, at the bottom of the mountain slope, the bus veered away from the new portion of the I-5 Freeway and turned at the junction leading into town. It was here that Mom and Dad had dropped us off to begin hitchhiking, sixteen months before, at the beginning of the circle. The bus rolled over the icy streets of Ashland, past Omar's dinner house where I had met one of the original motivators who had inspired me to travel the world.

Finally, the Greyhound eased up to the curb of the bus depot, stopping with a loud hiss of the brakes. Excited, I stepped onto the sidewalk of my hometown. It was only a few days before Christmas, and the streets displayed the decorations of the season. It was early morning, and the town was just coming to life.

Intent on preserving the element of surprise, I decided to walk the last several miles, first through the town itself and then up the long hill to my parents' house. I paused for reflection at the old Varsity Theater, pondering all those Saturday matinees that expanded my world as a youngster. A few years later, that same location became the designated pick-up point for the newspapers I delivered on my early morning paper route. Passing the grocery store that Dad once owned and my grandfather Hardy before him, I recalled sweeping sidewalks and stocking shelves with canned goods to earn money for my first bike. I turned up Gresham Street next to the ivy-covered library where "story time by the fireplace" had sparked my childhood imagination for so many delightful hours. Then there was the street to Mrs. Hartley's house where I had taken the piano lessons that so tested my patience and consumed some of the magical time of my youth.

Ashland residents, bundled up snugly in winter garb and shoveling their walks, waved as I trudged up the hill with my backpack, the frozen snow crunching loudly under my feet. Over an hour had passed since I had gotten off the bus. The house was in sight, sitting at the far end of the extended driveway leading up the hillside. The air was crisp and smelled of the conifers that dressed the slope just under the Mt. Ashland Mine Road. A soft layer of morning fog had rolled out in a smooth white blanket inundating the town, now far below. The Oregon I had left behind was reaching out to greet me. A neighbor's dog barked, then, recognizing me, began wagging its tail.

At last, I reached the top of the hill. I walked across the front of my parents' house, eagerly scanning the large windows for a glimpse of movement inside. Walking closer I saw indistinct figures, moving. There were images of Mom in her housecoat making coffee and of Dad walking down the hallway combing his hair as he always did in the mornings. My heart was in my throat. Setting my worn backpack down on the front porch, I took a deep breath and rang the doorbell. For just an instant time stood still. An instant between two worlds, the one I had just passed through and the new one that I was about to enter. Then the door opened.

Afterword

My return brought with it a sense of completion to a remarkable chapter of my life, laying down a sturdy foundation for the new episodes to follow. Within a week of my homecoming, I found employment in the wood products industry, and followed this line of work for the next fifteen years. For an additional seventeen years after that, I built a home improvement business in Northern California. In the more than three decades that I pursued these two careers, I did not leave U.S. shores.

Then, thirty-five years after my homecoming from the around the world trip, at the age of sixty, my retirement afforded me the opportunity to realize my dream of traveling the globe once again. I felt liberated and reborn as those old feelings of independence reemerged and flooded my being.

Understandably, my correspondence with Helen had ended when I was married in 1971, and our contact was lost. In a stroke of good fortune, and with the aid of the internet, I was able to locate her in the winter of 2001. She was still residing in the Melbourne area. I booked single passage in the spring of 2002 on a container freighter, the *America Star*, and sailed thirty-two days at sea, out of Savannah, Georgia, through the Panama Canal for Melbourne to see her once again. I was overwhelmed with anticipation.

Helen met the ship, thirty-five years after seeing me off from the very same port! We had many wonderful afternoons together, sharing the direction our lives had taken since parting in October of 1967. She had traveled the world extensively, inspired by some of the stories I had read to her at my apartment house. The car wash was gone, but St. Kilda was alive and well, having become a most fashionable district with galleries and fine sidewalk restaurants. My old apartment house still remained, in much the same dilapidated condition as when I had left.

Helen and I continue to maintain a very special friendship. We cannot help but occasionally speculate on how different our lives might have been had I complied with her requests in the radiograms to my ship, the *SS Australis*, and returned to Australia.

My old friend Kirby, traveling companion as far as Greece, retired as head of the English Division of Cabrillo College, in Aptos, California, where he taught fiction for some thirty years. He has published several books. We touch base occasionally, but there never seems to be enough time to sit down and review the good old days as we both would wish.

Traveling enriched my life beyond comprehension. The experiences from my around-the-world journey continue to influence me even today. Many of my loyal customers from the business life hailed from countries where I had traveled. My neighborhood grocer is a Sikh and he never tires of hearing the reflections of my stay at the Golden Temple of Amritsar. Every newspaper, book, and travelogue I see, brings to life those many precious memories. The journey became a large part of me and I am so grateful I took the risk, so long ago, to walk a different path for a while, and see the world.

June 12, 2008   RVH

Picture Credits

Cover .... ©iStockphoto.com/Steve Dibblee

Sketches based on the following photos

Chapter .... Credit

A Return to Europe .... Oleg Kuznetsov
Autumn in Munich .... ©iStockphoto.com/Jonathan Greaves
The Brenner Pass .... Linda Keller
Canals of Venice .... ©iStockphoto.com/Bill Grove
The Yugoslav Route .... ©iStockphoto.com/ Michael Cavén
My Greek Island .... ©iStockphoto.com/ Toon Possemiers
Voyage to Egypt .... ©iStockphoto.com/ Paul Kline
Beirut to Jerusalem .... Premasagar Rose <http://premasagar.
com>
Pipeline to Baghdad .... (Petra) ©iStockphoto.com/Gemma
Ivern
The Caspian Sea .... ©iStockphoto.com/ Klaas Lingbeek-
van Kranen
The Golden Temple .... ©iStockphoto.com/ Ondrej Cech
The Mercenary .... ©iStockphoto.com/ Anne de Haas
Road to Singapore .... ©iStockphoto.com/ Grace Tan
Down Under .... ©iStockphoto.com/ Linda & Colin
McKie
Kalgoorlie & the Frozen
Chickens .... ©iStockphoto.com/ Linda Stewart
Hitching the Nullarbor .... ©iStockphoto.com/ Linda & Colin
McKie
Into Melbourne .... ©iStockphoto.com/James Thew
Back to the Beginning .... ©iStockphoto.com/Dan Higgins